IN ACTION

Performance Analysis and Consulting

TWELVE

CASE STUDIES

FROM THE

REAL WORLD

OF TRAINING

JACK J. PHILLIPS

SERIES EDITOR

ASTD

Linking People,
Learning & Performance

Ordering information: Books published by the American Society for Training & Development can be ordered by calling 800.628.2783 or 703.683.8100, or via the Website at www.astd.org.

Library of Congress Catalog Card Number: 00-100861
ISBN: 1-56286-134-4

Table of Contents

Introduction to the *In Action* Series v

Preface...vii

How to Use This Casebook xi

Performance Consulting: A Trend Is Becoming a Reality...................1
Jack J. Phillips

Drivers of Employee Satisfaction...25
Arthur Andersen
Julie E. Mann and *David P. Boizelle*

If You Build It, They Will Come..39
Retail Banking
Neil Cerbone

Measuring the Impact of Career Development
    on an Organization 53
Sun Microsystems Inc.
Ron Elsdon and *Seema Iyer*

Workforce Education: A Staff Development Program 67
Pennsylvania Community Colleges
Barbara A. Frey and *Gary W. Kuhne*

The Phone Company (TPC) Case...75
Telecommunications
Kenneth H. Silber

Enhancing Job Performance through Performance
   Analysis and Consulting...93
Electric Service Company
J. Patrick Whalen

Using a Performance Analysis to Influence Employee
   Turnover..109
Jeans, Inc.
Tim Hatcher and *Kit Brooks*

Performance Analysis: Field Operations Management.............135
Steelcase, Inc.
Mike Wykes, Jody March/Swets, and *Lynn Rynbrandt*

Fish See the Water Last: Organization Effectiveness
   Assessment..155
Financial Management
Katherine Donahue

Managing the Information of an Executive Development
   Program...167
Arthur Andersen
Jerry F. Luebke and *Susan E. Bumpass*

Using AMIGOS to Improve Mentoring Relationships.............181
Sandia National Laboratories
Linda K. Stromei and *Patricia E. Boverie*

Reinventing the HR Function..199
Redwood Stone Products Company
Jack J. Phillips and Patricia P. Phillips

About the Series Editor..223

Introduction to the
In Action Series

Like most professionals, the people involved in HRD are eager to see practical applications of models, techniques, theories, strategies, and issues relevant to their field. In recent years, practitioners have developed an intense desire to learn about the first-hand experiences of organizations implementing HRD programs. To fill this critical void, the Publishing Review Committee of the American Society for Training & Development established the *In Action* casebook series. Covering a variety of topics in HRD, the series significantly adds to the current literature in the field.

The *In Action* series objectives are as follows:

- *To provide real-world examples of HRD program application and implementation.* Each case describes significant issues, events, actions, and activities. When possible, actual names of organizations and individuals are used. Where names are disguised, the events are factual.

- *To focus on challenging and difficult issues confronting the HRD field.* These cases explore areas where it is difficult to find information or where processes or techniques are not standardized or fully developed. Emerging issues critical to success are also explored.

- *To recognize the work of professionals in the HRD field by presenting best practices.* Each casebook represents the most effective examples available. Issue editors are experienced professionals, and topics are carefully selected to ensure that they represent important and timely issues. Cases are written by highly respected HRD practitioners, authors, researchers, and consultants. The authors focus on many high-profile organizations—names you will quickly recognize.

- *To serve as a self-teaching tool for people learning about the HRD field.* As a stand-alone reference, each volume is a practical learning tool that fully explores numerous topics and issues.

- *To present a medium for teaching groups about the practical aspects of HRD.* Each book is a useful supplement to general and specialized HRD textbooks and serves as a discussion guide to enhance learning in formal and informal settings.

These cases will challenge and motivate you. The new insights you gain will serve as an impetus for positive change in your organization. If you have a case that might serve the same purpose for other HRD professionals, please contact me. New casebooks are being developed. If you have suggestions on ways to improve the *In Action* series, your input is welcomed.

Jack J. Phillips
Series Editor
The Jack Phillips Center for Research and Assessment
Box 380637
Birmingham, AL 35238-0637

Preface

Performance analysis and consulting is a growing and critical topic. Most organizations struggle to find the best solutions to improve performance, yet they often fail to consider methodical processes to determine those solutions. Sometimes there is confusion about the degree of emphasis on performance consulting and the mechanisms for performance analysis to be successful.

Through this casebook, we hope to contribute to the understanding of performance analysis and consulting by offering a variety of systems, processes, and models. The authors, who reflect viewpoints from varied backgrounds, are diligently pursuing performance analysis and consulting projects in the HR, HRD, and performance improvement arenas.

This book should interest anyone involved in HR, HRD, and performance improvement. The primary audience is practitioners (or the performance consultants themselves) who are struggling to identify the most credible process to determine a performance deficiency and how best to address the deficiency. They are the ones who request more examples from what they often label the "real world." This same group also complains that there are too many models, methods, strategies, and theories—and too few examples to show whether any process really makes a difference. This publication should satisfy this need by providing successful performance consulting initiatives. Also, this book should encourage more practitioners to tackle this important topic and help them avoid some of the problems inherent in performance analysis and consulting projects.

The second intended audience is instructors and professors. Whether this casebook is used in university classes with students who are pursuing courses in HRD, internal workshops for professional HRD staff members, or public seminars on HRD implementation, it will be a valuable reference. It can be used as a supplement to a standard HRD textbook or as a complement to a textbook on performance analysis and consulting. As a supplemental text, this casebook will bring practical significance to the coursework, convincing students that there are systematic processes, methods, and models that can help determine performance deficiencies and the appropriate solutions.

A third audience is the researchers and consultants who are seeking ways to document performance analysis and consulting processes. This book shows the application of a wide range of processes, models, and techniques, most of which have their basis in sound theory and logical assumptions.

The final audience is the managers who must work with HRD on a peripheral basis—those managers who are asked to spend their time and offer the time of their employees to the performance consultants, are working to determine the real needs, and have offered what have been determined the best solutions to address performance needs. These are managers who participate in HRD programs to develop their own management skills, send other employees to participate, and occasionally lead or conduct sessions in these programs. In these roles, managers must understand performance consulting processes and systems and appreciate their value. This casebook should provide evidence of this value.

Each audience should find the casebook entertaining and engaging reading. Questions are placed at the end of each case to stimulate additional thought and discussion. One of the most effective ways to maximize the usefulness of this book is through group discussions, using the questions to develop and dissect the issues, techniques, systems, and processes.

The most difficult part of developing this book was identifying case authors to contribute systems, processes, and models that provide a methodical approach to performance consulting interventions. In the search, letters were sent to more than 10,000 individuals with an interest in performance consulting. To tap the global market, 1,000 of the individuals contacted were outside the United States. We had more than 100 requests for guidelines to the casebook. Based on the response, we selected 12 case studies to be presented in this publication. These 12 cases present a variety of approaches and represent several industries including banking, technology, telecommunications, higher education, and research and development.

In our search for cases, we contacted the most respected and well-known organizations in the world, leading experts in the field, key executives, and well-known authors and researchers. Whether best practices were delivered, we will never know. What we do know is that if these are not best practices, no other publication can claim to have them, either. Many of the experts producing these cases characterize them as the best examples of performance analysis and consulting in the field.

Although some attempt was made to structure cases similarly, they are not identical in style and content. It is important for the reader to experience the programs as they were developed and to identify the issues pertinent to each particular setting and situation. The result is a variety of presentations with a variety of styles. Some cases are brief and to the point, outlining precisely what happened and what was achieved. Others provide more detailed background information, including details on how the people involved determined the need for the process, descriptions of the personalities involved, and analyses of how the backgrounds and biases of the people involved created a unique situation.

There was no attempt to restrict cases to a particular methodology, technique, or process. It is helpful to show a wide range of approaches. We resisted the temptation to pass judgment on various approaches, preferring to let the reader evaluate the different techniques and their appropriateness in their particular settings. Some of the assumptions, methodologies, and strategies might not be as comprehensive and sound as others.

With regard to the individual authors, it would be difficult to find a more impressive group of contributors to a publication of this nature. For such a difficult and critical topic, we expected to find the best, and we were not disappointed. If we had to describe the group members, we would say they are experienced, professional, knowledgeable, and on the leading edge of HRD. Most are experts; some are well known in their fields. A few are high-profile authors who have made a tremendous contribution to HRD and have taken the opportunity to provide an example of their top-quality work. Others have made their marks quietly and have achieved success for their organizations.

As with any new publication, we welcome your input. If you have ideas or recommendations regarding presentation, case selection, or case quality, please send them to: ASTD *In Action* Series Editor, Box 380637, Birmingham, AL 35238-0637; phone: 205.678.9700; email: SeriesEditor@aol.com. These comments will be not only appreciated but also acknowledged.

Although this casebook is a collective work of many individuals, the first acknowledgment must go to the case authors. We are grateful for their professional contribution. We also want to acknowledge the organizations that allowed us to use their names and programs for publication. We realize this action may carry some risk. We trust the final product has portrayed them as progressive organizations interested in results and willing to try new processes and techniques.

We would also like to thank Kelly Perkins, director of publishing of the Chelsea Group. Kelly works with us to manage the *In Action* series process and keeps us on track. Kelly's willingness to put in whatever time it takes to see a project through is insurmountable.

As always, the staff at the American Society for Training & Development is a joy to work with. Nancy Olson, vice president of publications, and Ruth Stadius, manager of book publishing, are always supportive and willing to help ensure the success of each publication. Thank you.

Jack J. Phillips
Birmingham, AL
May 2000

How to Use This Casebook

The cases presented in this book illustrate a variety of approaches to performance analysis and consulting. Collectively, they offer a wide range of settings, methods, techniques, strategies, and approaches. Moreover, they represent a wide spectrum of industries, including telecommunications, finance, manufacturing, education, and high technology.

As a group, these cases represent a rich source of information about the strategies of some of the best practitioners and consultants in the field. Yet each case does not necessarily represent the ideal approach for the specific situation. In every case, it is possible to identify areas that could benefit from refinement or improvement. That is part of the learning process—to build on the work of other people.

There are several ways to use this book. Overall, it surely will be helpful to anyone interested in the topic of performance analysis and consulting, whether that person is a senior-level executive, an HRD professional, or a performance analyst and consultant.

Beyond that, four specific uses are recommended. To begin with, HRD professionals can use the book as a basic reference of practical applications of performance analysis and consulting. A reader can analyze and dissect each of the cases to develop an understanding of the issues, approaches, and—most of all—refinements or improvements that could be made.

In addition, this book will be useful in group discussions, during which interested individuals can react to the material, offer different perspectives, and draw conclusions about approaches and techniques.

Moreover, this book can serve as an excellent supplement to other management and training and development textbooks. It provides the extra dimension of real-life cases that show the outcomes of performance analysis and consulting.

Finally, this book will be extremely valuable to managers and executives who do not have primary training responsibility. These managers provide support and assistance to the HRD staff, and it is helpful

Table 1. Overview of the case studies.

Lead Author	Industry	Key Features	Primary Audience
Julie E. Mann	Business consulting; accounting	Five fundamental elements that drive employee satisfaction	HR practitioners
Neil Cerbone	Banking	Transformation of bank from operational to customer centricity	Organizational leadership
Ron Elsdon	High technology	Measurement of benefits from investing in employee career development	Management
Barbara A. Frey	Higher education	Presentation skills of instructors before and after staff development program	HRD professionals
Kenneth H. Silber	Telecommunications	Data network services' integration calls for new assessment of performance improvement needs	Performance consultants
J. Patrick Whalen	Utilities	Performance improvement program positively affects regional call center	Training and development professionals and consultants
Tim Hatcher	Textile manufacturing	Performance analysis uses qualitative, not quantitative, methods to address specific HR problem	HRD professionals

Mike Wykes	Furniture manufacturing	Improvement of business performance of field operations managers within a subsidiary	Performance analysts and consultants
Katherine Donahue	Financial management	Organizational effectiveness assessment actively involves employees	Performance consultants; HRD professionals
Jerry F. Luebke	Business consulting; accounting	Development and design of evaluation system for executive leadership development program	Performance consultants
Linda K. Stromei	Research and development	External consultant's experiences with implementing pared-down mentoring program	Performance consultants
Jack J. Phillips	Raw materials production	Results of thorough, comprehensive performance assessment process	HRD professionals; management; performance consultants

to them to understand the methodologies HRD professionals use and the results their programs can yield.

Space limitations have required that some cases be shorter than the author and editor would have liked. Some information concerning background, assumptions, strategies, and results had to be omitted. If additional information about a case is needed or desired, please contact either the lead author of the case or the editor. In most instances, the address of the lead author is provided in the biographical information offered by each person at the end of his or her case; the address of the editor is provided in the preface and in the biographical information at the end of the book.

The table in this chapter provides an overview of the cases by industry, key features, and intended audience. It can serve as a quick reference for readers who want to examine the cases by particular audiences, industries, and types or methods of consulting and analysis.

Performance Consulting:
A Trend Is Becoming a Reality

Jack J. Phillips

The training and development function is shifting its focus to performance improvement, a process by which a variety of solutions are implemented to improve performance in an organization. This paradigm shift represents a tremendous change in the way the training and development (T&D) function is structured and managed and the manner in which it provides programs and services. Training and development's roles, skills, and outputs are drastically changing as T&D staff members transform into a group of capable performance improvement specialists and consultants.

Consider, for example, the changes occurring at Rohm and Haas, a large specialty chemical company with production operations located throughout the world. The Rohm and Haas plant in Houston, Texas, created a network of performance consultants and charged them with the formidable task of changing the plant's prevailing paradigm of training and experience on the job. This was the key to driving adequate performance with a new approach, which considered all the factors that influence human performance (Miller, 1997).

Each unit in the plant now has a performance development implementer (PDI), who reports to the unit manager and addresses performance issues in the plant. All PDIs are connected by a network, which allows them to share information, address plant-wide initiatives, and build their own knowledge and skills. A performance development manager coordinates the network.

This shift required developing new knowledge, skills, and competencies for each PDI. The organizational structure changed significantly, and through a variety of communication strategies and action items, productive relationships were established between the PDIs and key employees throughout the plant. The services provided changed dramatically from traditional T&D programs to a variety of performance improvement services and solutions.

The result is a network of highly skilled performance specialists and consultants who understand and can address common needs of the plants as well as specific needs in each unit. Basically, the network provides a new lens for examining performance issues.

This example illustrates the tremendous shift in focus for the traditional T&D function as it provides a range of services to improve performance of a work unit, department division, plant, or entire organization.

Increasing Influence

In a global survey of practitioners, the shift to performance improvement received one of the highest scores for agreement to the existence of the trend, with a rating of 4.25 out of 5 (Phillips, 1999). The same practitioners rated the trend 4.37 out of 5 in terms of importance. Practitioners view this shift as important and visible. Moreover, perhaps no trend has been more publicized than this one. Books, articles, and studies describing the process have been plentiful (many of them are noted at the end of this chapter). Every T&D agenda contains the topic, and a special workshop has been developed by the International Society for Performance Improvement to prepare training and development staff members for this transition.

One of the most important studies of this shift is a major research project conducted by the American Society for Training & Development (ASTD) under the leadership of a panel of experts in the training and development and performance improvement fields (Rothwell, 1996). In this project, ASTD sought to develop a model for roles and competencies reflecting performance improvement. This model was intended to replace an earlier model of training and HR development. The expert panel concluded that most major organizations around the globe were making the transition from traditional training and development to performance improvement. After drawing that conclusion, the team developed an official ASTD model for human performance improvement, defining roles, competencies, and outputs. The study also addressed a variety of other issues necessary to make the transition a reality.

A survey of a sample of HRD executives around the globe confirms the transition. In regard to a question about the transition of training to performance improvement, 42 percent of respondents strongly agreed and another 42 percent agreed—84 percent total—that the training department was rapidly changing to fill a performance improvement role (Bassi, Benson, and Cheney, 1997).

Training and Development magazine, which is published by ASTD, reported the results of a survey among readers of the magazine. The survey reflected that 40 percent of the respondents believed that changing their professional titles to performance improvement specialist would best describe the work they do. Many departments also are changing their names.

Several influences are driving this transition from training to a performance improvement role. The most significant and visible drivers are as follows:

- The pressures of competition and the emphasis on efficiency and cost control in all organizations require more efforts to improve employee performance. The need for formal methods to improve performance represents an important emerging role in businesses, which often ask their T&D departments to become involved in performance initiatives to improve or enhance employee performance.
- The analysis of training program failure often leads to the conclusion that nontraining solutions exist that should have been addressed or corrected for performance to improve. As part of continuous process improvement, the T&D function has addressed these issues. The result is a more formal performance assessment and analysis process.

  In most situations where a performance problem exists, training is not the solution. This leads to an awkward situation for most training staff members. Although nontraining solutions are needed to correct a problem, the only services they can provide are training programs, which makes it difficult to resolve the problem. The problem must be handed off to some other organization or individual, leaving the client with unmet needs and unsolved problems. The T&D functions have now broadened the range of services they provide to include nontraining solutions that complement training solutions.
- A significant amount of training is not transferred to the job, and often many other factors in the work environment must be altered, modified, removed, or minimized for the training to be applied properly. Because of this, many T&D functions have placed more emphasis on performance analysis and consulting. A performance improvement role requires more attention to the work environment, sometimes with changes focusing directly on modifications of the workplace, the environment, and support mechanisms. This essentially

causes the training department to reach beyond the traditional role of developing programs to a broader role of resolving issues and removing performance inhibitors.

- Key executives and managers in the organization are more accepting of the process of performance improvement as a concept of a one-stop source of performance problem solutions. The notion of a performance improvement function communicates that the emphasis is on improving organizational and departmental performance, something managers have desired for years.

- The implementation of a performance improvement department represents the integration of a variety of different issues, techniques, and elements to bring about radical improvements and changes in the organization. For example, the requirement for measurement and evaluation, including return-on-investment, causes some organizations to focus more attention on performance analysis to sort out the various causes of performance gaps.

These and other drivers have caused organizations to make the dramatic shift to performance improvement.

Models

Sometimes the first step in analyzing this trend is to examine a performance improvement model. In the ASTD study briefly described earlier, several important models were examined to arrive at what is ultimately labeled the ASTD Human Performance Improvement Process Model (Rothwell, 1996). Figure 1 shows the simplified model developed in the study, representing six critical steps in the performance improvement process. In the first step, the performance problem or opportunity is thoroughly analyzed to identify a specific performance gap. This step includes an analysis of present performance compared with desired performance, as well as an analysis of the environment, systems, procedures, and processes. The impact of this gap is explored, as well as the cost of continuing with the problem or ignoring the opportunity.

The second step addresses the cause of the gap and examines a variety of potential causes, including reward systems, information flow, capabilities of employees, motivational environment, compensation arrangement, support mechanisms, culture, and local practices. The result is an identification of the specific cause or causes of the performance gap.

The third step is to select the appropriate interventions. There are many possible ways through which performance problems can be resolved, and these possibilities depend on the specific cause, the resources available, and the situation. Job description modifications, policy changes, compensation adjustments, reward system changes, staffing level modifications, training and development, and implementation of new technology are all potential solutions.

In the fourth step, the performance improvement solution is implemented. The application of the solution may be as simple as changing practices and policies or as complicated as developing and enhancing skills and knowledge. Implementation is carefully scheduled with the appropriate resources, timing, and activities identified.

The fifth step involves managing the change process. The implementation is monitored and steps are taken to make sure the appropriate individuals receive necessary information and that key stakeholders are appropriately involved in the process. Building helpful support and buy-in from management and keeping the progress on schedule are critical issues for this step.

The last step, evaluation and measurement, is important and includes data collection through a variety of methods to measure the success of the performance improvement intervention. Different types of data are collected, both qualitative and quantitative, to determine the extent to which the performance improvement process has succeeded in implementing the performance improvement solution, changing job performance, and ultimately driving a positive business impact. Although the measurement and evaluation process is planned in advance, data is collected after process implementation, and the results are presented to key stakeholders.

This model represents a simplified version of the performance improvement process. It has the advantage of condensing a relatively complex process into a series of six steps. Also, it has the validity of development by experts in the field with input from many practitioners.

Performance Assessment and Analysis

A comprehensive performance consulting process involves at least 14 distinct steps:
1. Determine the specific purpose and type of needs assessment.
2. Identify and select the sources for information for the needs assessment.
3. Involve key management in the process and gain necessary commitment.
4. Begin with the end in mind, with specific business-impact and job-performance measures.

Figure 1. ASTD Human Performance Improvement Process Model.

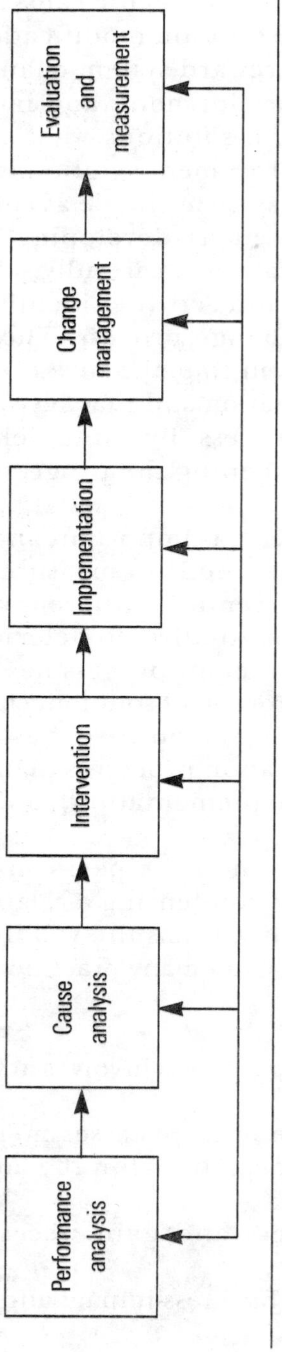

5. Use multiple sources of input and a variety of data.
6. Select the data collection methods appropriate for the situation, culture, and resources available.
7. Collect data according to a predetermined collection plan.
8. Link business needs to job performance needs, including tasks, behavior, and environment.
9. Identify the barriers to successful implementation of the solution.
10. Determine specific skills and specific knowledge deficiencies, if applicable.
11. Integrate and analyze all the data.
12. Prioritize specific need in terms of importance and cost to resolve.
13. Provide recommendations for specific solutions.
14. Communicate results of the needs assessment and analysis to appropriate target audiences.

These steps are comprehensive, and some may be omitted when a simple process is needed or when the stakes are not so high. A shortened version of this process is presented in figure 2, which describes a basic performance assessment and analysis process. This four-level process focuses on the business and job performance issues. The four levels in this model relate to the evaluation levels shown in figure 3. The evaluation levels are the traditional levels and represent the most common framework for evaluation (Kirkpatrick, 1994).

Information needed to determine the success of a program at each level is derived from specific objectives of the program. For example, the business impact from a training program is developed from measures contained in the impact objectives. The same process applies for application of training on the job and learning achieved in the program. Some programs even have reaction of satisfaction objectives, which outline the expected participant reaction to the program.

Program objectives at all four levels are derived from the needs assessment process. For example, the specific business needs uncovered via needs assessment will drive the impact objectives and identify the business impact. Also, the job performance needs assessment will uncover changes in tasks, behavior, and procedures needed in the job environment. This will determine the specific application objectives for the program. The skill, knowledge, and attitude deficiencies will determine specific learning gaps, which will appear as learning objectives in the program. Finally, preferences for the solution in terms of type of program, media, timing, delivery, and content will drive these issues and sometimes appear as satisfaction objectives. Thus, needs assessment is clearly linked to program objectives and evalu-

Figure 2. Performance assessment and analysis process.

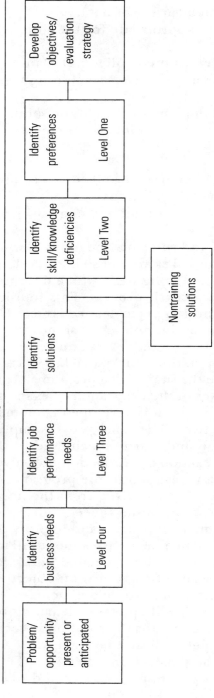

Note: Each level includes data sources, data collection, key questions, and key issues.
Source: Performance Resources Organization, P.O. Box 380637, Birmingham, AL 35238-0637. Used with permission.

Figure 3. Linking needs assessment with evaluation.

	Needs assessment	Program objectives	Evaluation	
4	Business needs	Impact objectives	Business impact	4
3	Job performance needs	Application objectives	Job application	3
2	Skill/knowledge/ attitude deficiencies	Learning objectives	Learning	2
1	Preferences *(Delivery need)*	Satisfaction objectives	Reaction	1

ation, and these linkages are often referred to as levels of needs assessment, objectives, and evaluation.

An example of this process is shown in figure 4, where an absenteeism problem has been linked to specific supervisory skill and knowledge deficiencies and a program has been developed to overcome them. In this example, the needs assessment and analysis levels clearly drive program objectives, and an appropriate evaluation method is used to collect data to satisfy the requirement for the particular evaluation level.

To develop this process effectively, several key questions need to be asked for each needs assessment level, as shown in figure 5.

Not every needs assessment should be conducted at all levels. The important point is that the value of the information obtained is higher at higher levels, with business needs providing the highest level of information. Frequency of use of needs assessment decreases with the levels (that is, the higher the level, the lower the frequency of use).

Preferences are a common type of needs assessment. For example, when a program catalog is distributed to the members of a target audience asking them to select the programs they would like to attend in the next six months, this is usually a needs assessment based on preference (level one). On the other end of the scale, the analysis of business needs is conducted infrequently, primarily because it is difficult and time consuming.

Figure 4. An example of linking needs assessment with evaluation.

	Needs assessment	Program objectives	Evaluation method	
4	An absenteeism problem exists	Weekly absenteeism rate will reduce	Monitor absenteeism data for six months	4
3	Discussions between team leader/supervisor are not occurring when there is an unexpected absence	Counseling discussions conducted in 95% of situations when an unexpected absence occurs	Follow-up questionnaire to participants to check frequency of discussions—three months	3
2	Deficiency in counseling/discussion skills	Counseling/ discussion skills will be acquired/enhanced	Skill practice session during program	2
1	Supervisors prefer to attend training on a one-day-per-week basis	Program receives favorable rating of 4 out of 5 on the structure of the program	Reaction questionnaire at the end of program	1

Figure 5. Key questions for needs assessment and analysis.

Business needs **Level One**	What business-level problems or opportunities exist that need to be improved? What business measures reflect this need? Where are they located? What are the historical values?
Job performance needs **Level Three**	What is preventing the business measures from improving? What is not being performed on the job as desired or as needed? What tasks should be performed What resources are needed?
Skills/knowledge needs **Level Two**	What skills and knowledge levels are needed? What gaps exist in skills and knowledge? How can skills and knowledge be acquired or enhanced?
Preference **Level One**	Which learning activities are preferred? Which delivery mechanisms are desired? What is the appropriate timing?

In reality, only a few requests for needs assessment should be taken to the level three and level four assessments—problems in which the scope is large and the impact or costs are great. The criteria often hinge on the following issues:

- the anticipated impact of the problem in costs or profit
- the perceived life cycle of the solution
- the importance of the solution in meeting operational goals
- linkage with strategic objectives
- the expected cost of the solution
- the expected visibility of the solution
- the size of the target audience involved.

Paradigm Shift

The shift to performance improvement represents a significant change for all involved in traditional training and development. Table 1 represents 15 important shifts often experienced when an organization transforms T&D into a performance improvement department.

These paradigm shifts represent several important changes in processes, practices, and procedures. A few of the major issues are briefly described next.

Performance Analysis

As described in the ASTD model, there must be a focus on the performance issues. Business needs—as well as the work performance issues—must be identified. Not only are the gaps identified, but the causes also are detailed. This is perhaps one of the most important elements of the performance analysis process, which represents a critical paradigm shift for the T&D staff. The result is a clear understanding of the business impact of the opportunity, the specific gaps that exist, and the causes of those gaps.

Solutions and Services

Because the T&D function is now preparing to offer a variety of nontraining solutions, services are expanding—shifting from the traditional products centered on structured learning experiences to a full range of performance improvement possibilities. The categories for potential solutions from a leading performance technology model (Rosenberg, 1996) are listed in table 2. For organizations making the switch in the early stages of the performance improvement process, the range of services often is limited.

Table 1. Paradigm shift to performance improvement.

Traditional Training Department	Performance Improvement Department
Characteristics	**Characteristics**
• No business need for the program	• Program linked to specific business needs
• No assessment of performance	• Assessment of performance and causes
• Most problems have training solutions	• Nontraining solutions are common
• Services organized around design and delivery of structure	• Full range of services to improve performance
• Specific objectives focus on learning	• Specific objectives for job performance and business impact
• No effort to prepare program participants to achieve results	• Expectations for results communicated to participants, clients
• No effort to prepare work environment to support transfer	• Environment prepared to support transfer
• Typical job title includes *designer* or *trainer*	• Typical job title includes *performance consultant* or *performance technologist*
• Work activities focus on preparation and teaching	• Work activities focus on collaboration, consulting
• No client relationship established; control outside the department is limited	• Process revolves around client relationships; contacts outside department are frequent and required
• No efforts to build partnerships with key managers	• Partnerships established with key managers, clients
• Department structure contains narrowly focused functions (development, delivery, administration)	• Department structure contains broad-based functions (analysis, consulting, design, facilitation)
• Departments have training label and usually report to HR executive	• Departments have performance improvement label and usually report to operations executive
• No measurement of results or cost-benefit analysis	• Measurement of results and cost-benefit analysis
• Planning and reporting on progress is input-focused or activity-based	• Planning and reporting on progress is output-focused or results-based

Table 2. Potential solutions from a performance technology model.

Training and Development Services

• Coaching	• Job/work design
• Compensation	• Leadership/supervision
• Culture change	• Performance management
• Documentation	• Performance support
• Environmental engineering	• Staffing
• Health/wellness	• Team building
• Job aids	• Training/education

Preparation and Expectation

Another important paradigm shift focuses on preparing for the actual intervention or solution, whether a training or nontraining solution. Part of the process comes from the specific objectives that are developed to focus on application and business impact. These objectives clearly define what specific changes must be made and what corresponding improvement is expected, moving the process beyond the traditional learning objectives of the T&D function. The designers of the solution, whether a training or nontraining solution, will clearly note what changes are expected and the subsequent impact desired. These expectations are communicated directly to participants, as well as clients and others who are directly involved in the process.

In addition, the environment is adjusted to support the transfer of the job, whatever the solution. The support groups in the environment are prepared to accept, support, and nurture what was learned so that on-the-job success ultimately will be realized.

Work Activities and Roles

Work activities change significantly with this paradigm shift. Traditional activities typically focused on conducting a needs assessment, developing and designing materials for a learning experience, and delivering the learning solution in an effective way. The new role focuses on collaboration and consulting. Consequently, job titles now include the words *performance consultant* or *performance technologist,* instead of *designer* or *trainer.*

Table 3 shows a complete listing of the competencies in the ASTD Human Performance Improvement Process Model (Rothwell, 1996). The table lists a total of 38 competencies, with the first 15 associated with the core competencies involving all human performance improvements. The remaining 23 focus on four key roles identified by the ASTD panel of experts: analyst, intervention specialist, change manager, and evaluator. These differ vastly from the traditional T&D roles and titles.

Relationships

Shifting to the performance improvement role results in more focus on building relationships. Inherent with the process is the relationship with the client who desires or needs the performance improvement. The client/consultant relationship flourishes throughout the process. The stakeholders, who have an important concern for or interest in the process, often are routinely involved in communication, information sharing, and problem-solving activities. Performance improvement team members build relationships and use them effectively to solve problems, provide analysis, and implement solutions. The performance improvement specialists must communicate effectively as relationships are built. Because the new roles involve new processes, key stakeholders must understand what the phrase performance improvement means and their role in the success of the process.

Structure

The structure of the T&D function shifts as the performance improvement role is undertaken. Figure 6 shows the structure of a traditional training and development department. This traditional department has analysts who often conduct needs assessments and evaluations, with designers and developers producing or purchasing structured learning programs. Facilitators conduct the programs and coordinators keep the programs organized.

In the performance improvement structure depicted in figure 7, the roles are different. The performance analysis and design group analyzes the gaps and causes, as well as designing or developing the appropriate interventions to solve the problem. Performance consultants implement the solution, sometimes facilitating the process and keeping the process on track throughout implementation. Evaluation is separate, containing the independent and objective evaluation team.

Evaluation

In the performance improvement function, evaluation operates similarly to that role in the T&D function. The primary difference is that an evaluation in a performance improvement function usually includes business impact and job performance data within a five-level evaluation framework (Phillips, 1997).

Table 3. ASTD core competencies.

	Competencies Associated with All Performance Improvement Work
1. Industry awareness	Understanding the vision, strategy, goals, and culture of an industry; linking HPI interventions to organizational goals.
2. Leadership skills	Knowing how to lead or influence others positively to achieve desired work results.
3. Interpersonal relationship skills	Working effectively with others to achieve common goals and exercising effective interpersonal influence.
4. Technological awareness and understanding	Using existing or new technology and different types of software and hardware; understanding performance support systems and applying them as appropriate.
5. Problem-solving skills	Detecting performance gaps and helping other people discover ways to close performance gaps now and in the future; closing gaps between actual and ideal performance.
6. System thinking and understanding	Identifying inputs, throughputs, and outputs of a subsystem, system, or suprasystem and applying that information to improve human performance; realizing the implications of interventions on many parts of an organization, process, or individual; taking steps to address any side effects of HPI interventions.
7. Performance understanding	Distinguishing between activities and results; recognizing implications, outcomes, and consequences.
8. Knowledge of interventions	Demonstrating an understanding of the many ways that human performance can be improved in organizational settings; showing how to apply specific HPI interventions to close existing or anticipated performance gaps.
9. Business understanding	Demonstrating awareness of the inner workings of business functions and how business decisions affect financial or nonfinancial work results.

continued on page 16

Table 3. ASTD core competencies (continued).

10. Organization understanding	Seeing organizations as dynamic, political, economic, and social systems that have multiple goals; using this larger perspective as a framework for understanding and influencing events and change.
11. Negotiating/contracting skills	Organizing, preparing, overseeing, and evaluating work performed by vendors, contingent workers, or outsourcing agents.
12. Buy-in advocacy skills	Building ownership or support for change among affected individuals, groups, and other stakeholders.
13. Coping skills	Knowing how to deal with ambiguity and how to handle the stress resulting from change and from multiple meanings or possibilities.
14. Ability to see "big picture"	Looking beyond details to see overarching goals and results.
15. Consulting skills	Understanding the results that stakeholders desire from a process and providing insight into how efficiently and effectively those results can be achieved.

Competencies Associated with Specific Roles

Specific competencies are linked to each role played by those involved in human performance work.

Role One: Analyst

16. Performance analysis skills (front-end analysis)	The process of comparing actual and ideal performance in order to identify performance gaps or opportunities.
17. Needs analysis, survey design, and development skills (open-ended and structured)	Preparing written (mail), oral (phone), or electronic (email) surveys using open-ended (essay) and closed (scaled) questions in order to identify HPI needs.

Role One: Analyst (continued)

18. Competency identification skills	Identifying the knowledge and skill requirements of teams, jobs, tasks, roles, and work.
19. Questioning skills	Gathering pertinent information to stimulate insight in individuals and groups through use of interviews and other probing methods.
20. Analytical skills (synthesis)	Breaking down the components of a larger whole and reassembling them to achieve improved human performance.
21. Work environment analytical skills	Examining work environments for issues or characteristics affecting human performance.

Role Two: Intervention Specialist

22. Performance information interpretation skills	Finding useful meaning from the results of performance analysis and helping performers, performers' managers, process owners, and other stakeholders to do so.
23. Intervention selection skills	Selecting HPI interventions that address the root cause(s) of performance gaps rather than symptoms or side effects.
24. Performance change interpretation skills	Forecasting and analyzing the effects of interventions and their consequences.
25. Ability to assess relationships among interventions	Examining the effects of multiple HPI interventions on parts of an organization, as well as the effects on the organization's interactions with customers, suppliers, distributors, and workers.

continued on page 18

Table 3. ASTD core competencies (continued).

Role Two: Intervention Specialist (continued)

26. Ability to identify critical business issues and changes	Determining key business issues and applying that information during the implementation of HPI interventions.
27. Goal implementation skills	Ensuring that goals are converted effectively into actions to close existing or pending performance gaps; getting results despite conflicting priorities, lack of resources, or ambiguity.

Role Three: Change Manager

28. Change impetus skills	Determining what the organization should do to address the cause(s) of a human performance gap now and in the future.
29. Communication channel, informal network, and alliance understanding	Knowing how communication moves through an organization by various channels, networks, and alliances; building such channels, networks, and alliances to achieve improvement in productivity and performance.
30. Group dynamics process understanding	Understanding how groups function; influencing people so that group, work, and individual needs are addressed.
31. Process consultation skills	Observing individuals and groups for their interactions and the effects of their interactions with others.
32. Facilitation skills	Helping performers, performers' managers, process owners, and stakeholders to discover new insights.

Role Four: Evaluator

33. Performance gap evaluation skills : Measuring or helping others measure differences between actual and ideal performance.

34. Ability to evaluate results against organizational goals : Assessing how well the results of HPI interventions match intentions.

35. Standard-setting skills : Measuring desired results of organizations, processes, or individuals; helping others to establish and measure work expectations.

36. Ability to assess impact on culture : Examining the effects of human performance gaps and HPI interventions on shared beliefs and assumptions about "right" and "wrong" ways of behaving and acting in one organizational setting.

37. HPI intervention reviewing skills : Finding ways to evaluate and continuously improve HPI interventions before and during implementation.

38. Feedback skills : Collecting information about performance and feeding it back clearly, specifically, and on a timely basis to affected individuals or groups.

Figure 6. A structure for a traditional training and development department.

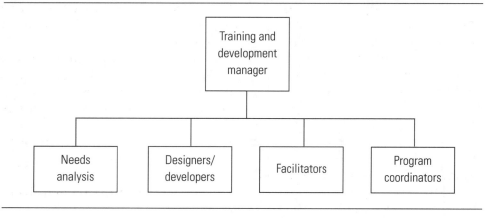

Figure 7. A structure for a performance support department.

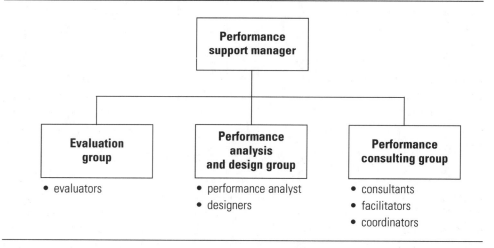

A traditional evaluation stops with reaction data (level one). Performance improvement evaluators track business impact measures, performance and implementation measures, learning measures, and reaction measures to provide a full range of evaluation information. They also must report these data to a variety of target audiences.

Impact on the Training and Development Department

This trend may be slow to develop in some organizations, and a few T&D managers actually resist it. The level of resistance is often a function of the current success and perception of the training and development function. In other words, if an organization perceives that its T&D department is ineffective, makes little contribution to the bottom line, and shows no measures of success, that department will have difficulty making a case to expand its role.

This trend often creates a dilemma for T&D departments. On a positive note, the training function expands its range of services to include a variety of nontraining solutions. Team members assume different roles with key managers in the organization. However, many training staff members are not equipped for these new roles and are not allowed to offer some of the nontraining solutions, such as compensation. Consequently, this process often involves gradual policy changes (Robinson and Robinson, 1995).

The most significant impact is that new skills must be acquired. A review of the competencies outlined in the ASTD model (see table 3) emphasizes the skills and knowledge the T&D staff needs to be successful with this process. The shift will require substantial training for the staff and, in come cases, may require employing new staff with the required skills. Above all, trainers must become performance technologists.

For some trainers, these new roles may be a radical departure from existing habits. To these seasoned trainers, every performance problem appears to have a training solution, and it may be tempting for them to continue to train when nontraining solutions are needed. Consequently, the transition often occurs slowly with much involvement from the staff.

The training and development staff members must learn more about the organization and its problems, opportunities, and performance issues. They must learn the language of operating managers and be able to converse regularly with this group. They must know case strategies, organizational goals, and the current status of many projects in the organization. They need to understand how various solutions can help or hinder certain problems and causes.

The T&D staff must communicate the new process to a variety of stakeholders, particularly key managers and clients who need to understand the new approach and framework and what it means to them. Without good explanations and understanding, as well as demonstrations, managers may become skeptical about the process and view it as a new fad floating through the organization (Rummler, 1996).

Because the shift from training to performance improvement represents a shift in mindset and attitude, as well as the development of a new process and set of skills, managers may resist the shift. When a manager asks for a specific training program and the response is an analysis that leads to a nontraining solution, some frustration may surface with the manager, particularly if he or she does not understand the process. The key is to communicate routinely and accurately so that resistance is minimized.

The Role of Case Studies

The challenge of this issue can be summarized in one preliminary question: Does the T&D department want to be in the performance improvement business? If so, the trend must be managed and coordinated with a decisive timetable. The following key questions can be helpful in reaching this decision.

1. To what extent do I agree this is a trend?
2. How important is this trend?
3. How much progress has been made with this trend in my organization?
4. Do I support this trend?
5. Do the key management groups support this trend?
6. What specific skills are needed? Will additional staff need to be added, or can the competencies be built through training and development?
7. What happens if I do nothing?
8. Does top management support this trend?
9. What additional funding, if any, is required to support this trend?
10. What barriers exist in implementing this trend?

In our search for cases for this new casebook, we specifically asked authors to provide examples of performance consulting in practice, showing a variety of tools to determine specifically the different issues and problems surrounding the situation. The cases presented offer a vast array of different approaches and illustrate the mix of techniques and tools that are available to analyze problems, uncover performance issues, and identify solutions.

We asked case authors to supply examples following the different levels of needs assessment as described in this chapter. In addition, we asked for explanations of how the specific solutions were developed or recommended from the analysis.

There is no attempt to show the actual success of the solution. Other casebooks in this series document the success of solutions. The important contribution for this publication is to illustrate the different ways in which the analysis, consulting, and assessment processes are conducted to arrive at a range of solutions for the specific request, problem, or opportunity. And that is what is delivered in this book.

Outlook

This trend will continue during the next few years as organizations look for new ways to improve productivity and boost competitiveness. Not only will the drivers continue to influence the shift to performance, but the benefits of implementing a performance improvement process also will be significant. In many cases, this shift reflects a more efficient process by avoiding unnecessary training programs when training is not the solution. Because the intervention focuses directly on business problems, the results are usually significant, desired, and welcomed by the key managers in the organization. Because the true causes of performance will be identified, the chances of improving or overcoming the performance gap are greatly enhanced.

This process also aligns the T&D function more closely with the strategic initiatives of the company and with the key operating executives, greatly enhancing the success of new efforts and initiatives. Additional significant benefits coupled with the increased drivers for the shift almost guarantees that this trend is here to stay.

References

Bassi, L.J., G. Benson, and S. Cheney. "Position Yourself for the Future: The Ten Trends Most Likely to Affect Your Future." Alexandria, VA: American Society for Training & Development, 1997.

Kirkpatrick, D.L. *Evaluation: The Four Levels.* San Francisco: Berrett-Koehler Publishers, 1994.

Miller, K. "Reinventing HRD: From Training to Performance Consulting." In *In Action: Leading Organizational Change,* E.F. Holton and J.J. Phillips, editors. Alexandria, VA: American Society for Training & Development, 1997.

Phillips, J.J. *HRD Trends Worldwide.* Houston: Gulf, 1999.

Phillips, J.J. *Return on Investment in Training and Performance Improvement Programs.* Houston: Gulf, 1997.

Robinson, D.G., and J.C. Robinson. *Performance Consulting: Moving Beyond Training.* San Francisco: Berrett-Koehler, 1995.

Rosenberg, M.J. "Human Performance Technology." In *The ASTD Training & Development Handbook,* R.L. Craig, editor. New York: McGraw-Hill, 1996.

Rothwell, W.J. *Model for Human Performance Improvement: Roles, Competencies, and Outputs.* Alexandria, VA: American Society for Training & Development, 1996.

Rummler, G. "In Search of the Holy Performance Grail." *Training & Development,* *50*(4), 26-32, 1996.

Additional Reference

Langley, G.J., et al. *The Performance Improvement Guide: A Practical Approach to Enhancing Organizational Performance.* San Francisco: Jossey-Bass, 1996.

Drivers of Employee Satisfaction

Arthur Andersen

Julie E. Mann and David P. Boizelle

This case study presents the work being done by Arthur Andersen to identify the elements that most impact employee satisfaction. Using the results of a worldwide employee survey, Arthur Andersen has identified five fundamental elements that drive employee satisfaction. These "drivers" provide the common ground on which a combination of centralized and decentralized improvement efforts are being built. This article reviews the methods used to identify those drivers and describes their significance and application.

Arthur Andersen is committed to improving employee satisfaction as it strives to meet its vision of "The Greatest Place to Do Great Work." But how does one of the largest professional services firms focus its employee satisfaction efforts given the diverse needs of more than 72,000 employees led by more than 4,000 partners spread over 382 offices in 84 countries? The answer lies in identifying the fundamentals of employee satisfaction and truly *living* the advice to "think globally but act locally."

Background

An employee satisfaction survey effort was undertaken at Arthur Andersen in 1994. A 140-question instrument, developed by an external vendor, was used to assess the state of employee satisfaction on a worldwide basis. Results from this survey led to the implementation of several large global initiatives that focused on HR processes, including

This case was prepared to serve as a basis for discussion rather than to illustrate either effective or ineffective administrative and management practices.

specific initiatives on performance feedback and mentoring. The decentralized nature of the partnership and global nature of the firm made large-scale, centrally driven implementation of these initiatives challenging. Considerable progress was made, but more was needed.

A slightly expanded version of the 1994 survey was conducted in 1997. Again, an external vendor developed the survey. A variety of global and local/regional reports were created. Responsibility for developing and implementing plans to address issues identified by the survey was placed largely in the decentralized hands of local office and country leadership. Most local and country leaders moved quickly to understand their offices' needs and to identify specific actions they would take to address issues. Not surprisingly, while some leaders were very effective, others were less so. Also, since actions were expected to be identified locally, they could not be applied consistently globally.

Three additional factors influenced the overall success of the decentralized approach:
- Global leadership had completely changed hands by the time the results from the survey were released. Subsequent leadership changes rippled through the firm for several months.
- The strongly decentralized organization had no means to monitor local action or share learnings.
- Some major issues (such as compensation and potential for international assignment) could not be addressed at an individual office level and needed country- or area-wide support.

Upon review, it was generally accepted that using the decentralized approach to address employee satisfaction in the absence of an overall strategy did not meet the desired expectations. Arthur Andersen needed an approach to address employee satisfaction that balanced local involvement and ownership of actions with strategic, global priorities and plans. The analysis eventually undertaken proved that behind the chaos of the vast number of reports and the unique needs of the different constituencies lay a common thread that truly bound them together in one firm.

Originally, there was no plan (and no specific funding) to carry out full-scale employee satisfaction research. Fortunately, another project was sponsored to identify Human Resource Best Practices in the United States. The project planned to use the 1997 employee survey data to identify offices with highly rated HR processes. Early in the project, the question of whether good HR processes drive (influence) high employee satisfaction was raised. A second question was whether a model should be developed to show which processes impacted employee satisfaction the most. These and other questions provoked a progressive research study that led to the identification of key drivers of employee satisfaction.

Research Approach

The following research process was used to identify the drivers of employee satisfaction. Steps in this process are not identified as "best practices," as true best research practices are clearly articulated in the academic literature. The steps in our process demonstrate *real* practice in which plans evolve, opportunities are created, and we try to make the best use of the data we have. These steps describe how the results were used to answer the question about the role of HR processes in employee satisfaction, to determine whether common themes existed, and to identify what most impacts employee satisfaction. Every effort was taken to produce statistically valid but also practical, meaningful results.

Establishing Sufficiency

Because the survey was not designed specifically for this research, it was important to establish sufficiency criteria. Did the survey address enough of the issues generally acknowledged to impact employee satisfaction to allow for meaningful conclusions? Before beginning any analysis of the data, a list of items that could impact satisfaction was created. This list was drawn from several sources, including Hackman and Oldham's material on the core job characteristics for intrinsically motivating work (1980), Maister's book on service professionals (1993), various employee satisfaction research articles, organizational systems models, and experience within Arthur Andersen.

The large number of questions (154) enabled the analysis to satisfactorily address the most critical issues. Most notably lacking in the data was the ability to consider an individual's positive or negative attitude and the exact nature of his or her work—for instance, amount of travel and extent of client interaction. These deficiencies were accepted given that we were looking for major organizational issues that extended across functions and across a large number of individuals. The results were determined to be sufficient to allow significant conclusions.

Establishing Hypotheses

The following items were hypothesized as potential influencers of employee satisfaction:
• Demographic variables:

— Office size. Do very large offices have fundamentally different issues than small offices?
— Service category (major service branches). Service categories function somewhat independently, and the nature of the work is different.
— Classification (job level). Previous internal studies have shown a relationship between satisfaction and classification. Does a different satisfaction model apply to the different classifications?
— Area. Arthur Andersen is divided among the four major geographical areas of North America; Latin America; Europe, Middle East, India, and Africa; and Asia/Pacific.
• Situational variables:
— degree of involvement in decision making
— type of work
— quality and frequency of performance feedback
— level of compensation
— sense of job security
— degree of office success, measured in terms of profitability and client satisfaction
— leadership effectiveness
— relationship with co-workers and support staff
— adequacy, efficacy, and believability of communication
— availability of tools, training, and skills for the job assigned.
• Employees themselves:
— personal career goals
— degree of intrinsic motivation
— skill level
— general attitudes.

Determining Demographic Priorities

One important goal was to be able to compare office-to-office performance. A key assumption was that there would be a greater difference in satisfaction between offices than there was between service categories or between classification levels.

Results from analysis of variance (ANOVA) showed small but measurable differences by service category, office size, and classification. The very large sample size ($n > 22,000$) enabled very small differences to be statistically significant. However, these differences were small enough that they did not suggest the presence of a vastly different population that could not be acceptably merged to create an overall model. Had the differences been large, all subsequent analysis would have targeted understanding the differences.

Issues regarding line and support functions proved more challenging. Although the difference in means between the two populations was acceptably small, there was a much higher nonresponse rate by support personnel (HR, accounting, secretaries) for several key questions. These questions were more targeted to line employee issues (for instance, amount of travel or desire to be partner). It was critical to retain these important questions; however, the data could not adequately represent the support functions. Rather than falsely suggest that this group was adequately represented, the decision was made to remove the support functions from the analysis. A recommendation was made that results for the support functions should be studied at a future date.

Establishing Guiding Principles

Two key principles guided our analysis:
1. *Look for themes and avoid drawing major conclusions from individual questions.* Because individual questions could not sufficiently represent an issue, we focused on identifying groups of questions that would each represent an aspect of the complex concepts we were seeking to understand.
2. *Apply systems thinking.* Organizational systems have many interrelated parts. Employees are impacted not only by leadership and HR practices but also by co-workers, support staff, formal and informal communication, and the work itself. In the analyses and subsequent recommendations, we considered the relationships and interdependencies between the elements in the organizational system.

Identifying Key Factors

The key technique used to group questions into themes was factor analysis. A factor analysis identifies patterns in the value of the variables (questions) in the data, producing question groupings or "factors." These factors describe an aspect of the phenomena being studied (Vogt, 1993).

The factor analysis was repeated many times, as questions that did not fit into a factor were removed and the analysis rerun. The Cronbach Alpha reliability test was used to remove questions that diminished the factor reliability. In addition, we set a minimum Cronbach Alpha value of .70 to be defined as a factor.

The initial analysis focused on U.S. data; however, prior to completing the U.S. factor analysis, the evolving analysis plan switched to a global focus. Factor analysis results for the global organization and for each geographical area were compared in each sequential set of the analyses as questions were removed.

Several very strong, consistent patterns emerged, while other patterns were suggested. Several tests and criteria were used to guide deciding whether a single set of global factors could be created and to determine the exact content of those factors. This assessment included reliability tests, factor weightings, and conceptual consistency among the questions in the factor along with a review of the initial hypotheses and published theories about likely drivers of employee satisfaction.

A single global set of 18 factors that incorporated 94 questions was identified. Because most of our audience would never view the questions within the factors, great care was taken in naming these factors since the names would convey great meaning to our audience. The 18 factors, known internally as "scales," are listed in table 1.

One scale requires a special explanation. The *trust and respect* scale was a valid, unique factor for every grouping except the Asia/Pacific geographical area. For Asia/Pacific, the questions in this scale were diffused among the *partners, motivating work,* and *resources* scales. Presentations of the findings emphasize the global nature of the model but also include a comment about this exception. Additional analysis and discussion are needed to understand the implications of this result.

Creating the Satisfaction Model

Stepwise regression was used to identify those groups of questions (scales) that best predicted satisfaction. The following four questions were used to represent the satisfaction outcome variable. This group

Table 1. Key factors.

The 18 Scales

Career development	Motivating work	Resources
Career objectives	Ability to impact	Supervisor
Fair burden	Partners	Training
Information	Performance reviews	Trust and respect
Fair rewards	Premier firm	Work/life balance
Long-term focus	Office/team support	Work management

was established as the key outcome variable prior to the factor analysis but was subjected to the same reliability criteria as the factors.

- Overall, how would you rate Arthur Andersen as a place to work compared with other companies and firms you know about?
- If you could begin working over again, in the same occupation as you're in now, how likely would you be to choose Arthur Andersen as a place to work now?
- I am proud to work for Arthur Andersen.
- Overall, how do you feel about your relationship with Arthur Andersen?

Two key criteria were used in analyzing our data. To be included in the final regression model, a scale must have increased the R-Squared by at least .01. Also, the overall model required a minimum R-Squared of .40; thus, the model would explain at least 40 percent of the variance in satisfaction. The scales in the resulting model were called "drivers" to emphasize their role as leverage points for employee satisfaction improvement efforts.

Regression analyses were completed on the global data set as well as on several key subsets, including geographical area, employee classification, and service category. The results were conclusive, with R-Squared ranging from .62 to .69. The results were also consistent across various groupings, with the same five drivers identified for virtually every grouping. The sequence of the drivers varied slightly across the analyses; therefore, the model does not emphasize relative strength. The five drivers identified were: *premier firm, career objectives, trust and respect, motivating work,* and *fair rewards.*

As noted above, the key exception to this list was that *trust and respect* was not identified as a driver in the Asia/Pacific area. This result is consistent with the fact that the scale itself was not strong for Asia/Pacific. *Trust and respect* was retained as a global key driver with the continuing caveat that its role in Asia/Pacific must be better understood.

The final test of the model was a review by key leaders and HR professionals within the firm. They said the model "felt right" and were excited about its potential applications. The following phrase was created to summarize the model in a simple, easily remembered format: Our employees want to work for *a premier firm* where they can pursue their *career objectives* in an environment of *trust and respect* in which they have *motivating work* and are *fairly rewarded.*

Understanding the Five Drivers

To better understand the meaning and potential application of these results, each driver is reviewed below. The introductory portion of the questions is left off for brevity.

- *Premier firm.* Arthur Andersen is recognized internally as a firm that hires the best to work for the best. Therefore, it is not surprising that employee attitudes about Arthur Andersen as a premier firm have a strong impact on their satisfaction with Arthur Andersen as a place to work. The statements for response in this scale include the following:
  — partners demonstrate a positive attitude about Arthur Andersen as a place to work
  — cooperation between partners
  — Arthur Andersen insists on high-quality work by its personnel
  — meeting client needs and expectations
  — the ability of the firm to attract high-quality people
  — the reputation of Arthur Andersen compared with other similar firms in the marketplace
  — quality of service provided by Arthur Andersen to clients of the firm.

- *Trust and respect.* This scale was the driver that best predicted satisfaction in the United States. It was somewhat correlated with several other scales, suggesting that trust and respect are broad concepts that permeate many aspects of the organizational system. Statements for response in this scale include the following:
  — creating an environment of openness and trust
  — treating you with respect as an individual
  — responding to your concerns, complaints, and ideas
  — listening to your concerns, complaints, and ideas
  — applying policies and procedures consistently for all personnel
  — trusting management in your office.

- *Motivating work.* Arthur Andersen seeks to hire bright, motivated people who want to be challenged. The fact that this scale is a key driver supports the important role of the work itself in employee satisfaction. Statements for response in this scale include the following:
  — a chance to have your ideas adopted and put into use
  — a chance to do challenging and interesting work
  — the authority to make decisions in the context of your role and responsibilities
  — the opportunity to work with clients who value your contributions
  — a chance to learn new skills and develop your talents.

- *Fair rewards.* Compensation and information about compensation are important issues for employee satisfaction at Arthur Andersen. For the question on the survey about why employees leave the firm, the top response was "salary." This linkage between compensation and opinions about retention was supported by the results of the factor analysis that produced a scale combining these issues. While Arthur Andersen actively endeavors to provide market-appropriate salaries, Andersen alumni may be able to command significantly higher salaries elsewhere. In part, this may be because their years of experience at Arthur Andersen are highly valued. The statements in this scale include the following:
  — satisfaction with your compensation
  — salary increases adequately reflect performance
  — satisfaction with the information you receive about compensation policies
  — the ability of the firm to retain high-quality people
  — the actions of partners demonstrate that they are committed to retaining high-quality personnel at my level.
- *Career objectives.* This driver includes questions that emphasize the importance of the employees' role in their own satisfaction. Arthur Andersen seeks to hire talented, driven people who often have very well-defined career objectives. Some people see working for Arthur Andersen as an important stepping stone in their career and do not plan on staying more than a few years. These people may tolerate misalignment between their immediate desires and what the firm provides. Conversely, other people expect their career objectives to be appropriately addressed by Arthur Andersen. Results from questions on this scale could signal a need for the firm to develop additional career path options and to discuss individual career objectives with employees in a consistent manner. The statements and questions for response in this scale include the following:
  — I want to become a partner at Arthur Andersen.
  — Given your choice, how long are you likely to work for Arthur Andersen?
  — I am committed to the future success of Arthur Andersen.
  — My goals and objectives are aligned with my office's goals and objectives.
  — I believe I am on a defined career path at Arthur Andersen.
  — What do you think your chances are of achieving your personal career objectives by continuing to work for Arthur Andersen?

Application of the Model

The Drivers of Employee Satisfaction Model has a wide range of potential applications. The key benefit of this model is that it helps to focus attention and energies on the most important leverage points to improve employee satisfaction. Current plans for application at Arthur Andersen focus on educating leaders about the findings and working with them to integrate our findings and potential action steps into current initiatives. Several examples of how the model and findings are being used are described below.

Use the Drivers as Benchmarks to Guide Decisions

The model articulates dimensions of people management that have the greatest leverage over employee satisfaction regardless of culture, office size, or employee level. The simplest application for line management and HR practitioners is to use the drivers as benchmarks by which they can evaluate and guide decisions.

For example, in a decentralized scenario, a local management team may decide to make a change in the compensation process. Local office management could evaluate the change against the backdrop of the model, using the drivers to prompt key questions, such as: Is this decision going to be perceived as a decision that a premier firm would make? Will the change be managed in such a way as to increase the trust and respect between employees and management? In what ways might the decision change employees' perceptions about their ability to achieve their career objectives?

Educate Leadership and HR Practitioners

Arthur Andersen's Drivers of Employee Satisfaction Model was presented to the partners in November 1998. Partners were informed that the global HR team had used the model to help develop action plans for addressing the strategic people needs within the firm. Partners were then challenged to use this model to guide *their* communications with employees and were asked to "continuously act as though we are recruiting our people all over again, every day." A key next step will be to identify ongoing communication and training opportunities to educate leadership and human resource practitioners about ways to apply the Drivers of Employee Satisfaction Model.

Establish Employee Satisfaction Performance Measures

Employee satisfaction is one of the elements of the "balanced scorecard" used to evaluate the firm's performance. The model provides a helpful framework for choosing which aspects of people management should be measured at Arthur Andersen. It also provides a framework within which to construct a short, simple employee satisfaction survey that will yield targeted information.

Previous surveys were too massive to assess satisfaction as an ongoing measurement method. The model enables the selection of a subset of targeted questions that can best measure satisfaction and its drivers. Our goal is to create a 20- to 25-question survey that will be conducted electronically on an annual basis. We believe this will provide us with good data that we can use to evaluate the effectiveness of activities focused on improving employee satisfaction. Additional sampling methods may be used for more frequent feedback as needed. A systematic process is being developed for monitoring overall satisfaction on an ongoing basis.

Identify Key Leadership Behaviors

Using the key driver model, the firm is in a better position to identify people-management behaviors that will directly impact employee satisfaction as well as to acknowledge leaders who consistently demonstrate these behaviors. These desired behaviors could be incorporated into leadership development training, performance feedback tools, and even into a leadership scorecard.

Efforts to link the key driver model with findings from partner 450-degree feedback (from employees, peers, leadership, and clients) are under way.

The *partners* scale, which rated several partner behaviors, was the strongest "driver" of *trust and respect* in every grouping analyzed. Results from other internal studies showed that both partners and clients feel that "establishing trust and mutual respect in working with others" is one of the most important partner behaviors. These results emphasize that the ability to establish trust and respect is a core competency for partners in their dealings with employees, clients, and one another.

Encourage Broad Ownership of Employee Satisfaction

The HR function has the responsibility to monitor and champion employee satisfaction; however, we must consciously focus on expanding the *ownership* of employee satisfaction to all employees and leaders. Most drivers of employee satisfaction are impacted by actions of the entire organization and are not tied to specific HR practices. Partners and employees need to be educated about the drivers and encouraged to apply them constructively.

Every individual within the organization can impact employee satisfaction, positively or negatively. Messages that encourage broad ownership include the following:

- Partners, employees, and supervisors must all work to keep hiring and work performance standards high.
- Marketing should market to employees as well as to clients.
- Partners should be aware of the impact their morale and behaviors have on employees.
- Engagement teams should evaluate ways to keep work motivating.
- Everyone should take responsibility for listening to each other and building trust and respect.

Conclusion

The Drivers of Employee Satisfaction Model provides a significant advancement in understanding employee satisfaction at Arthur Andersen. Application of the model can be used to improve employee satisfaction and support Arthur Andersen's vision to be "The Greatest Place to Do Great Work." The model can also impact overall client service, since the firm's primary "products" are the services delivered to clients by employees. Employee satisfaction can significantly impact the quality of those services.

As a management tool, the Drivers of Employee Satisfaction Model has the following strengths:

- It articulates which people-management issues have the greatest leverage over employee satisfaction.
- It provides a framework to use in discussing management decisions that impact employees and for evaluating the effectiveness of decisions.
- It suggests specific areas of people management to better focus the work of HR practitioners.
- It gives guidance to management teams to help optimize people-management investments.

Arthur Andersen is optimistic that conscious attention to employee satisfaction and application of the Drivers of Employee Satisfaction Model will help the firm better manage its greatest asset—its people. The firm must now focus attention on applying the model and educating partners and employees about employee satisfaction. Key next steps include the following:

- Develop communication and training plans to help our leaders and HR practitioners use the results to better understand employee satisfaction issues and focus their improvement efforts.

- Identify those aspects of employee satisfaction which can be managed best locally or centrally.
- Evaluate the unique relationship of the trust and respect questions in the Asia/Pacific area and understand the implications for application of the model in that area.
- Evaluate the survey results for the support groups.
- Continue to advance and refine the understanding of what drives employee satisfaction through discussion and future survey efforts.

Questions for Discussion

1. What would you do to engage a new leadership team in driving the organization to respond to a survey sponsored by the previous leadership?

2. What challenges does using question groupings ("scales" in this example) present when discussing the results with clients or developing performance measures based on the survey? What are the benefits of using question groupings?

3. Causal relationships were suggested between the "drivers" and employee satisfaction. Consider the ways in which employee satisfaction can be a driver of the satisfaction with other aspects of the organization, such as satisfaction with compensation.

4. Global organizations are naturally complex and often contain mixes of centralized and decentralized leadership. How would these complexities impact the way you conduct the survey, communicate the results, and encourage action?

5. Office size in this study ranged from 20 to 2,000 people. In what ways could office size impact satisfaction? Why was it important to test this impact prior to the analysis?

The Authors

Julie E. Mann is an organization development manager at Arthur Andersen. She works as an internal consultant supporting a variety of improvement efforts, including employee satisfaction, customer satisfaction, cost reduction, process improvement, and strategic planning. Before joining Arthur Andersen, she worked as an independent management consultant and spent eight years as a manufacturing engineer. Mann holds an M.S. in management and organization behavior and a B.S. in chemical engineering. She can be reached at 1405 North 5th Avenue, St. Charles, IL 60174; phone: 630.444.4029; fax: 630.377.3794; email: julie.e.mann@us.arthurandersen.com.

David P. Boizelle is director of HR for the Central Region Business Consulting Practice within Arthur Andersen. He has responsibility for recruiting, performance management, professional development, compensation, promotion, and key HR initiatives. Previously, Boizelle worked in a world headquarters capacity developing the capability of Arthur Andersen's worldwide HR community. Boizelle holds a B.S. in administrative systems and an M.S. in instructional technology.

References

Hackman, J.R., and G.R. Oldham. *Work Redesign.* Philippines: Addison-Wesley, 1980.

Maister, D.H. *Managing the Professional Service Firm.* New York: Free Press Paperbacks, 1993.

Vogt, W.P. *Dictionary of Statistics and Methodology: A Nontechnical Guide for the Social Sciences.* London: Sage Publications, 1993.

If You Build It, They Will Come

Retail Banking

Neil Cerbone

This case study focuses on a midsize retail bank in the Northeastern United States with 5,000 employees and 350 branches. It examines the five-year transformation of the bank from Operational Centricity to Customer Centricity. It pays special attention to some of the highly effective—albeit unorthodox—techniques utilized by its leadership to facilitate the transition. All numbers and percentages are accurate, as is the course and scope of the actual intervention.

Background

This bank's parent company was experimenting with an American presence. Widely represented across the globe, the company began its U.S. business in 1985 and believed that by acquiring the "right" smaller banks it would turn a profit. By 1990, it was deeply in the red, and management began to realize that its merger and acquisition plan was not working.

The European corporate hub was about to begin seeking a buyer for the U.S. venture. It began by sending a very senior representative from the home office to survey the landscape and decide how best to dismantle the American fiasco. When he arrived, he discovered two strikingly contrasting circumstances:

- The senior U.S. leadership team was deeply ensconced in a "good old boy" management style. Extreme emphasis was placed on cen-

---

This case was prepared to serve as a basis for discussion rather than to illustrate either effective or ineffective administrative and management practices. All names, dates, places, and organizations have been disguised at the request of the author or organization.

tralized controls and rigid policies and procedures. Innovation and creativity were discouraged, and corporate conformity was rewarded.

- The line workforce was a highly spirited (if misdirected), energetic, optimistic group that reluctantly acquiesced to the autocratic bureaucracy of the senior leadership but seemed quite able and bright.

The senior executive returned to Europe and made a business case to keep the U.S. business but to replace the entire leadership team. He even agreed to take on the role of CEO of the entire U.S. bank (retail and commercial) in order to control its progress toward profitability. His first task was to find the right person to lead the retail bank. He believed this person had to be a charismatic leader with a strong background in sales. He found such a person at one of the large U.S. banks and brought him into this American experiment to see if he could "make it right."

Enter Rocco Cruz

Rocco Cruz was a dynamic iconoclast who had developed quite a reputation within the industry for producing spirited teams, focused change initiatives, and, best of all, revenue. His methods were known to be unorthodox, but no one could argue about the results. Global changes in the banking industry clearly indicated that customer centricity was the key to market dominance. He knew what he had to do.

Upon accepting his new position, Cruz's first task was to create his senior leadership team. The first position on which he focused was his head of HR—or, as Cruz referred to the position, his "chief people person." He saw this role as critically strategic and was determined to fill it from within the organization he inherited. He did not wish to hit the streets to fill the slot, because he could not risk losing touch with the line and its perceptions of the world.

Cruz found Carol Haines, a senior HR generalist who had managed to stay afloat during the bureaucratic years by managing a team of fiercely loyal direct reports. They were determined to make life easier for customers and employees even if they had to navigate dangerous and political waters to do it. Haines was street smart and savvy. She could walk into a room of strangers and give you the low-down in less than 10 minutes. She had an instinct that was almost eerie. She was exactly what Cruz needed; they met, and within 10 minutes, they both knew it. Their partnership became the mechanism that took the organization from an interesting experiment to the eighth-largest bank in the Northeast—all in five years.

Planning

Cruz and Haines were on a mission. They saw the future, and they were determined to make it happen. In hindsight, they were slightly ahead of their time.

Their planning process had a spontaneity that many confused with no planning at all. In essence, their plan was to create an organization in which every decision was made from the customer's perspective. It was the range of decisions that actually provided the plan's structure.

Decisions needed to be made regarding people, infrastructure, policies and procedures, work-flow processes, technology, and products. Virtually no stone was left unturned and no question was left unasked, even if the answers were unwieldy, unpleasant, or just plain unknown. Cruz and Haines adhered to a strict hierarchy of priorities:

- *People.* Customers were at the top of the food chain, no matter what. Much attention was paid to defining a customer experience that was able to embrace all customers, all the time. Employees came next on that list. This included all employees. The plan was to tie every individual to the customer, even those employees who worked in back office functions and typically saw themselves as removed from customers.
- *Infrastructure.* This was flattened to enable easier access for and closer proximity to the customer.
- *Policies and procedures.* These were streamlined. Risk was to be reinterpreted to include anything that compromised customer loyalty.
- *Work-flow processes.* These were reengineered to facilitate every employee's ability to consistently exceed customer expectations.
- *Technology.* This was to play an enabling role and never to become the star of the show itself. Its value was to be measured strictly by the impact it would have on the customer experience.
- *Products.* These were moved to the bottom of the food chain. Cruz understood that products could easily be replicated. In and of themselves, they were not able to differentiate his bank from any other. He expected the products to be well designed and priced competitively, but he considered that a given.

The structure of this plan was revolutionary within financial services. For instance, Citibank had put technology at the forefront of its business, and it seemed as if the rest of the industry would follow. Cruz saw it differently. And while banks historically had competed on issues of product and pricing, Cruz eliminated these issues from his vision for the bank.

As for policies and procedures, these were typically the guardians at the gate. They served to protect the bank from fraud, to minimize revenue loss, and, in general, to protect the bank from risk. Cruz's leadership suggested that lack of customer loyalty was a greater risk than failing to maintain a neat, tidy, and rigid operating framework.

With regard to work flow, historically, it was designed to provide convenience and cost savings for the organization. Cruz insisted that it be reengineered to make life easier for the customer.

Last but not least, the employees who had been previously pressured to be good corporate soldiers were Cruz's not-so-secret weapon. He absolutely believed that if he could unshackle them, he would capture their minds, hearts, and spirits—and then they would put the bank on the map. They did.

His plan took one week to structure. He and Haines worked behind closed doors and emerged after five days with the structure pictured in figure 1, along with a long list of "to do's" grouped under every component.

Figure 1. Hierarchy of priorities.

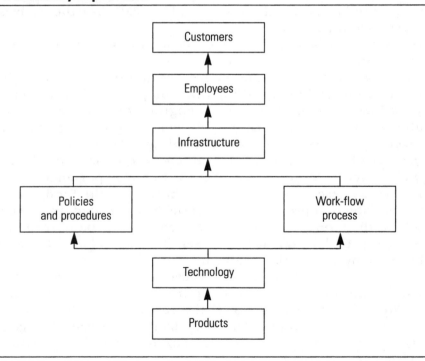

Performance Analysis

If we look to the five-level framework of performance analysis, we can see that Cruz and Haines were working on all five levels.

Level Five: Payoff

As set forth in the background section of this case study, the pay-off was to be found in a continuing U.S. presence for the bank. If Cruz and Haines could not turn a profit, the U.S. business was to be discontinued.

Level Four: Business Needs

As revealed in the planning section of this case study, virtually every component of the business was to be measured according to its impact on the customer's experience. Customer loyalty replaced customer satisfaction, and mechanisms were designed to measure that relationship. If any business unit could not prove its value to the customer, it was dismantled.

Level Three: Job Performance

Cruz and Haines enlisted the aid of three specialty consulting firms to help quantify and measure job performance expectations. They drew up a code of behavior called "the 34" because it consisted of 34 personal attributes critical to success in the new organization.

These attributes extended to all levels of the organization. Competency models, job descriptions, compensation, and incentive and recruiting processes were redesigned to emphasize "the 34." Many of these attributes, such as those listed here, were completely unheard of within the banking industry:

- courageous
- creative
- entrepreneurial
- flexible
- heroic
- independent
- information sharing
- innovative
- passionate
- perseverant
- problem solving
- optimistic

- outrageous
- self-initiating.

These attributes were then connected to behaviors within every job category so that tellers, check processors, branch managers, HR officers, and credit analysts all knew clearly what those attributes meant to them.

This process was unprecedented for virtually every employee. In many cases, it challenged the actual value systems that had defined not only their professional lives but also their personal lives. Internal pressure was increasing. That was part of the plan.

In addition, the workspace of each branch was redesigned around the customer's comfort. Permanent workstations were eliminated. All platform people staffed a "front desk," which was filled with marketing and sales materials in beautifully lit, appealing formats. The customer service representatives (CSRs) would greet each customer, and then one of them would take the customer to a space that was set up as a smaller version of the front desk. Everything had a strong focus on the customer.

CSRs were expected not only to conduct the customer's transaction but also to make recommendations and demonstrate the newly expanded capabilities of the automated teller machine (ATM) and call center services. To enhance those recommendations, the branches and call centers were required to work in harmony and partnership. Many programs were put in place to foster these relationships, including temporary job swapping. This was clearly not the bank the employees knew.

Level Two: Learning Needs

This level—uncovering the truth about the employees—was the most delicate piece of the process. Were they able to operate successfully in this new arena? If not, where were the gaps? If they were able but not willing, how would that information be revealed?

By this time, Cruz's team had extended beyond Haines and the small cadre of consultants to include Cruz's direct line reports as well as an extended HR team that included generalists, training specialists, and compensation specialists.

They decided the best way to begin was with a climate analysis and needs assessment. The assessment used traditionally managed questionnaires, focus groups, and one-on-one interviews and was conducted by one of the consulting firms to ensure nonbiased information. The results were disturbing. Although virtually everyone reported a complete endorsement of the customer centric strategy—and the data reflected complete support of Cruz and his vision—his or her behavior did not reflect that to be true.

When presented with these results, Cruz smiled and said (more than once), "If this is true, why are their knuckles so white?" Cruz, working with one of his consulting colleagues, decided that what his people needed was a solid blow to their emotional solar plexus. If Cruz could crack their smiling, rigid exteriors, his team members could uncover any underlying skill deficits and incongruities in attitude and perception. They could then go about addressing those issues accordingly.

Level One: Preference

From this point on, every exchange of information between the leadership and the line was permeated with visceral messages and objectives. How the line members *felt* was more important than what they *thought*. Cruz frequently spoke of his own fears and his insecurities. He was openly affectionate and frequently kissed his male and female colleagues hello and goodbye.

All questions were encouraged; nothing was forbidden. For instance, in a large meeting of over 1,000 branch employees, Cruz encouraged the crowd to be utterly candid. A new part-time teller stood up in front of everyone and asked, "If we are supposed to be so important—the personality of the bank—why are we so poorly paid?" The room fell silent. Cruz laughed and applauded the young man's spirit. He then gave an easy-to-understand, utterly candid explanation of comparative teller pay and the way work is valued in the marketplace. Finally, he invited the teller to meet with his "chief people person" if he wanted to learn more about pay scales and how they are determined. The audience stood and cheered.

Cruz insisted on many kinds of meetings to share information, from events designed to raise awareness and generate excitement or to boost learning and build skills to his "Ask Cruz" series, during which he visited with 30 to 40 people at a time and answered any and all questions. Cruz also installed a permanent hot line, which was accessible to everyone in the bank. Its only restriction was that all calls had to be based on customer issues.

As a result of these efforts, changes began to happen across the organization. Policies and procedures were rewritten to be more customer centric; work flow was streamlined by the people who actually did the work; product design was a collaborative process that included marketing, advertising, the back office, the branch staff, and the customers themselves; and unnecessary expenditures were reduced in many areas.

In addition, Cruz created a customer mythology, in print and verbally at meetings, by collecting and sharing "heroic" acts of customer care, such as the following:

- the area director who, when the ATM was down on a Saturday night, took money out of his own pocket to help a customer in need
- the branch manager who, during inclement weather, ran transactions to and from cars
- the teller who walked transactions to and from an elderly couple's home and bought them lunch
- the loan officer who approved an emergency loan on the spot by acting as the temporary co-signer.

Stories such as these went on and on and were often repeated. In part, this was because the structure of Cruz's intervention was built on people talking to people in informal settings as often as possible.

Methods Utilized

In addition to the meetings mentioned above, Cruz sought other, more unorthodox mechanisms—mechanisms rooted in the theater—for change. Cruz and his inner circle suspected that some sort of theatrical endeavor might provide a shortcut to the employees' emotions. As a result, three original one-act musicals were written and produced especially for the large event that ended each fiscal year:

1. The first, *If You Build It, They Will Come*, focuses on the travails of a branch manager as he struggles with the bank's changing climate. Although there are humorous components to the piece, the overall mood is somewhat dark. The manager is angry and feels disillusioned by these changes; his colleagues, each of whom is struggling as well, offer him support and perspective. The musical ends not with the manager jumping on the bandwagon but rather with him agreeing to hold on a bit longer and try to reinterpret these challenges as opportunities to do "Something Remarkable" (a song in the show).

2. The second, *Welcome to the Club*, was written to attend to the issues that originated from a major reorganization that Cruz engineered to make the bank more customer centric. While the general consensus was that the changes represented a definite improvement, there still were organizational bruises with which to contend.

Two songs in particular provide powerful reflections of the employee experience. The first, "Look What We've Done," takes a moment to look back over the year and applaud the tremendous achievements of the group, even as it acknowledges that the group is nowhere near the finish line. The second, "Easy," focuses on the incredible difficulty of committing to the changes ahead.

3. The last show, *Awakening the Magic,* refers to the next obstacle for the employees. Once the organization had recognized the value of the customer, it was time to "make the cash register ring." This was yet another daunting challenge to employees who had never seen themselves as salesmen—a term that conjured up images of smarmy people in loud sports coats foisting shoddy goods on unsuspecting dupes called customers.

The musical centers on one assistant manager as he stumbles through the learning curve only to realize that his resistance to selling is linked to factors in his personality that have plagued him throughout his life—specifically, a lack of initiative, a fear of failure, and unrealistic expectations. As he comes to terms with these issues in songs with his father, his estranged college roommate, and his ex-wife, he begins to understand that his success as a salesman is a metaphor of his success in his whole life.

Awakening the Magic was presented in conjunction with a 3.5-hour awareness-raising event called "The Simple Connection." It focused on the obstacles to selling as a primer to actual sales training, which the employees were about to begin. Cruz, Haines, and the team believed that if they just began sales training, it would be like throwing seeds on rocks. "The Simple Connection" was intended to serve as the fertile soil in which the seeds could take root.

The program was a multimedia one that utilized an audience response system (ARS) to track the employees' immediate reaction. It had a cast of eight actors and a facilitator, a role for Cruz, a starring role for actor and dancer Ben Vereen, nine basketballs, 24 slides, a live onstage drummer, and a square dance. Each piece was directly linked to a visceral learning point, which was linked to the tactical sale process they would encounter in the classroom in the coming year.

Cruz and his colleagues produced another 3.5-hour multimedia awareness raising event titled "Moment of Truth," based on the tenets set forth by Carlzon (1989). It too relied on a broad range of presentations, including an ARS, a cast of six, interactive video, and Disney and Nordstrom live case studies.

Results

The five levels of performance analysis provide a framework for analyzing the results of Cruz and his colleagues.

Level Five: Payoff

The bank remained in business for another seven years. At that point, it was sold domestically due to political machinations at the mother company that were completely unrelated to these initiatives.

Level Four: Business Needs

Overall, the bank rose from the 16th to the eighth-largest retail consumer bank in five years. Other measures of success included the following items:

- Customer complaints dropped 90 percent in the first two years.
- Channel distribution increased significantly, giving customers more opportunities to do more business more of the time.
- Wallet share rose from 12 percent to 40 percent.
- Product penetration rose from .8 percent to 2.1 percent.

Level Three: Job Performance

The focus on the customer began to permeate meetings at all levels of the organization. Friendly competition began to develop around who could come up with the strongest evidence of customer care. Managers harnessed that energy by praising not only the heroics but also "doing 100 small things right all the time." Promotions arose surrounding the number of ATM demonstrations in a day, the efficiency of customer profiling, or problem ownership and solution. People were able to see and articulate their roles as customer relationship specialists.

Level Two: Learning Needs

The most significant learning was the repositioning of sales in the mindset of the employees. Their paradigm shifted, and they began to recognize products and services as solutions that were of value not only to the bottom line but also to the creation of strong, endurable relationships with their customers.

More specifically, they learned the art of meaningful conversation. (Phrases such as "consultative selling" were avoided.) Through meaningful conversation, any gaps between sales and service were eliminated. Conversations focused on improving the relationship with the customer and often combined problem resolution and sales of products and services. It was seamless and invisible to the customer. To the employees, it was extremely empowering because they saw customer relationships as theirs to create.

Employees also developed a deep respect and empathy for each other. Because of job swapping and cross-functional learning opportunities, the gaps that had "siloed" branches, call centers, and back office support functions were virtually eliminated. Formal opportunities for these historically antagonistic groups to show their appreciation to each other were developed, such as breakfast celebrations, small tokens of gratitude, and the like.

Level One: Preference

First came the exodus. When people in the retail bank began to recognize that this was not a "flavor-of-the-month" initiative but actually a pervasive operating strategy that would require an entirely new paradigm for conducting business, a significant percentage of people (approximately 20 percent overall, with that running somewhat higher at the manager level) decided to leave. The first 18 months saw this activity across virtually every level and department.

These positions were then filled almost entirely by people whose experience came not from banking but from industries that traditionally focused on the customer (for instance, retail, service industries, and catalog companies). It was understood that the technical learning curve would be steep, but it was agreed that the benefits outweighed the risks.

After the first 30 months, the atmosphere of the bank had altered. While outposts of the old school (for instance, areas such as foreclosures and security) still existed, they were now explicitly seen as "old school," and Cruz referred to them as "the final frontier." The customer experience had replaced the operational experience, and whatever didn't follow suit stuck out.

Most measurable was a dramatic increase of customer referrals. Branch-posted revenues increased by up to 50 percent over two quarters due to customer word-of-mouth. (The employees now knew enough to ask, "What brings you to us?" based on their experience in meaningful conversation.)

You could walk into most branches and see customers and staff laughing and talking; you could monitor call center calls and hear relationships and partnerships being nurtured.

Problems and Concerns

The most significant problem in this transition was the schism that developed between the bank's retail and commercial sides. The commercial side—still run according to traditional banking practices— saw Cruz and his team as egomaniacal cowboys. The fact that they were so successful fueled the fire instead of quenched it. Their success seemed to challenge the bedrock upon which the commercial bank was based. This, coupled with a less-than-stellar performance by the com-

mercial bank, resulted in truly hostile camps. Anyone—including consultants—who tried to bridge that gap was seen as a traitor.

The commercial camp began seeking opportunities to reveal anything that even faintly suggested that the retail camp had made a
mistake. Certainly, there were things to cite. At times, Cruz endorsed
expenditures with unclear return-on-investments, and the musicals
were the target of much criticism. Cruz also recognized that in order to truly empower his people, he had to let them fly, with the
understanding that a certain number of "falls" would occur as a result. He was prepared to use those losses as learning opportunities
as well as proof of his support of all efforts exerted on the customers'
behalf—even less-successful ones. The commercial side saw it quite
differently.

On the other hand, Cruz *was* a cowboy. He didn't learn, until
well into the third year, the value of strong relationships with "those
guys." He would provoke them in meetings and challenge their conservative strategies and tactics with a fair share of arrogance. By the
time he fully recognized the damage that resulted from the missed
opportunities, it was too late. He had alienated them.

Recommendations

Recommendations must be focused on the top leadership of the
parent company. A transformation of this proportion must balance
all constituencies of the organization. Unfortunately, little activity at
the top level occurred to facilitate the relationship between the retail and commercial organizations.

Lessons Learned

The lessons learned in this case study are found not in what went
wrong as much as in what went right.

Organizations trying to implement changes such at those illustrated
here are often trapped by overly academic and overly intellectual
processes. Short-term measurements are put in place, and any performance slippage results in knee-jerk "remedial rethinking." But
the transformation to customer centricity is inherently unwieldy. Measurements will be felt in the long term. There will inevitably be short-
term losses, both in staff and revenue, because this transformation
is as much a visceral process as it is a strategic and tactical one.

There is an intuitive, amorphous component to this process that
relies on clarity of vision, perseverance, and personal and business
risk propositions. Any organization considering such a transforma-

tion would be well served to anticipate the natural tendency to overquantify the process. The shift to customer centricity must allow the somewhat nerve-racking process of trial and error, intuition, and operational flexibility.

Finally, the importance of personal fortitude and courage cannot be underestimated. People will need to behave in unfamiliar ways—and there's nothing more intimidating than that.

Questions for Discussion

1. If the company had not been sold for unrelated reasons, what impact would the schism between the retail and commercial banks most likely have had on the success of the greater organization?
2. Do you believe that a transformation such as the one described in this case requires a charismatic leader like Cruz? Why or why not?
3. If you had to conduct a similar transformation without a charismatic leader, how would that process differ from the one described here?
4. One of the programs that was developed as people began to leave the organization was called "Leaving with Dignity." Given what you've learned in this case, how would you design that program?
5. How ready is your organization for a change of this dimension? Where would you begin?

The Author

Neil Cerbone, author and cultural transformationist, founded Neil Cerbone Associates (NCA) in 1983. With his roots solidly planted in training and development, Cerbone realized early that helping his clients deliver a truly differentiated customer experience would take more than a better customer service program. As a result, NCA evolved into an organizational development firm that supports its clients through the arduous adventure called "customer centric transformation." The NCA team has worked with a number of leading companies, including Chase Manhattan, Motorola, Johnson & Johnson, Prudential, and Avon. Cerbone can be reached at 25 West South Orange Avenue, South Orange, NJ 07079; phone: 973.761.7722; email: neil@cerbonegroup.com.

Reference

Carlzon, J. *Moments of Truth*. New York: HarperCollins, 1989.

Measuring the Impact of Career Development on an Organization

Sun Microsystems Inc.

Ron Elsdon and Seema Iyer

In the fast-paced world of high technology, raw people talent separates the winners from the losers. Skilled employees can move easily from company to company. Organizational survival depends on securing and retaining this talent. One key motivating factor that connects employees to the organization is their career development. This helps align employee fulfillment with the organization's needs. This case looks at measuring how the organization benefits from investing in employee career development—as well as the paradox of how equipping employees with greater self-determination enhances retention.

Background

At the core of high-technology development today are those organizations that create hardware and software products to enable network computing. This industry sector is growing rapidly. For example, revenue growth averaged 18 percent per year from 1993 to 1998 for Sun Microsystems Inc., a major player in this sector and the subject of this study.

The heart of this industry is in Silicon Valley, California. As with many concentrated industries, a local infrastructure has developed that includes companies up and down the supply chain, competitors, and support service organizations.

The competitive stakes are high. Sun is in an intense battle with Microsoft over system standards and proprietary software applications. There are major pressures to recruit and retain employees. In 1998, Sun hired more than 5,000 new employees, many of whom were in

This case was prepared to serve as a basis for discussion rather than to illustrate either effective or ineffective administrative and management practices.

high-demand areas such as software development. Few barriers block the movement of people from one organization to another, and competitive strength comes from the knowledge of the workforce. As the chairman and CEO of another company—3Com—observed, "I'm much less worried about one of our competitors stealing the designs of our latest product than I am about one of our competitors stealing our best minds" (Benhamou, 1998).

Companies that successfully develop processes that aid in employee retention enjoy competitive advantage. This case describes the evolution of such a process and the measurement of its benefits. It also explores the issue of how to predict the optimum amount to spend on such activities.

Organization Profile

Sun Microsystems Inc. was founded in 1982 by four people in their mid-20s, who recently had graduated from college. According to Scott McNealy, one of the four founders (and now chairman and CEO of Sun), they didn't know what they couldn't do, so they went into this competitive arena and succeeded. "Kick butt and have fun" is McNealy's message to employees. Sun's culture is about having fun while employees work hard at innovation and at creating the future.

Sun's global headquarters are in Palo Alto, California. At the time of the study, Sun employed more than 28,000 people in 55 countries. Sun is a global leader in enterprise network computing, with almost $10 billion in revenues. While Sun's name is synonymous with Java, its products range from workstations and servers to software services.

More than a decade ago, Sun copyrighted its slogan "The Network Is the Computer," a vision that is now ubiquitous. Sun provides enterprise-wide solutions to businesses, enabling them to leverage information resources in a stable operating system environment. This is an area where competition for employee talent is fierce.

Currently, Sun is organized into product-based divisions, which are independent yet aligned. Supporting these divisions are core HR, finance, legal, and information technology services provided by a corporate resources group. The role of HR is constantly refined to add greater value to the organization and to keep up with the fast pace of change. HR at Sun promises to deliver a competitive workforce, a competitive organization, and a competitive workplace, commonly referred to as the "WOW strategy" within the company. HR provides a gamut of services, from conventional compensation and benefits to fitness programs and—of primary interest here—Career Services. Measuring the outcomes of delivered services and their refinement is an important element of the Sun culture.

From mid-1996 through mid-1998, while the high-tech industry experienced high employee turnover, Sun maintained single-digit voluntary turnover, despite the fact that its workforce grew by 20 percent worldwide each year.

Sun has invested in understanding what attracts people to the organization and what will retain them. Top contributors to attraction and retention include *work challenge, career development, financial opportunity, work variety,* and *commitment to people.* The importance of *career development* has been reiterated by a number of satisfaction surveys and by comments from employees.

In an environment of rapid change and little hand-holding, it is a big challenge to provide a middle ground between defined career paths and a "figure it out for yourself" approach. Working with the Career Action Center, a not-for-profit organization based in Cupertino, California, Sun developed an approach to support employees in becoming more self-reliant with regard to their careers and to identify measurable benefits to the organization.

Career Development in Organizations

The relationship between employees and organizations has evolved from the paternalistic, job-for-life corporate model in the 1960s, 1970s and early 1980s to today's free-agency model. Responsibility for career development lies first with the employee; the organization is responsible for providing support and growth opportunities. Most Silicon Valley companies, including Sun, have embraced this change, as it matches the preferences of those who have entered the workforce since the late 1980s.

In this new world, the question arises as to how the organization can best provide support. In Sun's case, McNealy views career development as "51 percent the responsibility of the employee and 49 percent the responsibility of the company." But what goes into the 49 percent, and how does the company track the value from this investment? Sun sought the support of the Career Action Center in answering these questions.

Career Services at Sun Microsystems

A great strength of Sun's approach to employee development is long-term commitment. This means continuous evolution and improvement in the process. Within Sun, the primary support resource for employees' career development is called Career Services. This consists of career counseling provided as a benefit to employees by Career Action Center counselors.

The current approach evolved from the first career center, which opened at Sun in 1991, with an initial focus on the manufacturing area and on equipping employees to deal proactively with redeployment. The center provided employees with career counseling, built around the concept of employees taking primary ownership of their career direction, supported by the organization.

This led naturally to the next evolution. Within 18 months, the focus of the center and its counseling moved firmly to ongoing career management, providing a benefit to all employees. At this point, responsibility for the center moved to the HR department, with the Career Action Center continuing to be responsible for advising on and delivering the services. The reach of the counselors was broadened; services now were offered at multiple Sun locations around Silicon Valley. Primary activities shifted from items such as creating resumes to supporting individuals in exploring their career aspirations. This included expressing those aspirations in development plans, aided by assessment instruments and workshops.

The evolution of Career Services continued, with an increase in the number of counseling sessions available as a benefit to employees (from two sessions to four); inclusion of telephone counseling to reach a distributed population; dispersion of five counselors to separate Silicon Valley facilities, as well as one on the East Coast; and increased emphasis on tracking the ability of the services to reach the Sun population and on measuring outcomes.

Today, Career Services is designed to help employees make well-informed career choices and match their aspirations to opportunities within Sun. The primary delivery approach is career counseling coupled with supportive resources and events such as one- to two-hour presentations tailored to employee needs.

Employees are informed about Career Services through a variety of channels. These include Sun's Website, career talks, email, orientation sessions for new hires, and counselors' presence at employee events. Counselors' offices are located close to high-traffic areas, and counselors are closely linked with local HR representatives. According to Carol Guterman, Sun's manager of Career Services, employees seek services that are comfortable to use, confidential, and accessible. The current arrangement addresses these elements.

The Assignment

Career Services was clearly helping individuals in their development based on their feedback to level one questionnaires. However, how was the organization benefiting, and what was the return-on-investment for this service?

Sun's vice president of HR was anxious to know the answer to these questions in order to decide where Sun's HR dollars could be best spent. At the same time, the Career Action Center saw the benefit to the career field and the community of gaining better understanding of the links between individuals and their work, as well as the impact of those links on organizations. Consequently, the organizations decided to begin a joint study to look at the impact.

The Participants

Seema Iyer brings much experience in demographics to her position as HR metrics specialist at Sun. By creating this position, Sun showed a commitment to using measurement to inform practice and a willingness to step outside the conventional box. Iyer contributes not only analytical skills but also, as a recent hire, an outside perspective that encourages and supports new approaches. Iyer is well supported by her boss, Lora Colflesh, who continually seeks to understand how her resources can be applied most effectively. Ken Alvarez, Sun's former executive vice president of HR, strongly supported using metrics to enhance the effectiveness of HR. Guterman, recently appointed Sun manager of Career Services, also is very open to new ideas and encouraging of the project, as were her bosses Gloria Debs and Susan Solat.

Ron Elsdon, of the Career Action Center, brings a combination of analytical knowledge gained in technical and business settings and career and counseling knowledge from his recent move into this area. His goal was to develop an analytical approach that supported Sun's needs and informed the career field. Elsdon's boss, Diane Saign, supported the project and assisted in securing funding, recognizing that this represents a new arena for the Career Action Center and an opportunity for the center to establish a new area of expertise. Cynthia Brinkmann, the Career Action Center's manager of the account relationship with Sun, and a member of Elsdon's organization, has been a driving force for the Career Services activity and also wishes to explore the measurable effect of the work.

Overall, both organizations supported the project, and the principals (Elsdon and Iyer) were committed to developing and implementing an effective design. The greatest difficulty was that this project was a step into the unknown with little to draw on from previous work.

Defining the Problem

The study began with the intent to understand the connections among *alignment, satisfaction, retention,* and *performance.* The purpose was to explore the chain of cause and effect between employee alignment with best work, satisfaction, retention, and business performance and measures that could describe these links. Over time, the following objectives were developed for the study:

1. Examine the rationale that by enabling people to seek greater fulfillment in their work through career development, you create value for the organization.
2. Enhance understanding of the complex linkages between employees' alignment with their best work and business performance.
3. Explore the impact of organizational career development support as one element of a high-performance work system.
4. Examine the impact of HR commitments (including Career Services) on business performance.
5. Begin exploring predictive methods to guide the future commitment of resources.
6. Explore the population demographics within a high-technology organization and the effectiveness of Career Services in addressing workforce diversity.
7. Communicate results in a graphical format that clearly shows important relationships among different elements.

Sun was ideally positioned for this study, as the organization routinely captures much of the needed data. The plan was to examine existing data sources, which would be linked together for the first time. Elsdon and Iyer examined the various types of data needed for the analysis, as shown in figure 1.

Traditional measures of business performance examine return on hard assets. In contrast, this analysis focused on employees as the primary asset of the organization. Consequently, financial measures were developed on a per-employee basis with operating income per employee the proxy for overall business performance.

The analysis began with three business units. It was soon evident that these results were valuable, so three additional business units were added. All six business units accounted for 90 percent of the organization's workforce, which averaged 18,000 people worldwide and 12,000 people in the United States during the time of the study.

Figure 1. Components of the analysis.

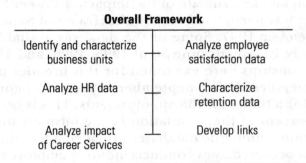

Overall Framework

Identify and characterize business units	Analyze employee satisfaction data
Analyze HR data	Characterize retention data
Analyze impact of Career Services	Develop links

Of these six business units, five were profit centers and one was a cost center. The units covered a wide range of activities, from services to advanced chip design to marketing and sales. In total, they are likely representative of high-tech organizations today.

Given the wide range of activities, the business characteristics among the six units were very different. To capture this, measures of research and development, sales and marketing expenses, revenue, assets, and operating income were developed on a per-employee basis. This required several iterations with the financial group to fine-tune the data and to ensure that the correct financial information was included.

It was necessary to define the reference population in each business unit. This was used to calculate financial information on a per-person basis and to calculate attrition, transfer, and Career Services activity rates. As some of the information was available on a worldwide basis and some was available for the United States separately, reference populations were defined for both areas in each business unit. It then was possible to relate performance and activity measures to the right reference group. When averages were needed, the midyear population number was used.

In addition, it was deemed important to assess employee demographics for the general population and for those people using Career Services. The population was characterized by ethnicity, gender, age, years of service, and grade level.

Another important aspect of the study was to look at the movement of people. This meant accessing HR databases covering transfers, promotions, and voluntary and involuntary terminations. Because retention is particularly important, this was examined in detail.

These measures provided both a base level reference for the general population and an estimate of the impact of Career Services. Detailed tracking was performed for the timeframe of September 1996 through September 1997. Some of the data was available for three fiscal years (July 1 through June 30 of 1995, 1996, and 1997); where possible, relationships were examined for this broader period.

From September 1996 to September 1997, 1,033 people used Career Services for a total of 2,138 appointments. This is between 6 percent and 11 percent of the population in the business units studied. Cross-correlation among the databases provided a measure of people movement that occurred. Sun conducts monthly employee satisfaction surveys, which cover many areas, including career development opportunity satisfaction. This information was averaged for the 1997 fiscal year for each of the business units to examine relationships that might exist.

Analyzing the Data

When the study began, it was not clear what relationships, if any, would be identified and what the strength of the relationships would be. Consequently, an analysis tool was needed that would allow manipulation of quite large data sets (several thousand records), easy visual display of results, and access to basic statistical analysis tools.

In addition, since basic mathematical modeling was planned, an analytical tool to handle nonlinear systems was needed. The systems chosen were Microsoft Excel for the data analysis and for visual display capability and Mathsoft's Mathcad7 for modeling.

Elsdon and Iyer met every two to four weeks during the two-month definition period and four-month analysis period. In the early stages, the focus was on defining data needs and checking the data for validity. In the latter stages, the focus was on the results and their meaning. The results of the study then were reviewed with various levels of management in Sun during a five-month period, and nonproprietary parts were reviewed outside Sun during this time.

A number of challenges arose in the data analysis and reporting. Discrepancies were noted between the Career Services data and the termination data; this was ascribed to some duplication and reporting differences in the Career Services data. The data source considered most reliable for a given analysis was used. Later study—a year after this work was completed—validated the approach and confirmed the conclusions. Moving the large data sets around was a challenge and required use of a zip drive. Incorporating the graphical results into reports required breaking the approximately 60 graphs into multiple separate files to allow tasks such as saving to occur in a reasonable time. Both Excel and Mathcad7 proved to be strong tools for data manipulation, modeling, and display.

Connection to Other Studies

Early on, Elsdon and Iyer addressed the question of the nature and extent of prior studies. A literature search turned up little quantitative work on the organizational impact of career development work. However, they did find a broad range of work on the impact of HR practices on business performance. The studies ranged from an academic to a practitioner focus and from an organizational to an individual, psychological perspective. Taken as a whole, they underlined the importance of this area due to the size of resources committed and the potential impact.

In addition, Elsdon made contact with others in the field who provided input on the use of frameworks, such as the five-level model, which provides a useful approach to framing the analysis (Phillips, 1997).

Summary of Results

The study addressed three primary questions:
1. How effectively does Career Services reach into the employee population?
2. What outcomes do career and HR services provide, and what is their value to Sun?
3. How is it possible to predict what to spend in HR?

One concern about reaching Sun's population was whether Career Services addressed the needs of different ethnic groups. This is particularly important given the growing diversity of Sun's employee population. As shown in figure 2, the Caucasian population, as expected, is the greatest user of Career Services, at 62 percent of the total. However, there is higher usage of Career Services by other ethnic groups, at 38 percent of the total, compared with their constituting only 33 percent of Sun's workforce. We can therefore conclude that Career Services is a valued resource used by ethnic minorities.

Another question was whether Career Services would be used by employees at all levels. By comparing profiles by grade level of those who used Career Services with the general population, it was clear that employees at all levels—from administrative to middle management—actively used the service. Similarly, when usage was eval-

Figure 2. Use by ethnic group.

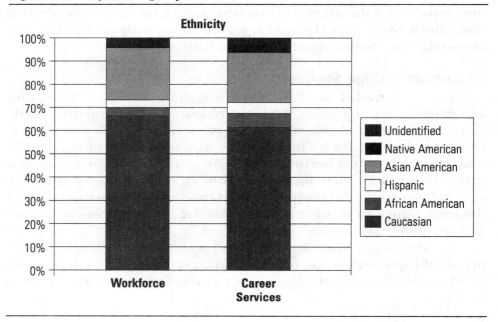

uated by years of service and age, the Career Services population closely tracked the overall population. This analysis also revealed how many employees have three or fewer years of service—and how important it is to pay particular attention to those with five or fewer years of service, as attrition is highest here.

In terms of gender usage, female clients accounted for 59 percent of all appointments, the reverse of the overall population, which is 40 percent female.

This information indicated that Career Services was used representatively. Moreover, it revealed where the focus of retention efforts should lie.

This brings us to the second question about outcomes and organizational value. The employee overall satisfaction data provided little discrimination from one business unit to another. This shows how important it is to carefully tailor satisfaction surveys to address specific areas of interest. For example, employee career opportunity satisfaction did increase significantly in those business units that spent more on HR (including Career Services). Again, however, the measures were not strongly differentiated.

Attrition provided a much more direct outcome measure. The overall attrition rate in the six business units fell noticeably as more people used Career Services, even though only about 10 percent of employees used the service during the period studied. More striking was the difference in the attrition rate for those who used Career Services and the overall population in the six business units. The attrition rate was lower by 1 percent to 3.5 percent for the group using Career Services, a large reduction for an attrition rate that is below 10 percent overall. The uncertainty in the range represents possible uncertainties in the data. The measured reduction over 13 months was 3.5 percent, and data analysis a year later confirmed that the attrition rate was lower by 1 percent on an annualized basis.

The reduction in attrition due to the use of Career Services' counseling shows how helping people align with their best work translates into a direct benefit to the organization. Moreover, the rate of attrition also fell as more resources were invested in the overall HR activity. Sufficient data was available to show a linear relationship.

This brings us to the third question: Is it possible to predict the right amount to spend on HR? Given the fact that attrition is so important to Sun and a clear outcome measure, the analysis focused on this characteristic. At this point, the study focused on possible approaches to mathematically modeling the impact of HR spending on business performance. Prompting this work was the thought that very low attrition rates increase the likelihood of stagnation in the organization, while at high levels, the costs are very high. There is likely to be an optimum somewhere between these extremes. Elsdon and Iyer developed a simple model that predicted an optimum and then looked to see whether the data supported it. The results are shown in figure 3.

While data is limited on the five profit centers studied (the diamonds in figure 3), business performance expressed as operating income per employee does peak at a midrange attrition rate. The line is a good fit of the model to the data. The model then was combined with the earlier relationship between attrition and HR spending to project an optimum spending level for HR.

Financial Impact

What does this mean financially? There are two parts to this question: the impact of Career Services and the impact of HR spending.

With regard to Career Services, it is estimated that the cost to the organization of losing one person is at least 1.5 times that person's annual salary. This includes the cost of recruiting a new person, training costs, and lost productivity. The average salary at Sun

Figure 3. Impact of HR spending on attrition.

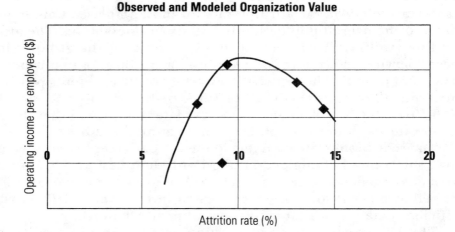

Observed and Modeled Organization Value

during the study period was $70,000 per year, which means the cost of attrition per person was about $100,000. Today, it is much higher. Thus, if you take the reduced attrition of 1 percent and apply it to the population using Career Services (about 1,000 people per year), you could expect the annual costs saving due to reduced attrition to amount to approximately $1 million.

Furthermore, for those employees in transition, the use of Career Services provides a cost-effective means of support. This is estimated to contribute another $100,000 per year relative to the use of outplacement services. As the fully loaded cost of Career Services is estimated at $600,000 per year, the return on investment is ($1,100,000/$600,000)×100, which is equal to 183 percent.

Clearly, Sun is capturing value from its investment in Career Services. This value would be further increased when improved effectiveness is taken into account. A similar analysis of the benefit of investing in HR shows this to be in the tens of millions of dollars each year based on reduced attrition.

Communicating Results

The results of the study were reviewed in graphical form with multiple levels of management at Sun. They were well received, confirming for Sun the value of the investment and providing the basis for continued support of Career Services. This analysis also helped identify those employees, such as new college hires, who could particularly benefit from focused attention.

With confirmation that Career Services was adding significant value, Sun's management now asked how the role might build in the future to further enhance Sun's competitive position. The results were also reviewed outside Sun in the career development field. Again, there was great interest in quantitative support for the impact of Career Services, although mathematical modeling is not a primary area of interest for most counselors.

Questions for Discussion

1. What are the critical issues in this study?
2. How transferable are these results to other industry sectors?
3. What are the implications for a follow-up controlled study over time?
4. What are the pros and cons of employee satisfaction surveys as a measure?
5. What other elements of value could be captured?
6. What other cost elements could be captured?
7. How could the uncertainty in the measured value be reduced?
8. How would you go about validating the model?
9. What skills are needed to implement such a study?
10. How can quantitative analyses be best communicated in the HR community?

The Authors

Ron Elsdon specializes in the career field and speaks at national conferences, publishes, and lectures in the field. He is a principal in New Beginnings Career and College Guidance and led the Career Action Center's services practice, providing career development support for individuals and organizations. Elsdon currently is an account executive with Drake Beam Morin. He has more than 20 years of experience working with U.S. and international corporations in a broad range of industries and in various senior management capacities. Elsdon holds an M.A. in career development from John F. Kennedy University and a Ph.D. in chemical engineering from Cambridge University, England. He can be reached at 61 Milano Court, Danville, CA 94526; phone: 925.838.5448; email: newbeginnings@elsdon.com.

Seema Iyer is an HR metrics specialist for Sun Microsystems. She joined Sun in 1997 and has been working on various metrics projects on staffing, compensation, and employee services for the HR operations group. Before joining Sun, Iyer worked for Adonis Medical Equipment as an HR representative and then as a demographer for the Child Welfare Research Center at the University of California, Berkeley. She holds an M.A. in demography from the university.

Note

Some of the content in this chapter is reprinted with permission from the Human Resource Planning Society from "Creating Value and Enhancing Retention Through Employee Development: The Sun Microsystems Experience," by Ron Elsdon and Seema Iyer, in *Human Resource Planning*, vol. 22, no. 2, pp. 39-47, © 1999, The Human Resource Planning Society, 317 Madison Avenue, Suite 1509, New York, NY 10017.

References

Benhamou, E. "Building a New Kind of Company for 'The New Economy'." Keynote address, given at the Career Action Center's 16th Annual Pinnacle Luncheon, 1998.

Phillips, J.J. *Return on Investment in Training and Performance Improvement Programs.* Houston: Gulf, 1997.

Workforce Education: A Staff Development Program

Pennsylvania Community Colleges

Barbara A. Frey and Gary W. Kuhne

As the community college system increases its focus on workforce education, its culture shifts to servicing the customer, marketing to area businesses, and meeting short-term learning goals. Instructors are delivering their courses to a new type of learner. This case study assessed the presentation skills of instructors before and after the intervention of a staff development program that addressed presentation skills. It is unique in that it provides empirical data on the benefits of presentation skills training to both the instructor facilitators and their adult learners.

Background

In recent years, Pennsylvania community college systems have assumed the role of providing workforce skills training to adults. According to the American Association of Community Colleges, the average community college student is 29 years old and works full-time. The fastest-growing segment of the community college enrollment is the "reverse transfer"—that is, a college graduate who is attending the institution to obtain a marketable skill. In order to fulfill this occupational role, the community college needed to reinvent itself. In short, this is not the old education system.

Many community college instructors believed that subject matter expertise was not enough to be effective trainers. Their desire was to deliver programs in a clear, engaging, and enthusiastic manner. They recognized that the ability of their participants to listen was both

This case was prepared to serve as a basis for discussion rather than to illustrate either effective or ineffective administrative and management practices.

limited and selective. Participants choose to listen—or not to listen— to the facilitators of their training. Even in the most learner-centered classrooms, facilitators must use public speaking skills in delivering content, leading discussions, and directing small group activities. When asked how they developed their presentation skills, the majority of instructors responded, "through trial and error."

In spring 1997, Ann Kozlowski of the Community College Women's Group asked for volunteers to participate in this study on presentation skills training. Eight female instructors volunteered to participate. Susan Barger, a communications expert and external consultant, was the trainer and project coordinator.

Population

Eight female instructors and their 352 adult learners participated in this study. The instructors taught full-time, had at least five years of teaching experience, and taught the same course in fall 1997 and spring 1998 to similar groups of learners. All the instructors were white, and between 40 and 59 years of age. They taught courses in math, science, and communications.

HRD Program Description and Delivery

Barger limited this pilot study to same-gender instructors in order to control variables that might influence the results. (The differences in male and female communication styles have been documented by several researchers.) Barger conducted the project in four phases over a 10-month period.

Phase One

Barger audiotaped six random hours of each instructor's classroom teaching in fall 1997. She used the audiotapes for five pretraining speaking qualities: volume, pitch, words per minute or rate, fillers per minute, and length of pauses (wait time) after instructor-generated questions.

SoundEdit 16 software was used to determine the instructors' average volume and pitch ratings. A typed transcript of the audiotapes provided ratings on the instructors' words per minute or rate, number of fillers, and length of pauses. Barger also measured the achievement and satisfaction of the learners. These measurements consisted of learners' final course grades and their scores on a satisfaction survey.

Phase Two

Following the fall semester, Barger met individually with each instructor for about three hours to review her performance data. She took a coaching role, guiding each participant through sample presentations until the individual's performance met the required standards. Each instructor established goals for improvement. At the end of the sessions, the instructor participants completed a training effectiveness survey to measure their satisfaction with the experience.

Phase Three

In spring 1998, Barger gathered the same data. She audiotaped each instructor for six hours. The audiotapes were analyzed for posttraining ratings on volume, pitch, words per minute, fillers per minutes, and length of pauses. Adult learners completed the same satisfaction survey and the achievement assessments.

Phase Four

At the end of the study, quantitative data was collected to examine the perceptions of the instructors. In a focus group with Kozlowski, the instructors discussed their motivation for participating in the training, the costs and benefits of the training, and their confidence in applying the training skills.

Costs

As a pilot study, the intent of this research was to determine the value of presentation skills training for all instructors. The study was relatively inexpensive to conduct because the volunteer instructors were not paid for their time outside of the regularly scheduled hours. As project coordinator, Barger devoted approximately 80 hours of her time toward this program. The expenses incurred in collecting and interpreting the data are shown in table 1.

Table 1. Data collection and interpretation costs.

	Amount
Tape recorder and high-bias tapes	$475
Transcription clerical worker	$260
SoundEdit 16 technician	$625
Statistician	$225
Total	$1,585

Data Analysis

The purpose of this study was to determine whether speaking skills of instructor facilitators affect the achievement and satisfaction of their learners. Barger worked with a statistician to compare the speaking qualities of the instructor before and after the training intervention by t-tests. This comparison was to show a transfer of the presentation knowledge and skills from the training workshop to the classroom. T-tests also were used to compare the adult learner achievement and satisfaction before and after the instructors' training.

Results

Overall, the instructors had a favorable reaction to the presentation skills training. Their satisfaction measured 4.68 on a 5-point scale. To determine the extent to which instructors applied their training, Barger compared the instructor speaking ratings before and after the intervention. Instructors had a tendency to improve in two qualities: the number of fillers per minute and the length of pauses. The number of years of experience, the level of education, nor the age of the instructors influenced their ratings on the speaking qualities.

When Barger compared the learner data between the fall and spring semesters, there was an improvement in learner achievement and satisfaction, but it was not statistically significant. One subgroup of learners—the younger adults—did reflect a significant increase in satisfaction. Learners who were younger than 26 were more satisfied with their instructors' teaching after they participated in the presentation skills training. A comparison of learner satisfaction scores by demographic variables is presented in table 2.

Discussion

When instructors demonstrated improved presentation skills, there was an increase in satisfaction among younger adult learners. This increase in satisfaction supports what we know of Generation X. Members of this generation grew up with the stimulation of cable television, video games, and computer technology, and they tend to crave stimulation and seek immediate answers. Therefore, they may tend to expect an engaging, animated delivery style from their instructors.

Some instructors already were exceptionally good presenters; therefore, they had less opportunity to improve their ratings. Volume, pitch, and rate were qualities that instructors had difficulty changing. They may have changed for short periods of time, but eventually they re-

Table 2. Comparison of satisfaction scores.

Demographic Variable	Fall Semester		Spring Semester		df	T
	Mean (n)	Standard Deviation	Mean (n)	Standard Deviation		
Age						
Younger than 26	4.4 (87)	0.5	4.5 (97)	0.5	182	−1.99*
26 to 50	4.7 (38)	0.4	4.6 (28)	0.5	64	0.75
51 and older	4.9 (1)	—	4.2 (2)	0.4	—	—
Race						
Non-White	4.4 (25)	0.4	4.4 (13)	0.6	36	−0.11
White	4.5 (99)	0.5	4.6 (112)	0.5	209	−0.96
Gender						
Male	4.4 (50)	0.5	4.5 (41)	0.5	89	−0.40
Female	4.5 (77)	0.4	4.6 (85)	0.5	160	−0.87
Enrollment status						
Full-time	4.5 (91)	0.5	4.6 (104)	0.5	193	−1.23
Part-time	4.4 (22)	0.5	4.5 (22)	0.6	55	0.25
Grade-point average						
3.4 to 4.0	4.6 (46)	0.4	4.7 (56)	0.4	100	−1.66+
2.7 to 3.3	4.4 (53)	0.5	4.5 (46)	0.5	97	−0.27
2.0 to 2.6	4.4 (18)	0.5	4.4 (16)	0.4	32	0.33

+ =$p<.10$; * =$p<.05$; — = results not statistically significant.

turned to their old pattern of speaking. Their rate of speaking and the length of their pauses for think-time were easier qualities to change once the instructors were aware of them.

Interestingly, the two instructors who showed the greatest improvement in their presentation skills had learners who showed significant improvement in their achievement and satisfaction. Goal setting was a particularly successful strategy used in the performance improvement process. During the individual training sessions, instructors identified speaking goals they wished to achieve in the spring semester. The goals focused on one or two of the speaking qualities that were measured in the fall. Six of the eight instructors (75 percent) changed the behavior they identified as their goal.

The instructors who volunteered for this study seemed to possess above-average levels of confidence and speaking skill. Reviewing the audiotapes, transcripts, and SoundEdit 16 printouts created awareness in speaking habits. One instructor commented, "It was so useful to have things I have been doing for years validated by someone else."

Instructors participated in this study for a variety of reasons. Most appreciated the individual coaching, which was scheduled at their convenience. One instructor stated that her motivation was "the opportunity to improve what I do." Another said, " I was excited to have an expert tell me I did this and I did not do that." The only cost associated with the training was time, but a third instructor commented, "It was time well spent."

Following the training, most of the instructors felt confident in applying the skills that they learned. One instructor said, "What I had to work on was wait time (pauses). I've been working on that and I think I've improved." A second instructor stated, "I was more than willing and I felt confident that I could go to the classroom and use the skills." An instructor who had doubts in applying the new skills said, "I almost feel I would need a coach in my classroom once a week to reinforce the skills. I don't know whether I changed much at all, although I wanted to."

Conclusion

According to the U.S. Department of Labor, the typical worker to receive training in 1995 was white, middle-aged, and working full-time and had earned a bachelor's degree or higher. Coincidentally, that describes the workers who volunteered to participate in this study. HRD professionals still need to "level the playing field" in training and development initiatives.

The two instructors who showed the greatest improvement in their skills saw significant increases in their learners' satisfaction and achievement. Therefore, it seems that additional research on presentation skills training is needed to determine its value to facilitators and learners.

This study needs to be replicated with male facilitators to determine any difference in their training needs or style. The instructors requested a follow-up study to determine their use of the presentation skills on a long-term basis. A long-term study would also allow for study on the cost-effectiveness of training. An improvement in faculty skills may affect student persistence, attendance, or enrollment. Due to the expense of individualized coaching, administrators recommended group training sessions. However, Barger strongly believed the individual coaching sessions were essential to the instructors' performance improvement.

Teaching Note

This case study appeals to the HRD practitioner. Oral communication competencies for eight community college instructors are analyzed in a logical, easy-to-understand research design. It is a quasi-experimental study with a pre- and posttraining performance comparison. In a quantitative analysis, instructor presentation skills are related to adult learner achievement and satisfaction. In a qualitative analysis, instructors' perceptions of the training are discussed.

As training is examined for the benefits it provides to facilitators of learning and the learners, students can relate to both roles. In a classroom setting, focus groups may be formed to discuss how instructor presentation skills have affected their learning or their facilitation of learning.

Questions for Discussion

1. Discuss the facilitator's role in engaging learners.
2. How does facilitator confidence affect his or her job performance?
3. What other methods could be used to measure a facilitator's presentation effectiveness?
4. Discuss the importance of participant satisfaction in creating a positive learning experience. Can a participant with a negative reaction to training still learn to improve his or her job performance?
5. What training strategies may be used to enhance transfer of training?
6. Discuss the threat of performance analysis to reluctant staff members.
7. What techniques could be used to improve long-term job performance?
8. Discuss the influence of the Hawthorne Effect in coaching and training.

The Authors

Barbara A. Frey received her M.Ed. in vocational education from the University of Pittsburgh and her D.Ed. in adult education from Pennsylvania State University. As a consultant for Cranberry Training and Development, she designs, develops, and facilitates management and professional development courses for business and not-for-profit sectors. In addition to consulting, Frey teaches HRD graduate courses in the adult education department at Pennsylvania State University. She can be reached at 100 North Pointe Circle, Suite 102, Seven Fields, PA 16046; phone: 724.772.4848; fax: 724.772.4888; email: bhf104@psu.edu.

Gary W. Kuhne received his D.Ed. in adult education from Pennsylvania State University, where he currently serves on the graduate faculty as assistant professor of adult education and coordinator of graduate programming in southwestern Pennsylvania. Kuhne is an author, educator, and consultant to both industry and government; his research and consulting focuses upon needs assessment, program evaluation, the nature of professional knowledge and expertise, leadership development, organizational analysis, and HRD in the public, private, and not-for-profit sectors. Kuhne, who is listed in *Who's Who in American Education,* won the 1995 Award for Excellence in Research and Publication from the National Continuing Education Association.

The Phone Company (TPC) Case

Telecommunications

Kenneth H. Silber

The Phone Company (TPC) decided to electronically integrate all of its data network services into a single service. This change led to a change in work process, job design, and technology. Outside consultants conducted a needs analysis to determine performance improvement needs for successful implementation of the new service. Data was collected from all groups involved in the work process through interviews, observations, focus groups, and extant data. Although the analysis initially addressed four evaluation levels, no data was available on business measures. Needs emerged in areas of information and communication, organization, performance support, skills and knowledge, and attitude. The consultants recommended that all five categories of needs be addressed for successful implementation of the new service—and that the recommendations be considered a complete systematic package of interventions. Five contracting and management problems occurred during the project.

Background

The Phone Company (TPC) provides managed private data networks to *Fortune* 1,000 companies. In the past, it provided four different kinds of services to customers. Each service had separate work groups to handle ordering, installation, maintenance, and repair. This led to the existence of 16 separate work groups that reported to four different directors, were located in several cities, and used different work processes and up to six separate computer systems.

This case was prepared to serve as a basis for discussion rather than to illustrate either effective or ineffective administrative and management practices. All names, dates, places, and organizations have been disguised at the request of the author or organization.

Customers who wanted to install new data networks or were having a problem with their data networks had to contact the correct work group. Customers who had more than one type of network might have to contact four to eight groups to get changes and repairs done to their networks.

Drivers of the Intervention

TPC decided to electronically integrate all of its data network services into a single framework. Technology would now allow all types of data networks to operate in an integrated fashion. From the customer's perspective, there would only be one TPC network transporting data. From TPC's perspective, the data would be automatically passed along the appropriate TPC network or networks according to speed and security requirements.

This change of product and service led to a change in work process, job design, and technology within TPC. Now one group, rather than four, would handle all ordering; the same consolidation would also occur within installation, maintenance, and repair. Further, those four functions would work together as a team to service customers from beginning to end. Finally, the team would use one computer system to track all of a customer's data network information, from ordering through maintenance.

At the request of the director of Integrated Data Services (IDS) and the manager of training, Silber Performance Consulting (SPC) conducted a needs assessment to determine training and other performance improvement needs for implementation of IDS. We designed and conducted the analysis project under the following charter:

- identify gaps in skills/knowledge and performance in potential IDS process/tool users
- recommend training and nontraining interventions to reduce gaps
- recommend strategies and delivery media for the interventions
- recommend implementation plan and change strategy for the interventions.

Planning for the Performance Consulting Intervention

The director of IDS, his project manager, the director's IDS tool development coordinator, the manager of training, and SPC met to develop a project alignment document. We agreed on project goals, boundaries of analysis, deliverables, measures of success, project action plan and timetable, and access to participants and subject matter experts.

Framework

The needs assessment/performance analysis collected data that fit into the following levels of the five-level evaluation/analysis framework:

- Level four. An attempt was made to collect data on the following business measures: quality (number of errors in installing a data network, number of customer calls to resolve problems); time (install a working network, repair problem); cost (installing and repairing a network); and customer satisfaction.
- Level three. Data was collected on the current and projected workflow processes, current and projected job designs, organizational structures, communication about and understanding of the projected change, and motivation for change.
- Level two. Data was collected on specific learning needs related to the work process and work flow, the relationship among different jobs and work groups, the technical skills and knowledge required to perform each job, and the skills and knowledge required to use both existing and proposed computer tools.
- Level one. Data was collected on how satisfied all participants and immediate stakeholders were with the current work process and tools, with the impending change of work process and tools, and with how the change should be structured and implemented.

Methods Utilized

We collected data through interviews, observations, and focus groups in two locations with 46 members of the following groups: core team, marketing, system development, customer care (enablement, installation), circuit design, warehouse, provisioning, problem resolution (first- and second-level and backbone).

The interviews, observations, and focus groups used a data-gathering instrument with questions related to the following issues:

- purpose of IDS
- IDS process
- IDS toolset
- roles in IDS process
- tasks performed in the role and how they are performed
- information and tools used to perform the role
- knowledge and skills needed to perform the role
- business measures
- attitude toward change.

In addition, documentation was collected as available. Documents included IDS process flow diagrams and task lists; IDS toolset diagrams, manuals, documents regarding requirements, and screen prints; current toolset manuals, screen prints, and outputs; and IDS training courses either delivered in the past or currently under development. The interview, focus group, observation, and documentation data was analyzed in terms of both high-level patterns and specific details.

Results

Although the analysis started out focusing on four levels, no data was available on business measures. Significant needs emerged in the categories of information and communication, organization, performance support, skills and knowledge, and attitude.

Level Three: Information and Communication

The following problems with communication were uncovered:

- *Incomplete picture.* Only a few people have a complete picture of the IDS process, toolset, and implementation plan. Most have only a partial (and skewed) picture or none at all.
- *Inadequate communication.* There is no adequate, frequent, universal, consistent, top-down, and cross-functional communication about the IDS process, toolset, and implementation plan.
- *Lack of opportunity for input.* Most staff members feel that they haven't had adequate input into the design of the IDS process and toolset. In addition, they feel that they haven't been listened to about how the changes in process and toolset as currently planned could negatively impact their work
- *Transition.* People across the organization don't have clarity on what is happening now; what will happen (phase one) when; and which of the computer languages used in the different locations will be used in the future.

Level Three: Organization

The following organizational problems were uncovered:

- *Corporate culture.* Four aspects of TPC's corporate culture impede the successful implementation of IDS:
  — the "hero" mentality (succeeding in spite of impossible odds, tools, and processes)
  — the "silo" organization (thinking that every customer group and every network technology is completely different and requires different people, processes, and tools to work with)

— "vertical, not horizontal organization" (almost complete lack of cross-functional communication and teamwork)

— "he's responsible, not me; here are the names of three other people you can talk to who might know" (not accepting responsibility/ownership for work results and knowledge).

- *Customer/service/platform/geography.* TPC's organizational thinking does not leverage the economies of scale of consolidation allowed by the technology, and the same tools, database, and process (with minor modifications) are used across all customers and services. As a result:

  — Groups continue to function as if their separate organizational cultural heritages still exist and make a difference.

  — Groups don't accept that each service, customer category, or service delivery platform does not require a completely different process, toolset, and organization.

  —Groups don't see that, with the new services and technology, there are no more standard offerings; all orders are some custom combination of services/platforms.

  — Different geographic locations behave differently in how they implement the process, interface with the new tools, handle role assignments, build different interfaces to the new tool set, perceive their roles and autonomy in the IDS process, and perceive the integration of their location with other locations.

- *Cross-functional blockages.* At present, TPC is not organized the way the IDS process works. For instance, there are no channels for work groups to work together in cross-functional teams. Moreover, there are no channels for work groups to communicate with each other about IDS issues (such as the IDS process, their roles in it, how one group's work impacts the work of another, and the tool set requirements and operation).

- *Change management.* There doesn't seem to be a clear process to roll out IDS phase one; deal with redundancies and incompatibilities between the current and new processes and toolsets; address the different ways groups are planning to implement the IDS process; or decide how to deal with legacy systems.

Level Three: Performance Support

There is little support for performance. Most tools are still in development; the requirements for the tools call for very little to support the performance of those using them; and conventional help is either missing or minimal.

The following specific items are missing: field description and format, job procedure steps and decision aids, context-sensitive help, process diagrams of steps, auto-task performance, legacy system translators, online documentation, gateways to Websites, people contact information, and gateway to training.

Level Two: Skills and Knowledge

The following problems were uncovered regarding knowledge level, skill level, and training:

- *Knowledge level.* People have little understanding of what IDS is and where they fit in the whole picture. Their confusion encompasses the following:
    - what IDS is, how the entire IDS process works, and how it differs from the current process
    - what the IDS services offered are, to whom those services are geared, and how IDS services relate to other TPC services
    - what their new roles in the new process will be, how that role will be different from their current ones, and how working this new way is different
    - handoffs in the process (where the information they receive comes from; where their information goes, how it is used, and by whom)
    - consequences down the road of their work (including errors and omissions)
    - whom to call for help
    - what each IDS tool is, what its function is (and how that differs from current tools), which tools it replaces (and which tools will stay), which tools it interfaces with, and how that interface takes place.
- *Skill level.* People cannot perform new job tasks, perform current job tasks differently as required by the new process, or use new tools to perform job tasks.
- *Delivery approach and mode.* Current training is generic (rather than job specific), is mostly classroom-based (rather than delivered at the workstation or work location), is scheduled (rather than delivered "just-in-time"), and doesn't differentiate between training of new hires and retraining of existing personnel.
- *Current and transition training.* No coordination exists among the different TPC groups currently doing IDS training.

Level One: Attitude

TPC is plagued by considerable attitudinal problems, including the following:

- *Workarounds.* People have grown accustomed to using—and developing—"workarounds" for current processes and systems.

  For instance, they have adapted to switching among five sessions on the screen; copying information from system to system; handwriting information on paper, Post-it notes, and file folders; making several phone calls to obtain or check information; and "throwing work over the transom" for some other work group to worry about.
- *Anxiety.* There is anxiety about any changes in the roles people play in the process; the thinking process about work; the work procedures they use now; and the tools they use now, as described above.
- *Legacy tools.* There is resistance to giving up legacy systems and tools.
- *Transition.* People felt that they did not have the information or tools they needed, as demonstrated by comments such as "We sold it before we had it" and "We get calls now, and we in the support groups have no answers. We look bad with customers."

Problems and Concerns

Five project problems occurred—one during data analysis, two just as the analysis results were presented, and two resulting from the project alignment meeting.

First, TPC did not collect any data on specific business measures. Although they had a vague feeling that it took too long to install a network and too many customer phone calls to repair a network, no data was collected about errors, costs, time, complaints, or customers lost. This made it impossible to objectively demonstrate the impact of the performance improvement interventions recommended and implemented. Fortunately, the absence of data did not stand in the way of management's approval and implementation of the analysis and the recommended interventions.

Second, just as the results were presented, and implementation was begun, TPC was acquired by another company. This created a great deal of organizational uncertainty in addition to that which already existed. It distracted senior management's attention and complicated the already existing organizational issues.

Third, since the acquiring company had internal consulting divisions that could implement the communication, organization development, performance support, and skill training components of the recommendations, a rivalry developed among consulting organizations. The internal organizations took over the project, and SPC's involvement was limited to development of a small piece of the overview training.

A key piece of information failed to emerge during the alignment meeting, causing a fourth problem. It took most of the analysis to discover that several other people in the TPC's Internal Systems (IS) department were really the key people driving the tool development, not the director's coordinator. This created the need for another series of alignment meetings to obtain buy-in for the project, information about system status, agreement to implement the recommended interventions, and delivery of the promised system.

Finally, the IDS director's project manager, the director's tool development coordinator, and the director of IS did not share the IDS director's vision of the service or belief in the importance of this study and this project. The IS director was interested in getting the system completed by a date imposed by her boss, rather than meeting the IDS director's needs. The director's two key people on the project felt threatened by the change, the involvement of the training department, and the involvement of an outside consultant. They felt they could handle this "simple training task" and didn't need any help with the training, and that the analysis study and recommendations weren't necessary for the new system and process to succeed.

As a result, they attempted to hide information or to make it unavailable during both the analysis and training design phases of the project. They sowed dissent on the project team and eventually aligned themselves with the acquiring company's internal solution teams.

Recommendations and Recommended Solutions

All five categories of needs that emerged must be addressed for successful IDS implementation. IDS will not produce the desired performance efficiencies, increased number of orders processed, reduced number of errors, increased customer satisfaction, and increased profits, given the current performance support, attitude, information, and organization of TPC.

The following recommendations should be considered a complete systematic package of interventions working together to produce the desired result—*not* a smorgasbord of ideas from which a few favorites can be randomly chosen and the more difficult or distasteful ones ignored.

Level Three: Information and Communication

There are seven recommendations under this section.

With regard to *communication*, frequent, multichannel communication is needed to give everyone the same clear picture of the IDS process, toolset, and implementation plan. Recommendations are as follows:

1. Communication should be frequent—that is, some communication every day.

2. Communication should be multichannel—that is, more than plain email-based newsletters.

Specifically, it should include all of the following: broadcast or cassette audio or video messages; in-person formal presentations by the director; informal lunchtime get-togethers; weekly group staff meetings for all work groups focused on some aspect of IDS; mailings to people's homes; presentations by work-group managers or members; presentations by certified IDS trainers; and posters showing IDS services, process, and toolset.

3. The message should be consistent—that is, everyone who talks about IDS says the same things.

4. The message should be universal—that is, any message is delivered to everyone in TPC, regardless of work group, geographic location, or organizational level.

5. Information should be delivered vertically—that is, from "top down" to the "troops." The IDS core team should generate several weekly messages and disseminate them to other directors, who in turn disseminate them to their managers, who then disseminate them to their staffs.

6. Information should be delivered horizontally—that is, from "group to group." Work groups who interact with one another during the IDS process should meet with each other to discuss IDS and how it will impact their interactions.

With regard to employee *opportunity for input:*

7. Cross-functional, cross-locational focus groups should be conducted. These groups should gather information about how the IDS process and toolsets will affect each work group, gather information for refining the IDS process and toolsets, create ideas for cross-functional work teams to implement the IDS process, create ideas for successful transition from the current to the new process and toolsets, and make people feel they are included in—rather than left out of—the design and implementation of IDS.

Level Three: Organization

The 12 recommendations in this section address a wide range of organizational issues.

With regard to *corporate culture:*

1. The "hero, silo, personal, vertical, he's responsible" thinking of TPC management needs to be changed. This can be accomplished

by making work groups responsible for their outputs tied to the bottom line and ensuring that work groups work, are responsible, and communicate cross-functionally.

2. TPC's organization should be changed to reflect what is now known about high-performance organizations.

Specifically, the following qualities should be incorporated: a shared sense of purpose, open communications, trust and mutual respect, an organizational structure that matches work process, shared leadership pushed down to level where work gets done, cross-functional teams to do work and solve problems, effective work procedures, authority and responsibility for required outputs, building on differences, flexibility and adaptability, and continuous learning.

With regard to *customers, service, platform,* and *geography:*

3. TPC should create a unified organization that leverages the economies of scale of consolidation allowed by the technology using the same tools, database, and process (with minor modifications) across all customers and services.

As part of this, separate organizational cultural heritages should be eliminated. In addition, TPC should be clear that each service, customer category, and service delivery platform does not require a completely different process, toolset, and organization. Moreover, TPC should make it clear that there are no more "standard offerings" with the new services and technology—all orders are some custom combination of services and platforms.

4. TPC should provide the entire organization a unified direction for implementation of IDS.

With regard to *cross-functional blockages,* TPC needs to create formal channels for different work groups to work with and communicate with each other. Specific recommendations are as follows:

5. TPC should be redesigned to parallel IDS process flow using cross-functional teams.

6. Team-building activities should be conducted to assist the cross-functional teams to work together.

7. Teams should be empowered to do the work they are responsible for.

With regard to *change management,* there seems to be no clear process to roll out phase 1 of IDS. This can be accomplished through the following recommendations:

8. TPC should develop an implementation plan that takes into account people's needs.

9. TPC should deal with redundancies and incompatibilities between the current and new processes and toolsets.

10. TPC should standardize the ways different groups are planning to implement the IDS process.

11. TPC should decide how to deal with legacy systems.

12. TPC should provide transition support as the organization goes through the change process.

Level Three: Performance Support

TPC needs to make one change for *performance support:* A real electronic performance support system (EPSS) should be added to underlie the IDS toolset.

Such a system has three primary strengths. First, it goes beyond help and documentation to provide support to people using tools to perform jobs. Second, it's cheaper, quicker to develop, and easier to use than training and reduces the need for training. Finally, it leads to consistent performance across workers and to fewer errors on the job.

The EPSS should contain the following elements: field description, format, and example; job procedure steps; job decision aids; context-sensitive help; process diagram and steps; auto-task performance; legacy system translators; online documentation; gateways to Websites; people contact information; and gateway to training.

Level Two: Training

The 10 recommendations in this section address training issues.

With regard to *knowledge level,* TPC employees need to know what IDS is and where they fit in the whole picture. This can be accomplished through the following three recommendations:

1. The focus of the training should be on understanding the IDS services, process, job role and task changes, and toolset changes.

2. The training should be the same for all TPC employees and provide a unifying experience for them. It should give high-level overview of IDS, including all the elements identified in the analysis as knowledge gaps.

3. For each element, individual users should be able to drill down to more detailed information.

In particular, there should be at least two levels of detail—the first for those who want a "deeper understanding" of a particular aspect of IDS and the second for those who need to know how each element will affect their job specifically. This second level of detail should be customized by new functional roles, and it should incorporate links or gateways to the EPSS and to Web-based computer-based skill training for each job.

With regard to *skill level,* this study was unable to identify specific job tasks and skills requirements for phase one of IDS or to define how they differ from current tasks and skills, as neither the toolsets nor the process flow was finalized during the study. A further task analysis is required as toolsets and process are finalized.

Once the tasks and skills are identified, the focus of the training should be on job tasks, and skill required to do them, not on the generic tools, as outlined in the next three recommendations:

4. Users should learn "how to do it" only for the job tasks they perform, instead of learning all about a particular tool.

5. The focus of the initial training for existing staff should be on the differences between the old and new ways to perform tasks. This approach is easiest to develop, shortest for learners to go through, and easiest for learners to learn.

6. How employees deal with the inputs to, and outputs from, their functions should be addressed using the overview training described in the first three recommendations in this section.

Wherever possible, skill training should be minimized, and the tools to facilitate good on-the-job performance should be included in the EPSS.

With regard to *training delivery:*

7. Training should be Web-based computer-based training (CBT) that can take place at an employee's workstation; be available on a just-in-time, as-needed, seven-day, and 24-hour basis; and allow employees to proceed at their own pace.

In addition, it should be modular (so that employees can learn just what they need and have time for); contain registration, progress reporting, and testing; be job-specific and based on job tasks; and incorporate both tutorial-based design (information, example, practice, and feedback) and simulation-based design (actual job problems to work through with coaching and feedback). Finally, it should have multiple levels; be based on entry skills and prior job and system experience so that new hires, experienced personnel, and experts can all learn something; and be hooked to the EPSS.

With regard to *current/transition training:*

8. All training efforts should be coordinated so that the same message (knowledge and skills) is delivered to everyone.

9. One set of training materials should be developed by a competent instructional designer.

10. One person from each work group should be designated to go through a train-the-trainer program that includes certification.

That person should then become the designated short-term, live instructor for the group; become the designated group coach once the Web-based CBT is on-line; and be allocated a significant portion of his or her job time to do training and coaching.

Level One: Attitude

The following seven recommendations address attitudinal issues.

With regard to *workarounds:*

1. Employees need to be made aware that the new toolset renders many workarounds unnecessary.

2. Rewards and consequences must be put in place to discourage the use of workarounds.

With regard to employee *anxiety:*

3. TPC must develop an attitudinal component that can stand alone as part of the information and communication process and be added as an introduction to the IDS overview course.

4. This component should take the form of an introductory video or Web-based program (whether in audio or print format) and should explicitly address attitudinal issues.

In particular, it should include statements by the director of IDS and various TPC employees representing all customer, service, platform, and geography groups. Moreover, it should explain why changing over to IDS is necessary for TPC's competitive edge, acknowledge the difficulties and anxieties associated with such a change, and explain how jobs will become easier and people at each level will become "more professional" in the long term.

Finally, it should explain what types of support the organization will offer to ease the transition. In addition, ongoing attempts must be made throughout the organization to offer consistent support (non-punitive coaching) through the learning curve of the new process, work procedures, thinking about their jobs, and toolsets.

With regard to *legacy tools:*

5. Sincere efforts must be made to gather input from everyone about how the IDS process and toolset will affect their jobs and to incorporate that input wherever feasible.

6. Clear statements must be made about what will happen with legacy systems (that is, whether they will remain, go away, be used in parallel, be used for *x* number of months and then go away, and so forth). These statements must be enforced uniformly across all TPC locations.

7. Clear statements must be made about what the new toolset will be, what its interfaces will be, who will use it, and how it outperforms

existing systems. These statements must be enforced uniformly across all TPC locations.

Eventual Outcomes

Management approved the implementation schedule shown in table 1. The communication and IDS product and service description videotapes were produced and incorporated into the IDS overview course. That course was developed and delivered to business unit trainers, who would, in turn, train all TPC employees. The EPSS was developed and run behind the IDS system tool. The Web-based skill training was developed and implemented.

Following the acquisition and the consultant power struggle, all additional work was done by the other consultants, and no further data is available on organization development recommendations and whether any level four and level five impact occurred based on the interventions.

Lessons Learned

SPC learned—or actually relearned—two key lessons from this project, one related to level of impact and the other to project alignment and building coalition support.
1. First, a lesson on level of impact: Despite the fact that TPC collected no quality, time, cost, or customer satisfaction data, SPC should have collected baseline data on key metrics in those four areas during the analysis study. That would have made the economic case for implementing the recommendations much stronger and provided justification for them should the project sponsor change in the middle of the project. SPC does this as standard practice today.
2. Second, a basic consulting lesson involving project contracting: SPC should have probed more deeply during the project alignment meeting about other key players and stakeholders involved in implementing IDS and about the attitudes of the director's staff toward involvement by training and the consultants. A second alignment meeting involving all key personnel should have been held to obtain project buy-in and access to resources. Further, at the first signs of resistance, SPC should have called a meeting of the entire project team and done team problem solving of the issues. This is SPC standard practice today as well.

Questions for Discussion
1. Given the problem as described initially, who would you have invited to the project alignment meeting? How would you have gotten their buy-in to the project?

Table 1. Suggested strategies for implementation.

The following strategy is most specific for the recommendations regarding training, performance support, attitude, and information.

Dates (All 1997)	Intervention	Implementation Activities
2/14 to 2/28	All	• IDS core team discusses, modifies, and approves the recommendations in this report, combining them with the organizational recommendations of the two other consulting groups • IDS core team appoints a process owner and project manager • IDS core team provides budget and other resources to support implementation of all interventions within the tight time frame required
3/1 to 3/31	Training (knowledge; skill; transition) Attitude (anxiety)	• Instructional developer develops IDS overview course and attitude video script prototypes for live delivery in classroom pilot test • Project manager identifies generic courses and instructors to address skill needs • Project manager schedules classes
3/1 to 12/31	Information (communication; input) Organization (corporate culture; customer/service/platform/geography)	• IDS core team conducts focus groups to gather input from all work groups affected by IDS • IDS core team begins and continues frequent, multichannel, consistent, universal, vertical, and horizontal communication • IDS core team begins organization interventions by communicating positions on these issues
3/1 to 4/30	Training (skill) Attitude (legacy)	• IDS core team finalizes toolset requirements • IDS core team decides which legacy tools will remain • Project manager, instructional developer, and IDS core team identify tasks and skill requirements for new process and roles • Project manager, instructional developer, and IDS core team identify gaps between current job skills and future job skills

continued on page 90

Table 1. Suggested strategies for implementation (continued).

4/1 to 4/30	Organization (corporate culture; customer/service/platform/geography; change management)	• IDS core team provides unified direction for IDS implementation • IDS core team makes appropriate organizational redesign changes (cross-functional; empowered) • IDS core team provides detailed implementation plan for IDS phase one rollout (technical and people)
4/1 to 4/15	Training (knowledge; skill) Attitude (anxiety)	• Instructional developer conducts pilot classes including attitude video (script only) and IDS overview course (live delivery prototype) with phase zero staff and one representative of each work group involved in IDS implementation • Instructional developer certifies demonstrated competence in group trainers (coaches)
4/15 to 8/31	Training (transition)	• Project manager oversees offering generic skills classes
4/15 to 8/31	Training (knowledge; skill; transition) Attitude (anxiety)	• Instructional developer develops IDS overview course for Web-based CBT and attitude video for delivery in appropriate final medium • IDS core team ensures that everyone has hardware and software access
5/1 to 8/31	Training (skill) Attitude (legacy)	• Project manager oversees several instructional designers develop Web-based skill training for the identified skill gaps in each job role
5/1 to 8/31	Performance support	• Project manager and EPSS development group selected by education manager develop EPSS underlying the IDS toolset, hooked to both the IDS overview course and skill training
5/1 to 8/31	Organization (cross-functional; corporate culture)	• IDS core team hires organizational development consultant to conduct team-building activities • IDS core team hires organizational development consultant to do organizational effectiveness work with team and upper management
9/1	Training (skill) Performance support	• Job incumbents begin to use EPSS underlying toolset • Job incumbents begin to take skill training as needed for their jobs via CBT

2. What baseline level four data would you have gathered during the needs and performance analysis?
3. What other questions would you have asked in the needs and performance analysis? Of whom?
4. Based on the situation, what other results might you have expected to find from the analysis?
5. Given the findings, what other recommendations would you have made?
6. How would you have aligned yourself with the other consultants to ensure your continued participation throughout the project?

The Author

Kenneth H. Silber is the founder and president of Silber Performance Consulting (SPC). Silber has contributed to the performance consulting and instructional fields since their inception 30 years ago, and his extensive experience has taken him worldwide to consult and advise corporate and not-for-profit organizations and to work with academia in designing and implementing performance improvement, instructional design, process redesign, and change management interventions at the organization and business unit levels. He specializes in the areas of analysis, design, the evaluation of change management, performance improvement interventions, and the transfer of skills to client organizations.

Silber holds a Ph.D. in instructional technology from the University of Southern California. He has co-authored three books, written more than 40 articles and monographs, and made more than 100 presentations. He is a life member and past president of the Chicago chapter of the International Society for Performance Improvement (ISPI) and served to redesign the HRD Institute for the Chicago chapter of the American Society for Training & Development. He can be reached at 1025 West Dakin Street, Suite 1-E, Chicago, IL 60613; phone: 773.248.0303; fax: 773.326.0673; email: wiseoldken@silberperformance.com; Website: www.silberperformance.com.

Enhancing Job Performance through Performance Analysis and Consulting

Electric Service Company

J. Patrick Whalen

This case study describes how performance improvement was achieved using comprehensive consulting and analysis coupled with various solutions. The program results demonstrate a positive effect on job performance and business impact improvements in a regional call center within an electric service company.

Background

The Electric Service Company (ESC) provides electricity service and power to several states in the southwestern United States. ESC employs approximately 6,000 employees across several states. In a recent organizational change effort, ESC closed all local offices that were open to the public for inquiries and payments. Instead, numerous pay sites (located in places such as local grocery stores, city offices, and post offices) were set up for easy payment options.

In addition, all customers now call one 800 number to handle all primary inquiries. This number feeds into one of three integrated customer call centers that employee approximately 85 customer service representatives (CSRs) each. The CSRs are responsible for helping customers with scheduling new installs and repairs, billing inquiries, credit and collection issues, complaints, outage reporting, and resident meter reads. To assist the CSRs in handling these calls, ESC implemented an integrated online reference system (ORS) that provided tutorial information on customer accounts, internal scheduling information, and procedural guidelines.

Drivers for the Intervention

One of the regional call centers was experiencing a high volume of customer complaints due to slow response time and reports of poor customer service on the phone. This call center also was experiencing a costly problem with the CSRs making credit and collection decisions with delinquent customers on an inconsistent basis.

Beth Simpson, the director of the Western Region Call Center (WRCC), contacted James Williams in the corporate training and development function (T&D), requesting customer service and credit and collections training for the 85 customer service associates. During the initial diagnosis, Simpson mentioned that she had attended the two-day customer service course designed by T&D a year ago. She said she really enjoyed it and felt it would be appropriate for all her employees. She didn't think that the credit and collections component would be difficult to customize and add in with the other training in order to keep the course at two days in length. Simpson wanted the training to begin the next month and offered in four sessions so that everyone could complete it.

Williams reassured her that this was indeed a problem that needed immediate attention. However, he requested that before they actually planned the training, he would like to investigate the causes of the performance problems further in order to implement the most appropriate solution that would have the greatest impact on her concerns.

During his initial diagnosis, Williams discovered that all CSRs received three weeks of training (including two days of customer service and one day of credit and collections) before actually being on the floor and taking calls. In addition, he found that the cost associated with the poor credit and collection decisions was approximately $13,000 per month in this one region.

As a result of these findings, Williams recommended that T&D conduct a comprehensive performance and needs analysis. This analysis would assist T&D in determining the most appropriate solution that would provide the biggest return. Simpson agreed to the analysis and requested that a very short timeframe be considered due to the presented problems. Planning began immediately.

Planning for the Performance Consulting Intervention

An essential element of a results-based analysis methodology is the up-front planning process. This planning ensures clear and concise communications and expectations of the consulting group and the client. T&D considered this planning process crucial to any program success.

For this project, the planning process included two primary up-front sessions with Simpson and selected team leaders of the phone center to establish the parameters of the analysis and discuss the primary issues that need to be analyzed. These sessions included discussions of expectations, needs of management, methods of analysis, communication schedule, preliminary costs, timeframes, and responsibilities. Based on the information gathered during these two sessions, the analysis would focus primarily on customer service skills, credit and collections, ORS utilization, and barriers to performance.

After completing these two sessions, T&D used an analysis-planning template to guide discussion topics and formulate a project scope report and contract. The report and contract were distributed to all stakeholders for signatures and final approvals. A sample of the planning template is included in table 1.

T&D used the planning document to map out the analysis project. As requested by the client, T&D implemented a rapid timeframe of 1.5 months for design, administering analysis tools, and reporting results. A sample of the document for the WRCC is presented in table 2 (please note that some of the proprietary data was not included due to management request). T&D facilitated one additional session to present the results, findings, and recommended solutions.

Framework

As in many other organizations, ESC's training budgets are increasing, development services are expanding, and upper management is requesting that corporate T&D demonstrate value-added service to the organization.

T&D recently contracted the services of an external consulting firm (Performance Resources Organization) to assist in the development of a comprehensive consulting, analysis, and evaluation methodology and strategy. T&D implemented this comprehensive results-based methodology to assist internal clients in providing the appropriate interventions and development activities that provide the biggest impact to their work units. This step toward value-added service and

Table 1. Performance consulting and analysis planning template.

Planning Categories	Information Needed and Gathered
Project scope	Problem statement Initial diagnosis information
Methods of analysis	How will data be gathered Who is responsible for what components
Communication schedule	What is to be communicated By when By whom
Client needs and agreements	What specifically is needed or agreed to By when Who is responsible for providing what
Consultant needs and agreements	What specifically is needed or agreed to By when Who is responsible for providing what
Preliminary costs and benefit projections	Labor and actual costs (including fringe and overhead) Expected outcomes and benefits
Deliverables	What is to be delivered By when By whom
Anticipated barriers	Possible causes of barriers Remedies
Project timeframes	Development and administration of analysis timeframes Data analysis and presentation of results

Source: J. Patrick Whalen, Performance Resources Organization.

accountability has demonstrated valuable returns to the organization. These returns are apparent in permanent improvement solutions, money not spent on unnecessary training, and buy-in from management.

The methodology implemented by ESC includes a comprehensive five-level analysis framework, matched with appropriate skills and impact objectives, and five postintervention levels of measurement

Table 2. Call center analysis planning document.

Project: Training and Development Needs Analysis for Western Region Call Center (WRCC)

Planning Categories	Information Needed and Gathered
Project scope	To investigate the performance issues and needs of the WRCC to determine appropriate solutions for performance improvement. Simpson made the initial contact with Williams in T&D. She discussed the need for customer service and credit/collections training due to a high level of customer complaints and poor credit and collections decisions by CSRs.
Methods of analysis	Questionnaire (from T&D); Simpson will send out memo requesting participation and importance of analysis. Interviews (T&D will design and conduct). The management team will allow participation.
Communication schedule	T&D will provide weekly status updates via email. Williams will send these updates to Simpson and the leadership team.
Client needs and agreements	WRCC will provide T&D access to their employees for the needs analysis questionnaires and interviews and will encourage participation. WRCC will meet with T&D to discuss results of needs analysis and evaluation methods and determine further courses of action. WRCC will provide an appropriate environment to ensure skill transfer (including postintervention discussions to set goals, skill application expectations) of the implemented solutions. WRCC needs to have immediate attention put on this analysis and a commitment by T&D with appropriate resources. WRCC needs to have a comprehensive report highlighting the results of the analysis and the proposed solutions.

continued on page 98

Table 2. Call center analysis planning document (continued).

Consultant needs and agreements	T&D agrees to create a needs analysis questionnaire to identify time usage of each application, level of proficiency/perceived importance, and preferred delivery style of learning intervention. T&D agrees to compile needs analysis data and formalize a report. T&D will need access to all call center employees and any pertinent existing data and records.
Preliminary costs and benefit projections	T&D salary costs for analysis = $11,120 (four consultants, daily salary of $278 each for approximately 10 days of work). Call center salary costs = $7,036 (2.5 days of meetings for leadership team at an average daily salary of $364 plus 1.2 hours for all employees at an average daily salary of $234). Costs of analysis = $18,156. Proposed benefits include cost savings (avoidance) of at least $25,000 in unnecessary training. The biggest anticipated benefit will be in reducing the costs of delinquent accounts. The dollar amount will be determined after the analysis. Additional benefits will be examined once solutions are accepted.
Anticipated barriers	Willingness of employees to provide candid data. Will have to keep process confidential and attempt anonymity. Rapid timeframe for analysis. Communication from management will assist in getting timely data.
Project timeframes	Development of analysis tools will be completed 5/19 and administration of analysis will begin 5/24. Data analysis by 6/20 and presentation of results 6/25.

to determine overall effectiveness and return-on-investment (ROI). This particular study included all five levels of analysis, as outlined in table 3.

Methods Utilized

As there was a pressing need to implement solutions to the presented problem rather quickly, ESC used three primary methods to gather data for this analysis: questionnaires, interviews, and existing records.

T&D designed the questionnaire to assess current levels of competence, causal factors of performance gaps, and support system (ORS) utilization. The call center management team and T&D created 26 detailed questions to send to all employees of the call center (a sampling of questions is presented in table 4). T&D also administered a customer service and credit and collections skill assessment along with the questionnaire to determine skill gaps. In order to ensure a high response rate, Simpson sent letters requesting participation and email reminders to all 85 employees. T&D recorded a very acceptable response rate of 88.7 percent.

T&D conducted interviews with a cross section of employees and team leaders to gain qualitative data on performance expectations, support needs, and communication issues. Two T&D employees conducted the 20 interviews following a prepared script in conference rooms at the client site. Each interview lasted approximately one hour, and the entire interviewing process took approximately one week to complete.

Table 3. Five levels of analysis.

Level	Analysis of Data
Level Five	The bottom-line impact of a problem, opportunity, or requested intervention
Level Four	The specific business measures/drivers that need improvement (such as sales or productivity; quality, excessive time, or cost)
Level Three	The types of job performance needs including workflow processes, work design structures, and dysfunctional behaviors
Level Two	The specific knowledge, attitude, and skill deficiencies
Level One	The preferences of the participants and immediate stakeholders

The management team of the WRCC provided T&D with existing data and records. This data included call volume, lost call ratios, call goals, financial reports of delinquent accounts, and customer satisfaction records.

Results

T&D categorized the results obtained from the data analysis for the four primary issues (customer service skills, credit and collections, ORS utilization, and barriers to performance) identified during planning. The corresponding analysis levels are in parentheses. The results are listed in order of importance or priority based on respondent input.

The analysis results for barriers to performance were as follows: 1. Regarding call answers, the goal was for 90 percent of calls to be logged off in 90 seconds. Respondents reported that this goal inhibits customer service, creates rushed calls, and impairs credit decisions, and 80 percent of CSRs interviewed indicated that the 90-second goal makes it difficult to provide quality customer service and make appropriate decisions. They also indicated that they are accountable and paid on the number of calls answered, the number logged off in 90 seconds, and the percent of dissatisfied callbacks (complaints), not for credit and collection decisions (level four).

Table 4. Sample of analysis questionnaire.

1. **Of the types of calls you receive, assign a percentage of time spent per day on each type:**
Scheduling new installs/repairs ____%;   billing inquiries ____%;   credit and collection ____%;
complaints ____%; outage reporting ____%; resident meter reads ____%; miscellaneous ____%

2. **How often do you access the ORS for help with each type of call?**
Scheduling new installs/repairs ____%;   billing inquiries ____%;   credit and collection ____%;
complaints ____%; outage reporting ____%; resident meter reads ____%; miscellaneous ____%

3. **The ORS could be more useful if . . .**

4. **List any barriers that could be inhibiting your performance:**

5. **How do delinquent customer accounts and poor credit decisions impact or cost ESC?**

6. **What additional skills training (if any) do you need to enhance your job performance?**

7. **Rate the level of effectiveness of communication with team leaders and management on performance issues:**

2. Data provided by the HR department and supplemented by interviews suggests that excessive turnover is a factor at approximately 19 percent per month and that it could affect monthly performance goals (level four).

3. Of CSRs interviewed, 56 percent reported a lack of effective communication from team leaders on performance issues. The data collected in interviews supported this, stating the primary focus is on performance factors other than credit and collections (levels three and four).

4. Team leaders reported that they are paid incentives based on call ratios, answer times, and customer satisfaction—not on credit and collection decisions (levels three and four).

5. Credit arrangement guidelines are not readily available for CSRs (level three).

The analysis results regarding credit and collections included the following:

1. Accounts that are in 90-day arrears and charge-offs cost an average $13,623 per month—$163,476 annually (level five).

2. CSRs are unaware of the impact of poor credit decisions on charge-offs and 60- to 90-day arrears (level two).

3. Information, deposit calculations, and guidelines are not readily available for commercial accounts (level three).

4. There is no apparent reinforcement for CSRs to make appropriate credit decisions based on ESC guidelines or expectations (level three).

5. When making a credit and collection decision, respondents refer to ORS 18 percent of the time and ask for assistance from a team leader 22 percent of the time (level three).

6. CSRs reported that the training they attended on credit and collections addressed 57 percent of skills needed to do the job, leaving a skill gap of 43 percent (levels two and three).

The analysis results regarding ORS utilization found the following:

1. All (100 percent) respondents reported that they use ORS for customer billing inquiries, and for scheduling work orders for new installs and repairs in at least 80 percent of situations (level three).

2. All (100 percent) respondents reported that they use ORS for credit and collection decisions in only 15 percent of situations, for an average of 18 percent (level three).

3. Of CSRs interviewed, 93 percent reported the lack of current updated information on ORS as the reason for underutilization (level three).

4. Of CSRs interviewed, 76 percent reported that it was easier to reference some of the information (such as routing number, codes,

and specifications) from paper reference cards on the their desks (level three).

The analysis results regarding customer service skills uncovered the following:

1. The respondents averaged skill assessment scores of 72 percent on customer service, which suggested a skill gap of 28 percent (level two).
2. One of the CSR performance evaluation components includes the number of complaints CSRs receive each month through callbacks or correspondence. Interviewees stated that they would rather appease a customer on credit and collection decisions than to have them call in a complaint (levels three and four).
3. Several respondents stated in the interviews that the 90-second log-off time inhibits their ability to provide good customer service and make good company decisions (levels three and four).
4. Existing data has shown an obvious increase in volume and the various types of calls handled by the CSRs since the local offices were closed (level four).
5. Customer complaints showed a slight trend increase since all calls were transferred to the call centers (level four).

Problems and Concerns

Presenting findings such as those listed above often raises problems and concerns.

In this instance, one area of concern involved making the case that ESC needed to readjust those deeply ingrained procedural issues that could be barriers to performance.

For example, one of the most prominent issues is the goal of logging off calls in 90 seconds. The employees in this one call center reported that 90 seconds wouldn't give them enough time to handle the variety of calls and still provide excellent customer service. As all three call centers have the 90-second goal, T&D had to collect data from the other centers on call volume and customer complaints to gain a benchmark.

Moreover, regional directors from the other call centers demonstrated reluctance to change the 90-second log-off goal even though they were experiencing similar issues. They were concerned with actual monetary value and savings to the company by raising the ceiling for the log-off goal. They stated that the goal had been in place for some time and weren't sure that it needed to be changed. One director added, "The problem isn't the goal but the amount of people. We need more people." Finally, one of the indicators for the performance incentives for call center managers is to maintain an average

90-second log-off time by employees. Unless the incentive was going to change, they were unwilling to change the time.

A second area of concern involved findings of problems with employee turnover and the lack of management skills in ESC's three call centers. In this case, turnover or management skills were not an initial concern for the scope of analysis. The data surfaced in the interviews and through existing staffing data. As a result, T&D made a request to explore these issues more thoroughly, in order to determine the impact on the day-to-day operations of the call centers and to implement appropriate solutions. In this instance, the difficulty lay in trying to determine which solutions to implement for WRCC even as additional time for further analysis was being requested.

Recommendations and Recommended Solutions

T&D recommended six primary solutions to WRCC based on the analysis data:

1. Restructure incentives paid to management and performance measures for the CSRs in order to reflect the various performance criteria that impact ESC (such as credit and collection decisions, customer satisfaction, and call volume). Eliminate incentives that are counterproductive to performance.

2. Investigate or pilot a change in log-off goals to give CSRs more time to work with customers and to enhance the value of their decisions.

3. Improve team leader performance coaching and communication with employees.

4. Update all necessary components of ORS with appropriate information. Investigate having at least one employee responsible for coordinating updates and similar changes. Analyze the ease of use of ORS compared to current time constraints. Analyze the option of upgrading the ORS to run on a different integrated platform that will be more efficient and user-friendly. (ORS currently operates on a mainframe system with the customer information screens.)

5. Implement a skill-specific half-day training module for call center employees to address the skill gaps on customer service and credit and collections.

6. Allow further analysis to determine causes and solutions to turnover and the specific skill gaps of management.

Objectives

It is standard business practice on consulting projects for T&D to create outcome objectives of any recommended solutions to provide the client with benchmarks and evaluation criteria. T&D and the management team of the WRCC created the objectives for this study based on the results of the initial analysis and needs of the client organization.

After implementing the recommended solutions, WRCC should:
- reduce wasted cost of unnecessary training
- reduce the cost of accounts that are delinquent or in 90-days' arrears by at least 28 percent within three months
- increase utilization of ORS in the different call type categories
- decrease callbacks and written customer complaints by 11 percent within three months.

Eventual Outcomes

One of the primary issues was the log-off goal of 90 seconds. Simpson agreed—for a three-month pilot program—to increase the log-off goal to 120 seconds. She had to agree not to penalize the management team's incentives based on the pilot results.

The pilot timeframe was also used to evaluate any hidden costs associated with increasing the time (such as backlog, lost calls or hang ups, customer wait time, and customer satisfaction). Of these hidden costs, customer wait time was the only one to show a significant increase (with an average of nine seconds). In contrast, the volume of lost calls remained the same, and customer callbacks regarding wait-time decreased during the three-month evaluation period.

Simpson considered this pilot a success. She is attempting to increase the log-off goal to 120 seconds as well to change the incentives.

The client requested that T&D calculate the eventual outcomes for this case based on cost avoidance of the original training request by Simpson versus the proposed training solution and analysis costs.

The cost for two days of training (on customer service and credit and collections) would have cost ESC $43,520 in employee time and materials with very little opportunity to evaluate the impact or isolate any other factors contributing to the problem. The proposed half-day skill-specific course will cost $11,045, and the analysis costs for this project were $18,156 (for a total of $29,201). Thus, the savings would be $14,319 ($43,520 − $29,201).

T&D provided this figure per the client request; it does not include postprogram evaluation data or any measurement data of implementing the other recommended solutions. However, it did support the value of up-front analysis—and in this case, this data helped obtain buy-in for additional analysis.

An additional objective was to reduce the cost of accounts that are delinquent or in 90-days' arrears by at least 28 percent. Three primary solutions were implemented during the three-month pilot program—the half-day training, the new log-off time of 120 seconds, and the new focus on credit and collection decisions by management. During these three months, the cost actually decreased 37.3 percent or $5,081 per month, for an annual projected savings of $60,977. Unfortunately, no attempt was made to isolate any of the other secondary factors that might have influenced this drop (such as providing job aids for credit guidelines, increased coaching and communication efforts of team leaders for credit decisions, and general awareness).

Customer callbacks and correspondence fell by 16 percent during the three-month evaluation period. This result exceeded the expectations of management. The data suggested the greatest source of this reduction (12 percent) was in the complaint categories of "not enough time spent with customer" or "employee did not adequately handle customer concern." This supported the WRCC management decision to increase the log-off goal to 120 seconds. The WRCC management team attributed the additional 4 percent reduction to the overall implemented solutions or improvements.

Simpson agreed for T&D to analyze the issues of turnover and skill gaps of the management team in the WRCC.

Unfortunately, WRCC was unable to update the ORS or restructure the management incentives during the three-month pilot program. ESC considered these to be corporate-wide decisions that would require further investigation. Thus, results regarding increased utilization of ORS or the benefit of restructuring incentives to bring them in line with performance expectations are not available.

Conclusion

Although this performance consulting and analysis project was successful, it was not without its challenges, and several lessons were learned.

Perhaps the most painful lesson involved confronting ingrained corporate issues that needed to be changed. As most consultants can testify, this is not an easy or favorable task. T&D might have been more successful initiating these changes if they had collected more corporate-wide data and had involved the additional stakeholders in the initial phases of the analysis. This might have helped gain the necessary buy-in up front and helped the additional stakeholders to see the potential benefits of the proposed solutions.

A second lesson involved the difficulty of recommending that the client carve out more time for additional analysis based on the results of a just-completed analysis. In this case, once the issues of turnover and management skills became apparent, T&D should have amended the analysis plan to include these components. Usually, the client either isn't patient enough or doesn't have the time to wait for any additional analysis.

Fortunately, Williams convinced Simpson to implement some of the various solutions so that some action could get under way. She could then see some tangible benefits before moving forward with an additional analysis project. The concept of "analysis to paralysis" is now a concern, and T&D will have to make every attempt to gather data in an unobtrusive way while still maintaining the integrity of good data.

One of the most important lessons involved the need to properly plan to isolate various factors that could influence the results. Several factors could have contributed to the increase in customer satisfaction and the reduction in the cost of poor credit and collection decisions. Unfortunately, no process was set up to gather evaluation data that could isolate and pinpoint each factor's impact. Therefore, T&D had to report the data in very general terms, which opened the door to greater error in analyzing each intervention's contribution to business results.

Questions for Discussion

1. What are the various factors that led to the success of this analysis?
2. What steps did T&D take to ensure management support in the process?
3. How could the processes and methods in this case be improved to isolate the additional influences on the recommended solutions?
4. How could the concept of "analysis to paralysis" be a factor?
5. What additional evaluation methods could be used to help measure the impact of this intervention?
6. How can consulting and training organizations gain the support of line management to assist them in analyzing, designing, implementing, and evaluating appropriate solutions?

The Author

J. Patrick Whalen is the senior consultant of learning and consulting services for Performance Resources Organization. Whalen consults with a broad range of organizations on evaluation methodology, establishing evaluation strategies, conducting business impact studies, identifying needs, and return-on-investment (ROI) projects. He conducts workshops on performance consulting, needs analysis, assessment, measurement, evaluation, and the ROI process. His primary experience has been as both an internal and external consultant of HR and performance enhancement programs across various industries. His principal consulting focus has been in measuring the performance of individuals, teams, systems, and the overall business impact of HR interventions. Whalen has authored and co-authored several articles and chapters on measuring ROI, improving job performance, results-based budgeting, and performance consulting. He has master's degrees in industrial organizational psychology and in counseling and sports psychology, and he is licensed as an HR professional. He can be contacted through Performance Resources Organization; phone: 918.760.7703; email patrickwhalen@worldnet.att.net.

Using a Performance Analysis to Influence Employee Turnover

Jeans, Inc.

Tim Hatcher and Kit Brooks

Many performance analyses use quantitative methods to identify general performance problems. Yet few performance analyses are implemented to address a specific HR problem using qualitative methods to collect and analyze data. This unique case describes a performance analysis that used qualitative methods to analyze and influence excessive operator trainee turnover in a midwestern textile manufacturer.

Background

Jeans, Inc., a textile manufacturing company located in a midwestern metropolitan area with a regional population of approximately 100,000, was one of several plants reporting to a large international corporation. Jeans, Inc. was plagued with an annual employee turnover rate that neared 90 percent.

The 35-year-old plant employed approximately 600 employees including managers, supervisors, maintenance workers, trainers, operator trainees, and sewing machine operators. About half of the employees were union members. The workforce was primarily female (83 percent) and ethnically diverse (approximately 70 percent Caucasian, 18 percent Hispanic, 9 percent Asian American, and 3 percent African American).

The regional employment picture included a low unemployment rate of 2 percent to 3 percent coupled with limited availability of skilled and semiskilled labor. General employment opportunities in the re-

This case was prepared to serve as a basis for discussion rather than to illustrate either effective or ineffective administrative and management practices. All names, dates, places, and organizations have been disguised at the request of the author or organization.

gion were low-wage, low-skilled jobs and limited technical and service-oriented employment. A recent influx of Hispanic workers into the region had placed additional pressure on an already saturated unskilled and semiskilled labor market. Thus, high turnover was a problem for all the low-skill, low-wage employers in the region.

Employee turnover is a costly performance problem, even in relatively low-skill-based industries such as the textile industry. It is estimated that the annual per-person cost of turnover ranges between $1,200 and $20,000, depending on the position, and may be as high as $40,000 (Mercer, 1998; Taylor, 1998).

While the plant's management team was concerned about the excessive employee turnover rates, no strategy existed to address the issue. The operator turnover rate of approximately 84 percent per year negatively impacted the plant's ability to meet the established efficiency ratios. Of greater concern to the plant manager, many operator trainees failed to complete their training probation. Thus, fewer new operators were available to replace those who left the company. The plant manager estimated that turnover cost the plant approximately $100,000 a year through increased overtime and the plant's inability to meet production and training targets.

The plant manager had discussed the turnover problem with a workforce literacy consultant who directed the in-house education program. During this discussion, they decided that the local university might have the resources to address the turnover problem. Consequently, a faculty member with expertise in performance consulting was contacted. As a result of initial meetings between the faculty member, the consultant, and the plant and personnel managers, a project was agreed upon that would analyze and identify the influence(s) of turnover. The following is a comprehensive description of this project, the performance analysis.

A performance consulting team consisting of six members and a team leader was created to conduct the performance analysis. The members consisted of a faculty member with performance consulting and applied research experience, an experienced workforce consultant pursuing a doctorate, and five additional doctoral students with varied experiences working in business and industry. All team members had varying knowledge of performance analysis methods and most of the members had knowledge of quantitative or qualitative research methods. Team members also received graduate-level credit for their participation in the project.

Planning for the Performance Analysis

Planning for the performance analysis resulted in a three-phase approach of preanalysis, analysis, and postanalysis and intervention. However, due to time constraints, the team decided not to implement phase three. Each phase contained several steps as outlined in table 1.

The planning process took approximately three weeks. The entire team met a minimum of two times per week for several hours. The team met with the plant personnel manager on three occasions, and the team leader (faculty member) met with the plant and personnel manager two additional times.

Team planning meetings used processes such as brainstorming and focus groups. Because team members were receiving graduate credit for the project, the project schedule was configured to coincide with semesters—that is, approximately 15 weeks. The project schedule consisted of two consecutive semesters, with the majority of phase one and two planned for completion during the first semester.

The initial project was designed and scheduled for completion within six to eight months. However, due to the transient nature of team members, complexity of the performance problem, and plant constraints in implementing interventions, the entire three-phase project extended over 30 months. After completion of phases one and two (approximately six months), the team disbanded and the faculty member continued as sole consultant for the duration and completion of phase three.

Framework of the Performance Analysis

The conceptual model or framework used in this study was a general performance improvement process with the following steps:
- performance analysis
- identify applicable intervention(s)
- design and develop intervention application
- implement
- evaluate the process.

The level four business measure that required improvement was the reduction of excessive employee turnover. Improvement of the measure was critical because it contributed to decreased plant efficiencies and fewer trainees completing the training curve (the time it took a trainee to achieve minimum efficiency on a given operation). For example, operators were given a two-week period to reach a 70

Table 1. Performance analysis plan.

Performance Analysis Phase	Steps
Preanalysis	1. Review of literature related to turnover 2. Review regional employment picture 3. Become aware of culture and turnover-related issues
Analysis	1. Collect data from various sources 2. In-process data analysis 3. Assure trustworthiness 4. Analyze all data
Postanalysis and intervention	1. Report results of phases one and two to plant key personnel 2. Draw conclusions and make recommendations from phases one and two 3. Analyze and decide on intervention needs 4. Sequence and implement interventions 5. Collect and analyze data from interventions 6. Draw conclusions and make recommendations 7. Report findings to key plant personnel

percent efficiency rate on simple operations, while more complex operations allowed a 21-week training period with a lower efficiency rate.

Additionally, level one preferences of stakeholders, such as the type of training preferred by the operators, were identified during the preanalysis.

As the performance analysis progressed and interventions were implemented, job performance needs, such as supervisor behaviors (level three) and learning needs of the trainers (level two), and additional preferences of stakeholders, such as trainees' preferences for a particular training method (level one), were identified and addressed. Thus, while the project was planned to include limited data collection, additional levels of performance were identified and required additional data collection as the project progressed.

A review of literature indicated that the traditional method to address excessive employee turnover was the application of a single intervention, such as increased wages or job redesign. A literature review uncovered no performance consulting approaches that addressed a specific performance problem through application of a performance analysis and multiple interventions designed to minimize or correct the problem.

Please note that interventions were implemented not during phases one and two but only in the third and final phase. Beyond the need to reduce excessive employee turnover, the performance analysis sought to answer the conceptual question of "How does a performance consulting process influence employee turnover?"

Data Collection Methods

Performance analyses generally use quantitative approaches such as surveys and questionnaires to collect data. There were three reasons why qualitative methods such as interviews, observations, and extant data reviews were preferred over quantitative methods for this project:

1. The nature of the work environment, the complexity of the performance problem, and its relation to training dictated a deeper level of understanding of the phenomenon of turnover than quantitative research might produce. A fundamental characteristic of qualitative technique is its in-depth exploration of a phenomenon and its context (Denzin and Lincoln, 1994).

2. Results of the literature review indicated less-than-satisfactory results on reduction of turnover using traditional quantitative measures.

3. Team members had qualitative methods expertise.

The primary qualitative method used in this project was the case study. The case can be an event or an entity that is explored (Yin, 1994). In this project, the entity or phenomenon under investigation was employee turnover. The context of the study was a textile organization and the employees who were affected by the phenomenon. Employee turnover in this study was defined as turnover of sewing machine operator trainees.

In addition to the observations, interviews, and document collection, a written survey was used to gather attitude- and reaction-level data from selected employees. This quantitative method was necessary to obtain an extensive amount of information from a large number of prospective employees. Thus, this project used both qualitative and limited quantitative methods.

The performance analysis used several different data collection methods. In the preassessment phase, plant extant (existing, historical) data such as personnel records and regional employment statistics were collected and analyzed. In the analysis phase, one-on-one formal interviews and nonparticipant observations were performed. During the postanalysis phase, formal and informal interviews and observations were completed. (Nonparticipant observation was defined as observation by an individual, such as an external consultant, who wasn't directly influenced by or involved in the phenomenon under investigation.)

Interviews and nonparticipant observations were conducted with employees who were directly related to or affected by the phenomenon of employee turnover. This purposive sample was necessary to ensure that information-rich cases would manifest the phenomenon and it is a common qualitative procedure (Patton, 1990). Over 45 employees were interviewed or observed, including the plant manager, plant supervisors, operator trainees, "leavers" (former employees), incumbent operators, maintenance employees, trainers, bargaining unit representatives, and the plant personnel manager and staff. Collected data was confidential and participants' anonymity was protected through a university-required "human subjects used in research" procedure.

Standardized open-ended and scripted interviews were conducted with leavers, the plant and personnel manager, personnel staff, trainers, operator trainees, and supervisors. The interview process was planned and piloted prior to actual interviews. Interviewers were coached on ways to minimize bias and ensure trustworthiness of the data. This included exploring the proper use of scripts, questioning techniques, methods to effect rapport between interviewer and interviewee, and methods to ensure data consistency.

With the exception of interviews with leavers, formal interviews were conducted either on the job site or in areas adjacent to the production floor. Leaver interviews were conducted over the telephone using similar methods to ensure data quality.

All interviews were audiotaped or documented (or both) and included information on the employee and the context of the interview (such as date, time, place, and surroundings).

In addition to standardized open-ended interviews, many informal conversational interviews were documented to support and validate the more formal standardized interviews. Informal interviews usually were spontaneous and unplanned. Team members used contact notebooks to document and summarize important issues or themes that emerged during the informal interviews and all subsequent employee contact. Using the same techniques, individual interviews and interviews and observations with small work groups were undertaken to enhance data trustworthiness. (The concept of trustworthiness is expanded below.)

Observation as a data collection method served to provide rich information on firsthand exposure to the day-to-day experiences and behaviors of employees and helped consultants recognize the activities and physical aspects of the situation. Observations were conducted during several situations, including during meetings, lunchtimes, breaks, training sessions, informal on-the-job conversations, and production work.

Observers neither actively engaged employees nor consciously interfered with routine or common activities and dialogues. Observation protocol was discussed with observers prior to observations. Thus, they were aware of the limitations and possible influences of observations on employees and conducted observations in an unobtrusive manner. For example, observers used the same "language" and clothing of the plant workers as much as possible without seeming contrived or patronizing.

Observation was continuous and occurred during all phases of the performance analysis. Several hundred hours were spent in the plant by the consulting team and the team leader. This prolonged engagement between the consulting team and the employees was essential to ensure trustworthiness of the data collected. Prolonged engagement also served to increase familiarity and build trust among the team and the employees.

The review of extant plant data included personnel documents such as turnover and absenteeism records. All personnel records were considered confidential, and the data collected or documented was not traceable to specific employees.

The most useful existing data was extrapolated from approximately 50 exit interviews completed by employees who left the company. These records contained written textual input from the former employees. This rich data provided insights into why people left and helped to identify the primary problems and issues that influenced their decision to leave. It should be noted that as part of the analysis phase, several leavers also were interviewed by the consulting team.

In addition to personnel records, extant data such as flyers, operations specifications, production records, safety reports, memos from plant management, various bulletin board documents, and memos and news from corporate headquarters were reviewed. Employee response to these documents was observed and documented.

Qualitative methods have been criticized as being somewhat subjective in data collection. Ensuring data trustworthiness is a common qualitative procedure that addresses the problem of subjectivity. Data trustworthiness is concerned primarily with credibility (the accuracy of the identity and description of the study's subjects), dependability (the extent that the research design or analysis fits the phenomenon under study), and confirmability (the extent that the data is consistent with the study's findings) (Lincoln and Guba, 1985; Patton, 1990).

Trustworthiness in this performance analysis was established through the following:

- the use of a variety of data sources, prolonged and persistent engagement of the consultant(s) with the phenomenon (in this instance, turnover)
- a clear audit trail that used a numeric coding system to ensure that data can be traced back to its specific source(s)
- triangulation of data, the use of multiple perspectives to interpret single sets of data
- member checks and peer debriefings, which included cross-checking the accuracy of findings and interpretations with the people giving the information and debriefing with team members who had knowledge of performance analysis methods and turnover.

In addition to qualitative data, quantitative data was collected using a written survey during the postanalysis phase as part of the pilot test of a realistic job preview (RJP). The RJP process was one of the interventions for levels three and four. An RJP is any method that gives prospective employees a balanced picture of the job that they would be expected to perform. The objective of the 13-item RJP survey was to obtain feedback from prospective employees on the extent to which they felt a 10-minute videotape, showing a realistic depiction of an operator's job, benefited them in deciding whether or not to continue the selection process. A total of 123 surveys were completed by prospective employees over a three-month period.

Results

Findings of the performance analysis are categorized and discussed following the three planning phases of preanalysis, analysis, and post-analysis. The framework for levels one through five are identified and discussed within each of the three planning phases. A brief review of how the data were analyzed precedes the discussion of results.

Results may refer to quotes and references to data sources. For clarity and traceability the following codes are used: I = interview data, D = documents, and O = observations. Numbers following letters refer to the line numbers of textual data. This coding scheme supported the audit trail mentioned above and ensured trustworthiness.

Data Analysis

The goal of qualitative data analysis was to identify patterns in the data. Interviews, observations, and extant data reviews were documented. All lines of qualitative data received a code to ensure traceability. All data was reviewed and reduced to identify categories, find connections between categories, and select core categories and validate others (Strauss and Corbin, 1990).

Open, axial, and selective coding were the three types of coding used to reduce raw data, such as transcribed interview data. Open coding is a process of breaking down, examining, comparing, conceptualizing, and categorizing data. Axial coding reconfigures data after open coding by making connections between categories. Selective coding requires selection of a core category and relating it to other categories (Hatcher and Ward, 1997).

Qualitative and quantitative data were put into and manipulated by either a qualitative software package or a statistics software package running on a personal computer. Descriptive and inferential statistics were calculated on the survey items, including demographic data such as gender, age, and ethnicity.

Preanalysis Phase

The preanalysis phase included activities designed to familiarize the consulting team with the context of the phenomenon under investigation. Results of the literature review related to turnover, review of the regional employment situation, and awareness of culture and turnover-related issues within the plant are discussed below.

The review of related literature conducted by the performance analysis team revealed that turnover was a common problem in the textile industry and that certain variables such as job satisfaction and work commitment were related to employee turnover. Few studies were located that examined the influence of training on turnover, and most of the research focused on a single intervention, such as an increase in pay or benefits, to reduce turnover.

Review of the regional employment data indicated that low unemployment, coupled with a recent recruitment of Hispanic workers into the region by a local business, had impacted many employers by increasing turnover in lower-paying, low- and semiskilled job categories. Interviews with plant and personnel managers revealed that they felt one of the contributing factors in the organization's high turnover was the "tight labor market in the region" (I-38). The plant personnel manager supported this by stating that "The labor market here is making it impossible to get good people and to keep them . . . they can quit us in the morning and go down the street and have a job paying about the same that afternoon" (I-139).

The review of employment data helped the research team better understand employee turnover within the textile industry in general and its immediate impact on regional employment. It also helped team members to analyze possible causes of turnover. The employment data and literature review were considered when the research team developed possible interventions during the postanalysis phase.

Prior to the actual analysis, the research team spent time in the textile plant talking with operators, trainers, and other key employees and observing key activities. These informal activities spanned a three-week period during the planning phase of the performance analysis. In addition to familiarizing the consultants with the plant culture, these activities enabled them to assess employees' attitudes toward the turnover problem and the performance analysis team's involvement in that problem. This period of familiarization served to build trust, a critical part of qualitative data collection.

The preanalysis activities provided a contextual framework for the analysis and postanalysis phases and uncovered level one needs of stakeholders. The participants in the analysis became more familiar with one another and with the turnover issues that were being investigated. An outcome of the preanalysis activities was the discovery that many employees had ideas about possible causes of turnover, and they seemed relieved that the analysis team was, according to a trainer, "finally getting something going . . . on turnover" (I-24). Suspected animosities or skepticism toward "university types" and their ability to produce meaningful results seemed to be reduced by the preanalysis phase. For example, the plant manager remarked on several occasions that members of the team were focused, professional, and "regular people." Conversely, not all participants seemed convinced about the team's competence or ability to change things in the plant during the preanalysis.

The preanalysis phase also served to augment the cohesiveness of the consulting team. As with many teams, the choice of members was somewhat arbitrary, in that members were graduate students at one university. Members had no prior experiences working together as a team. The preanalysis gave them opportunities to work through issues such as minor personality conflicts without jeopardizing the analysis.

As stated earlier, several meetings with management and other key employees occurred during the preanalysis phase. These meetings resulted in identifying the following key issues that were subsequently addressed:

- the employment situation in the local region should be examined
- confidentiality of all participants in the study must be ensured
- the effectiveness and role of the organization's orientation program should be investigated.

A secondary result of these meetings and several informal follow-up meetings was to gain management and employee commitment to the project and to provide a sense of urgency to the turnover issue. Plant turnover rates during the preanalysis averaged approximately 75 percent (D-111, D-119).

Analysis Phase

The analysis phase included collecting data from various sources, in-process data analysis, assuring trustworthiness, and final analysis of all data. It took place during the approximately 26-month period following the preanalysis. For example, as part of the RJP, the intervention identified in phase three, a review of literature and performance analysis was completed prior to implementation of interventions.

Using qualitative methods, data was collected on an ongoing basis. On two occasions data collection was suspended for a brief period while results were formally shared with the client. The first report was completed and presented by the entire team after phase one and the early stages of phase two. At the conclusion of phase three, when multiple interventions had been implemented and analyzed, the faculty member presented a second report.

Data was collected from various sources previously identified (plant management and so forth). Collecting data from such diverse sources is a dynamic process, and it doesn't occur in a linear or lock-step manner. Consultants must constantly alternate their attention between the data being collected and the various inferences and paradigms made during prior phases of the performance analysis. A paradigm is a mindset or way of viewing or making meaning of a phenomenon such as turnover. This data collection was primarily concerned with level four business measures that required improvement—that is, employee turnover and its effect on the plant's ability to meet production and training goals.

Coding of data allowed the consultants to develop an overall theoretical framework for the analysis that would otherwise be difficult or impossible to accomplish with such a large amount of textual data. For example, the axial codes in table 2 were the basis for selective codes that formed the theoretical framework of the project. This means that as data was collected, axial codes—the broad constructs of the study—were developed and reviewed constantly against selective codes that resulted from the axial code analysis. Selective codes included performance analysis, interventions, and organizational leadership and climate. Each of these codes were further defined and their relationships clarified.

Miles and Huberman (1994) suggested that data be displayed so that consumers of the data can draw their own conclusions, thus enhancing the trustworthiness of the data. For example, table 2 shows the relationship between the phenomenon under investigation (turnover), the various contexts under which it occurred (work and employment environment), the ongoing strategies that affected turnover, and the consequences of interventions.

The performance analysis was a causal condition that influenced the phenomenon of employee turnover and was a focal point for the plant's leaders and employees to finally begin addressing the problem of turnover.

Prior to the performance analysis, the plant manager had discussed turnover with the personnel manager, line supervisors, and key employees (D-5), yet no action plans or proposed solutions to the problem had emerged.

The data indicated that employees and management had perceptions about turnover, its impact on the company, and the proposed performance

Table 2. Relationship among axial codes.

Phenomenon	Context	Intervening Conditions	Action and Interaction Strategies	Consequences
Turnover	Regional environment	Labor market	Interventions	Train trainers
		Leadership	Redesign effort	Train supervisors
	Organizational environment	Corporate pressures	Rumor of plant closure	Job restructure
	Corporate and industry environment	Organizational climate		Change communication strategy

analysis. For example, a trainer remarked that "all you hear about is how the place is going to shut down" (I-87), and an operator said that trainees "don't stay long enough to make the curve" (I-49). Plant management remarked that the analysis might "help us figure out what's causing them to leave" (I-52), and a supervisor said, " I don't think studying it is going to help; it's an attitude problem" (I-10).

The performance analysis resulted in a general profile of the organization and of employee turnover. For example, employees felt that the "company is real good to their employees, benefits-wise" (I-63), and that pay was acceptable, even for leavers. Leavers cited other reasons for terminating employment, such as the following: "I didn't know what I was supposed to do" (I-142). "It was hard to get to the efficiencies they wanted . . . the trainer was never around to help when I needed it" (I-161). "My supervisor didn't help me and the trainer was always doing something else" (I-211).

Turnover-related results from the analysis phase revealed the following:

- overall turnover in the plant was approximately 7 percent per month, or 84 percent per year
- turnover was highest in two of the eight production lines in the facility
- approximately half of former employees ("leavers") were female Caucasians; approximately half were male Hispanics
- turnover occurred predominantly during the first 21 weeks of employment and orientation training was thought to be a possible contributing factor (Hatcher et al., 1995).

Results indicated several possible influences of employee turnover. The primary influences were operator and trainer training (a lack of skills and knowledge of operator trainees and operator trainers was identified). Additional influences included management and supervisory issues, such as lack of valid supervisor job descriptions, and organizational communications, such as plant-level communication from the plant manager to the workforce, and orientation training. Appropriate interventions for each of the possible contributors to turnover were considered and discussed with plant management.

As a result of the analysis to this point, the level four business need was expanded to include level one preferences of participants regarding the perceived influences and possible solutions to turnover and level two learning and training needs of supervisors and trainers.

Due to the trainers' identified lack of skills and knowledge and the suspected impact this deficiency had on operator training, it was decided that further analysis of this problem should "produce the best and fastest results" (I-70). Consequently, a more thorough analysis of all eight trainers was conducted.

The trainer analysis used the same performance analysis methods as previously discussed, but included an emphasis on on-the-job observations. Each of the eight trainers were observed and formally and informally interviewed by members of the performance analysis team over several weeks. In addition, operator trainees, trainer's supervisors, and employees such as maintenance workers who interfaced with trainers were interviewed. Data collected included written and audiotaped notes of observations and documented responses to informal interviews.

Analyses of transcribed and coded notes and interviews uncovered the following problems with training:

- Trainers were required to perform many other production duties besides training. For example, a trainer supervisor remarked that trainers were used for "a lot of things that don't have to do with training" (I-226).
- Trainers were not very competent, and some were not considered competent as operators. For example, a maintenance worker remarked, "Some of them don't have any business being trainers" (I-441).
- Trainers were not given enough time to perform required training duties. A trainer said, "I don't have time or even know the best way to train sometimes. A difficult person is hard to teach" (I-619).
- Trainers had difficult jobs because they not only had to train multiple individuals but also were expected to be proficient at various production operations within the plant.

The analysis phase served to identify possible influences of turnover that weren't identified by plant management or key employees. The analysis also served as a method to build trust between key employees and the consultants. This prolonged engagement facilitated trust-building and enhanced communication and understanding between all parties involved in the turnover issue.

Postanalysis Phase

The postanalysis phase began shortly after the team's report to management on the project's first two phases. The postanalysis phase included reporting results of phases one and two to key plant personnel, drawing conclusions and recommendations from phases one and two, analyzing intervention needs from the data, sequencing and implementing interventions, collecting and analyzing data from interventions, drawing conclusions and making recommendations, and reporting findings to key plant personnel.

During the postanalysis, the level four business need was again expanded to include level one preferences of participants regarding possible influences of turnover and how they might be alleviated through interventions. The postanalysis phase also identified level two learning and training needs of supervisors, trainers, and trainees.

The research team developed a report of findings that included preanalysis and analysis activities, up to and including the trainer analysis. A presentation of major findings was made to management and key employees and a written report of significant findings and recommendations was submitted to plant management (Hatcher et al., 1995).

Immediately following this report, the team leader (now the sole consultant) reviewed plant turnover data. Overall, plant operator turnover had decreased approximately 10 percent during the analysis phase (D-159-160).

Additional analysis was required to develop effective interventions from conclusions and recommendations generated during phases one and two. For example, upon completion of the report, the consultant asked key employees questions concerning the validity and usefulness of the performance analysis and what they thought should happen next. Results from informal interviews with employees both directly and indirectly involved in the analysis revealed the following perceptions:

- The analysis disclosed more information than many thought it would.
- Employees were surprised that "university people could do something that was real" (I-148) and not so theoretical.
- The results of the performance analysis were not surprising, in that several interviewed employees felt that they already knew the causes of turnover and thus the analysis activities to date simply validated those assumptions.
- The analysis should stop, and ". . . something's gotta be done to fix turnover, not just analyze it to death" (O-622).

As a result of the preanalysis and analysis phases and the emphasis that plant management placed on the identified primary influences of turnover, critical next steps of identifying and implementing interventions to minimize the turnover problem were completed.

As the trainer analysis had received prior attention, it was decided that management and supervisory issues and organizational communication would be examined next, followed by an examination of operator trainer interventions and orientation training. Plant management believed that the implementation of one or two interventions would provide the best and most expeditious return on investment and that the performance analysis had produced sufficient evidence to warrant the implementation.

Several interventions were identified and discussed for each of the four influences of turnover (supervisory issues, organizational communication, trainer issues, and orientation training). The consultant facilitated discussions using nominal group-type methodologies that resulted in consensus on which interventions to use.

The four influences of turnover and their implemented interventions are as follows:

1. *Management and supervisory issues.* Results of interviews with key employees revealed that supervisory-related interventions—such as identification and review of specific job responsibilities with each supervisor and reallocation of production responsibilities for key supervisors—should be addressed first.

The job responsibility review required an examination of job specifications by plant personnel staff followed by a brief review of job responsibilities by each line supervisor. Interviews with supervisors revealed that they seemed gratified at the prospect of providing feedback in establishing their own job responsibilities. One supervisor said, "I can't believe that they are finally letting *us* have a say in this" (I-210).

Supervisors revealed their beliefs that their job responsibilities needed to be revised to reflect actual tasks being performed. As a result, the consultant modified supervisor job responsibilities and had each supervisor review and give feedback on quality and validity. Revised job responsibilities were forwarded to the plant personnel manager. As overall turnover rates remained stable during this time period, this intervention did not appear to influence employee turnover (D-189, D-196).

The reallocation of production responsibilities for key employees may have affected turnover. Using the revised job responsibility data, key supervisor responsibilities such as reducing the dependence on trainers for production duties were carried out. Results of observations of and interviews with key supervisors and their subordinates revealed that they believed the intervention was beneficial and had an effect on turnover. For example, one long-time operator remarked that she could "tell a difference in how things were going . . . when she came over to our line . . . it was better almost from the start" (I-257).

The data supported the effect of this intervention for a short time, as the production line that implemented the intervention saw approximately a 15 percent reduction in turnover (D-210). However, within two months following the implementation, the turnover rate in this production line had returned to previous levels (D-220).

2. *Organizational communication.* Organizational communication, the second influence on turnover, required implementation of the following interventions: a reduction in the amount of communication-oriented paperwork; revision in the use of the plant electronic public address system; and increased use of supervisors and trainers as "communication conduits" between management and the plant workforce. Each intervention is discussed below.

Results of interviews with and observations of employees and supervisors revealed that the organizational communication interventions were considered worthwhile. Respondents perceived the introduction of the electronic bulletin board to be especially valuable. The new bulletin board had bilingual capabilities and all messages were transmitted in both English and Spanish.

Shortly after the electronic bulletin board was installed, the paperwork reduction and supervisor communications interventions were simultaneously executed. A microcomputer system had been installed recently in the plant offices. The system included intranet, internal and limited external email capacity; word processing; spread sheets; and access to corporate-related engineering, production, and quality data. Observations revealed that the computers had limited use by supervisors and trainers and were used almost exclusively by plant management and engineering personnel (O-429, O-501).

The intervention that focused on supervisors and trainers assuming the role of "communications conduits" was discussed with key employees and management. It was decided, that supervisors needed training in interpersonal and organizational communication skills in order to be successful in that role. Informal interviews with and observations of supervisors and trainers indicated that they disliked prepackaged training programs (I-791).

As a result of this negative experience with purchased training, increased production pressures, and consistent plant closure rumors (O-974), management decided that the supervisors' training should be developed specifically for their needs and that it should take place after the other interventions were implemented and their effects on turnover were evaluated. Unfortunately, due to timing and priorities for other interventions, supervisory training was not implemented and its effect on turnover was thus not applicable.

During the paperwork reduction and public address system interventions, overall turnover rates declined by approximately 3 percent (D-1229). However, because several interventions were carried out simultaneously, one was omitted, and there were limited observations and interviews, it was not possible to segregate the specific effect of any one intervention on employee turnover.

Overall labor market trends in the region fluctuated from a low of 2.2 percent unemployment to over 5.5 percent. This increase in unemployment may have had an impact on turnover in that more people were seeking employment, which may have affected employees' decisions to stay or leave.

3. *Operator and trainer training.* Interventions consisting of developing trainer job descriptions and "train-the-trainer" and skills training for trainers were discussed and implemented. The rationale for development of trainer job descriptions was that the data indicated that trainers, supervisors, and trainees were unclear on precise duties of the trainers.

Trainer job descriptions were drafted; all eight trainers were reviewed and their feedback regarding the draft was solicited. Several experts in HRD simultaneously analyzed the revised trainer job descriptions.

The plant manager hired an external consultant who specialized in operator skill development and train-the-trainer programs in the textile industry to develop a train-the-trainer and trainer skills training program. Comprehensive training in operator and train-the-trainer skills was conducted over a 20-week period.

Observations by the performance analysis consultant of training sessions and informal interviews with the skills trainer and operator trainers revealed that trainers were satisfied with the training program and "impressed with the trainer's knowledge" (I-610). Interviews with trainers focused on the extent to which learning new skills affected their trainees' abilities to learn and whether they felt the training program affected operator trainee turnover. For example, one trainer said about the trainer, "He's real good at making stuff easy to understand" (I-600), and another trainer said. "I thought I knew the specs, but I was doing some of them wrong . . . it helped me to teach them" (I-721). Trainers indicated that the training had an effect on turnover. One trainer said, ". . . my girls are getting it faster than before" (I-697); another said, "I've had them all week and I think they may all make it, with maybe one that won't" (I-688).

Interviews with and observations of the trainer/consultant revealed that he thought the trainers needed refresher skills training and some specific techniques for training "difficult" trainees (I-1120).

During the train-the-trainer program and for approximately one month after completion of the training, overall plant turnover fluctuated slightly (plus or minus 1 percent). However, one production line's turnover rate increased by approximately 10 percent (D-1330, D-1389). Observations by the consultant of the operator trainer assigned to this production line revealed that the trainer might not have been as comfortable with the transfer of skills training as the other trainers. Additionally, the production supervisor for this line exhibited fewer supportive behaviors toward the trainer than the other line supervisors (O-440, O-822, and O-579). Therefore, although trainer skill development was important to management and the trainers, it didn't appear to have an immediate influence on turnover.

4. *Orientation training.* Development and implementation of an RJP process to be used during orientation training was the final intervention addressed. Turnover within the first 21 weeks of employment was identified as an important issue during the analysis phase.

Further analysis was conducted prior to selection and implementation of the RJP intervention. These additional analyses included observations, extant data review, and formal and informal interviews with personnel involved in and impacted by the orientation process.

Results of these additional analyses revealed the following:

- the orientation process was inconsistent and conducted over a several-day period
- although approximately 50 percent of trainees were Hispanic and observations revealed that English was their second language, orientation was done primarily in English with a part-time Spanish interpreter
- participants perceived orientation training to be too lengthy (I-1230), objectives not clear (I-1303), and content too complicated (I-1342).

Prior to the orientation analysis, a review of literature on orientation training and turnover revealed several studies that suggested that an RJP conducted as part of an orientation program positively influenced employee turnover, especially within the first few weeks of employment (McEvoy and Cascio, 1985; Meglino et al., 1988).

Results of the analysis of orientation training, time constraints imposed by management, and knowledge of the workforce supported the use of a videotaped RJP. The video was developed and pilot tested as part of a planned overall revision of the orientation process, not as an independent intervention. That is, following results of the pilot test of the RJP videotape, the entire orientation training process would be revised, pilot tested, and implemented.

Upon completion of the videotaped RJP, a pilot test was planned and implemented. The pilot test consisted of a written survey completed by all prospective employees. Once prospective employees viewed the RJP videotape, they were given the option to self-select out of the hiring process or move on to the next phase.

The RJP survey was developed based upon the previous reviews of literature on RJP and turnover and was pilot tested and revised in English and Spanish. The original survey had 20 items; the revised survey used in the study had a total of 13 content items and four demographic items on gender and ethnicity.

Items on the survey asked questions about the videotape's objectives, clarity of information, quality, to what extent the videotape helped prospective employees make a decision about working for the company, and whether the videotape helped them understand the operator job. Each item included a five-point rating scale that ranged from high agreement to low disagreement.

The revised survey was used weekly for approximately six weeks. A total of 123 surveys were distributed, and 99 surveys were completed for an 80 percent response rate. An analysis of survey data revealed that the videotape was easy to understand, was of high quality, and its objectives were clear. In addition, it helped prospective employees understand that the company would be a good place to work, helped prospective employees know more about the company and the job, and helped reduce turnover.

Plant turnover rates during the RJP intervention activities declined approximately 22 percent (D-398-D-402). During this time, the majority of new hires were assigned to one production line that had a history of higher-than-average operator turnover (D-119, O-128). Employee turnover rates of trainees in this production line declined approximately 40 percent during this same time period (D-421). Again, however, unemployment rates in the region remained higher than average and may have had some effect on employee turnover.

The plant manager abruptly suspended the RJP process after only six weeks of use. Several external and internal events forced plant management to cease all turnover-related interventions, including the RJP process. These events included:
- escalation of an ongoing, large-scale redesign process within the plant initiated by corporate leadership
- several local and national labor-relations issues that required immediate attention

- a reinterpretation of immigrant hiring procedures that resulted in over 24 Hispanic workers simultaneously quitting, which drastically inflated turnover rates
- pervasive and persistent rumors of an imminent plant closure.

The action and interaction strategies mentioned in table 2 were evidenced in these internal and external factors. The plant manager discussed with the consultant on several occasions the impact of both the redesign effort and rumors of possible plant closures on the turnover efforts. The plant manager indicated that the redesign effort "was having some adverse effects on our ability to work with the bargaining unit" (I-3311) and that "the objectives of the redesign are not being made clear to everybody involved" (I-3337).

The issue of plant closures surfaced during several conversations around the future of the facility. The plant manager said, "I don't really know what will happen . . . I just hope we aren't doing all this effort for nothing. It just wouldn't be fair" (I-1238).

Further discussions between the consultant and the plant manager resulted in an understanding that the RJP videotape and other interventions would be reinstated when "things settled down" (I-2223). Unfortunately, it became clear to the plant manager that the issue of an imminent plant closure was "more than just a rumor" (I-2224). Finally, all turnover reduction efforts and interventions were indefinitely suspended by the plant manager in anticipation of the inevitable plant closure. The plant was permanently closed less than one year later.

In summary, the plant turnover rate at the beginning of this study was approximately 84 percent annually. During the study the turnover rate remained consistently lower. In some cases, for a short time period of time, it dropped to approximately 35 percent (D-2224). Overall, employee turnover averaged approximately 60 percent for the duration of the study. Therefore, turnover was reduced by approximately 24 percent (D-2229, D-4478, I-3173).

Problems and Concerns

No performance analysis or case study is flawless, and several problems and concerns arose during this analysis. The consultant and the employees involved in the analysis identified four concerns that may have influenced the project outcomes:

1. Participants were concerned about the possible outcomes of the analysis from the very start. Because this workforce was generally unaccustomed to "outsiders"—especially outsiders from a university—

they were wary of exactly why the consultants were there and questioned whether there might be some "hidden" management agendas.
2. Employees were fearful of possible repercussions from the results of the analysis phase. This especially worried the trainers. They interpreted the identified need for additional training as management questioning their abilities. In the work culture of this textile plant, ability was a highly respected attribute. To alleviate this attitudinal problem, the consultant explained to the trainers that if they had better skills in training and in performing operations they might be able to positively affect the turnover problem and their trainees would not be quitting all the time. Thus it was in their interests to enhance their skills. This seemed to ease the trainers' concerns that management felt they were not skilled workers.
3. Once the preanalysis and partial analysis phases were completed, the consulting team disbanded and the faculty member became the sole consultant. This caused some initial confusion for some plant employees who had developed a relationship with team members. The consultant made a point to enter into informal dialogues with these employees whenever possible and thus was able to eventually gain their trust and support. In addition, the shift from a team approach to a sole consultant caused problems with accessibility and workload on the part of the consultant. This reduction in consultant hours spent in the plant was one of the causes of the extension of the postanalysis phase. Even so, the change from multiple consultants to a single consultant may have improved the quality of results in that there was consistency in interviewing, observing, and maintaining uniformity in understanding the study's paradigms over a long period of time.
4. The consultant was especially troubled by the external events that may have had a mitigating effect on the performance analysis. For example, the rumor of imminent plant closure was rampant throughout the plant during the performance analysis project and was most tenacious during the postanalysis phase. It is reasonable to assume that this had an effect on the project outcomes. It not only served as a continuing intervening strategy but also appeared to be a psychological barrier for employees involved in the many change processes attempted during the postanalysis phase.

Beyond the concerns of the consultant and employees participating in the performance analysis, several methodological problems and concerns were identified:
1. One of the criticisms of qualitative methods is its lack of generalizability or the inability to generalize findings from a sample to a larger population or from one analysis or setting to another. How-

ever, due to the rigor by which this performance analysis was accomplished, results of this study may be transferred to similar contexts. That is, similar organizations with excessive turnover may experience similar results from a similar analysis using the same methods, if the other influencing variables, such as regional employment rates, are comparable.

2. In addition, there was concern over assuming a pure cause-and-effect relationship between implementation of interventions and a reduction in turnover rates. Because of the many intervening variables in evidence in this performance analysis, it is unwise to draw absolute conclusions that one or more interventions directly caused a reduction in employee turnover.

3. The final area of concern was that although organizational leadership and climate were identified as contributing factors in the initial coding, the data did not support these concepts as having a significant contribution to the phenomenon. These concepts were not actually grounded in the data and were not systematically conceptualized (Strauss and Corbin, 1990). These discrepant cases are based on inadequate amounts of evidence and nonconvergence of the data and should be isolated and studied.

Problems such as evidentiary inadequacy can cause erroneous assumptions and false interpretation of data. One explanation of this anomaly may be the effect of the performance analysis and the use of the RJP on the phenomenon under study. In other words, the strength of the performance analysis and the RJP may have overridden the influence of other concepts such as organizational leadership and climate within this particular time, place, and context. Another plausible explanation of the discrepant case may be that stresses caused by redesign efforts and persistent rumors of plant closure could have had an influence on employees' decisions to stay with or leave the company, although this notion was not fully supported by the data.

Lessons Learned

Several important lessons were learned as a result of this analysis. First, this performance analysis addressed employee turnover in a textile-related facility as a multifaceted performance issue. This means that performance was defined as the result of multiple actions or influences. It also identified various influences of turnover through a performance analysis and through the results of implementation of multiple interventions that were designed to alleviate high turnover of operator trainees over a relatively long period of time.

One-dimensional interventions should be avoided in performance analyses designed to address complex HR problems such as employee turnover. Multidisciplinary causes of turnover generally are addressed with single-pronged interventions. Beer (1996) found that limited methods resulted in a single intervention being applied with minimal results. Additionally, Swanson and Zuber (1996) found that a naive overreliance on employee surveys as a single data collection process resulted in a failed organization development intervention. Thus, multiple methods and interventions should be used to solve complex performance problems (Beer, 1990, 1996).

The analysis served as a catalyst for plant management and, especially, the plant manager to begin a plant-wide focus on the issue of employee turnover. As a result, the performance analysis served as a causal condition for the problem of employee turnover.

Prolonged engagement was an important factor in building trust and obtaining trustworthy data. The continued collaboration among the consultant, the plant manager, and several key employees over an extended period of time strengthened the relationship between analysis, development of interventions, and the performance analysis results.

Additionally, the consultant's ability to gain almost unlimited access to the plant for the duration of the long-term study was a constant reminder to concerned employees that the issue of employee turnover was unresolved. One possible conclusion is that a performance analysis may be a possible vehicle for consultants and others to study workplace issues requiring deeper and more meaningful investigations than surveys or questionnaires can typically produce.

In addition to prolonged engagement, the overall rigor of the methods used in this performance analysis may have mitigated some of the concerns around the cause-and-effect issue discussed above. Observing and constantly tracking quantitative data such as turnover rates during a performance analysis and implementation of multiple interventions may enhance the legitimacy of critically viewing the relationship between a given performance problem such as employee turnover and specific interventions.

Again, it is important to reemphasize that the causal relationships between a performance analysis, subsequent interventions, and employee turnover may be ambiguous if not misleading. It may be overly simplistic to assume that implementation of any intervention has an absolute, direct, and causal effect on a specific performance problem such as employee turnover. However, to disregard a qualitative, holistic approach to employee turnover as was accomplished in this project belittles alternative ways to view and solve ubiquitous HR problems that are absolutely necessary in complex and ever-changing organizations.

Conclusion

The results of this performance analysis have implications for HRD professionals interested in addressing employee turnover or any other specific HR problem as part of a performance improvement process. Since the multiple intervention approach applied in this project appears to have influenced turnover, HRD leaders should take note that primarily quantitative, cursory analyses coupled with single methods or one-dimensional interventions may have inconsistent and even unfortunate results (Swanson and Zuber, 1996). It also is interesting and meaningful to reflect upon this performance analysis in light of the many environmental variables—such as the labor market and rumors of a plant shutdown—that had a potent, albeit indirect, influence on the analysis and results.

Future performance analyses might focus more on environmental variables, both internal and external, and identify the impact they have on turnover and other HR issues. Finally, rigorous analyses and the use of multiple interventions may provide a better return on the extensive resources and efforts required to impact the dramatic financial costs of employee turnover.

Questions for Discussion

1. Within Jeans, Inc., trainee turnover was a symptom of what internal and external factors?
2. What was the primary factor identified by the performance assessment as contributing to trainee turnover?
3. Why was a qualitative research design appropriate for this project?
4. Why would a multiple intervention approach to a performance problem be preferable to a single-pronged approach?
5. What methods could be used to determine the impact that external events had on the project outcomes?

The Authors

Tim Hatcher is associate professor of HRD in the department of occupational training and development at the University of Louisville in Louisville, Kentucky. Hatcher is a frequent contributor to the training and HRD literature. His primary interests are in performance improvement processes that positively impact organizational social responsiveness. He can be reached at the University of Louisville, 348 School of Education Cardinal Boulevard, Louisville, KY 40292; phone: 502.852.0610; fax: 502.852.4563; email: Hatcher@UofL.edu.

Kit Brooks is principal owner of BrooksWorks, an organizational consulting firm. Her clients include international manufacturing organizations, institutions of higher education, service entities, and small businesses. Brooks also holds the title of visiting professor in adult and vocational education at the University of Arkansas, where she teaches HRD. Her primary interests include organizational change, performance improvement, and partnering with HRD students and practitioners to conduct applied research.

References

Beer, V. "All of the Intervention Eggs Were in One Basket: A Response to Swanson and Zuber." *Performance Improvement Quarterly, 9,* 79-81, 1996.

Beer, V. "Surveymania in HRD Program Evaluation." *Performance Improvement Quarterly, 3,* 2-11, 1990.

Denzin, N.K. and Lincoln, Y.S. *Handbook of Qualitative Research.* Thousand Oaks, CA: Sage Publications, 1994.

Hatcher, T.G. and Ward, S. "Framing: A Method to Improve Performance Analyses." *Performance Improvement Quarterly, 10,* 84-103, 1997.

Hatcher, T., Barry-Brooks, K., Crutchfield, E., Holt, B., and Kettle, S. *Employee Retention at ABC & Co: Research Findings* (ERIC Document Reproduction Service No. ED 392 887), 1995.

Lincoln, Y.S. and Guba, E.G. *Naturalistic Inquiry.* Thousand Oaks, CA: Sage Publications, 1985.

McEvoy, G.M. and Cascio, W.F. "Strategies for Reducing Employee Turnover: A Meta-analysis." *Journal of Applied Psychology, 70,* 342-354, 1985.

Meglino, B.M., DeNisi, A.S., Angelo, S., Youngblood, S.A., and Williams, K.J. "Effects of Realistic Job Previews: A Comparison Using an Enhancement Preview Approach." *Journal of Applied Psychology, 73,* 259-267, 1988.

Mercer, M.W. "Turnover: Reducing the Costs." *Personnel, 65,* 36-42, 1988.

Miles, B.M., and Huberman, M.A. *Qualitative Data Analysis.* Thousand Oaks, CA: Sage Publications, 1994.

Patton, M.Q. *Qualitative Evaluation and Research Methods.* Thousand Oaks, CA: Sage Publications, 1990.

Strauss, A.L., and Corbin, J. *Basics of Qualitative Research-grounded Theory Procedures and Techniques.* Thousand Oaks, CA: Sage Publications, 1990.

Swanson, R.A., and Zuber, J.A. "A Case Study of a Failed Organization Development Intervention Rooted in the Employee Survey Process." *Performance Improvement Quarterly, 9,* 42-56, 1996.

Taylor, D. "The High Cost of Turnover" in *Minding Your Own Business.* Available URL: http://www.webtex.xom/business/7-21-98.html.

Yin, R.K. *Case Study Research: Design and Methods* (2d edition). Thousand Oaks, CA: Sage Publications, 1994.

Performance Analysis: Field Operations Management

Steelcase, Inc.

Mike Wykes, Jody March/Swets, and Lynn Rynbrandt

This case study describes the process used to improve the business performance of field operations managers within a subsidiary of Steelcase, Inc. Steelcase analysts and consultants used a five-phased methodology to uncover operational and performance gaps, clarify the causes of poor performance, and recommend key solutions. The consultants delivered key information and guidance through specific reports, meetings, and work sessions. Implementation of the solution mix resulted in increased job performance that led to positive impacts on business metrics. The case study reviews the results of an evaluation performed after one year, and key lessons learned are discussed.

Background

Steelcase, Inc. is the world's leading manufacturer of office furniture and services dedicated to providing high-performance environments that will help people work more effectively. Its products and services include work settings, systems, seating, desks, and files, as well as the application of knowledge to help transform the ways people work.

Steelcase is a global company with headquarters in Grand Rapids, Michigan. It employs some 21,000 people worldwide who work in manufacturing and sales facilities in 15 countries, and its annual sales are approximately $3 billion dollars. Its products and services are sold and serviced through a worldwide network of nearly 700 independent office furniture system dealers (about 400 in North

This case was prepared to serve as a basis for discussion rather than to illustrate either effective or ineffective administrative and management practices.

America) who provide direct, primary contact with end-user customers. Steelcase's customer base includes many of the *Fortune* 500 companies as well as substantial portions of other market segments.

Performance Analysis at Steelcase

The performance analysis and consulting group is comprised of a leader/manager, several performance consultants, and two performance analysts who report to an organizational entity within the corporate quality function. This group was under the HR function at the time of the case study.

Within this team, the performance consultant (called "consultant" in this study) provides face-to-face, ongoing contact with internal clients, while performance analysts ("analysts") provide primary performance analysis support and human performance technology expertise.

The Process

Performance analysis at Steelcase follows the phases of partnership and entry, assessment, implementation, and evaluation (Robinson and Robinson, 1995; Rummler and Brache, 1995; Stolovich and Keeps, 1999). Its purpose is to help internal clients uncover key issues related to business and performance deficiencies and select the most cost-effective solutions. These solutions always involve an appropriate "mix" to ensure that all systemic factors and interdependencies that affect group and individual performance are considered. To ensure that appropriate variables are considered, analysts and consultants use a variation of the behavior engineering grid originally developed by Gilbert (1996) and revised by Dean and Ripley (1997) and Rummler and Brache (1995), as shown in figure 1.

The performance grid illustrates factors that affect performance into two basic categories:

1. *Environmental factors.* This comprises those factors provided by the organization, such as clear information and expectations; timely feedback; appropriate tools, processes, systems and resources; and incentives (rewards and consequences).

2. *Individual factors.* This comprises those factors that individuals "bring to the table," such as the right skills, knowledge, and attitudes to carry out what is expected of them; the right capacity to use the tools, systems, and resources they're provided; and the right motives (that is, internal and external motives that match the incentives the organization provides).

The extent to which these factors are aligned determines the probability that groups and individuals will produce appropriate

Figure 1. Performance grid.

Factors that affect performance

Environmental factors: (What the organization provides)	**1. Expectations** • clear performance and result expectations • clear "how tos"	**2. Feedback** • relevant and timely • reflects adequacy of performance	**3. Tools, systems, processes, and resources** • tools, resources, time, materials to do the job • access to leaders • work process, systems, organization	**4. Incentives and consequences** (Financial or nonfinancial) • clear performance consequences • consequences and criteria that don't conflict • development opportunities and so forth
Individual factors: (What the individual brings)	**5. Knowledge, skills, and attitude** • the right skills, knowledge, attitudes • opportunities to develop the right skills, knowledge, attitudes	**6. Individual capacity** • match between person and position needs • mental, physical, emotional capacities • includes augmentation to help individuals meet job needs and so forth	**7. Motives** • Intrinsic (internal) motivators match with incentives and consequences • extrinsic (external) motivators match with incentives and consequences	

accomplishments (what Gilbert termed "worthy performance"). This concept of aligning these factors to increase performance forms the core of Steelcase's performance analysis philosophy. A more complete discussion and explanation of this concept is beyond the scope of this case study, and the authors highly recommend the sources cited at the end of this article for further study. Other models and approaches are used by the consultant and analysts, depending on the situation. For example, the Rummler-Brache process improvement model (1995) is used when the major issue appears to be a process dysfunction.

The Steelcase Case Study

The performance analysis for this case study took about two months to complete. Results were evaluated after one year.

Background and Business Need

Steelcase's worldwide network of independent dealers work directly with end-users and customers. Because the business health of these dealers is directly related to the business health of Steelcase, hundreds of Steelcase employees devote their work efforts to helping the dealers remain successful.

The focus of the entire office furniture industry has broadened beyond just selling new furniture to being concerned with helping customers increase their office productivity through effective use of space and furniture. This includes the efficient management of existing furniture (maintenance, moving, warehousing, inventory control, and so forth). These "furniture management" services, when performed efficiently, can be a substantial profit center for dealers (referred to as "service providers" in this case study). However, because furniture management services is still a specialty area, most of these service providers need some help.

A Steelcase subsidiary company, the Furniture Management Coalition (FMC), helps selected Steelcase service providers provide furniture management services to their customers at profitable levels. FMC is composed of about 30 people who are located primarily within the continental United States. It is headed by a vice president, with a management staff of about six people.

A key position within FMC is that of field operations manager (FOM). FOMs are widely dispersed within the continental United States, and each one handles a broad—often a multistate—territory. FOMs work directly with selected service providers, and they recommend those providers who are capable of providing furniture management services. They also help maintain profitability by assessing service provider development needs and by coaching them.

Moreover, FOMs help resolve (customer) problems with service providers and act as the "voice of the service provider" with Steelcase corporate entities. Thus, the FOM role is a demanding, complex one that requires highly skilled, multifaceted people.

Phase One: Partnership and Entry

The first step was to figure out where to begin. The FMC vice president asked the consultant to help fix several problems related to the FOM position. These problems included the following:

- FOMs were not communicating regularly with one another to share ideas and best practices.
- Each FOM performed procedures differently.
- FOMs were spending up to 80 percent of their time fighting fires and tracking down problems.
- While FOMs were measured on the same metrics (the profitability of their service providers' furniture management services), the application of these measures was not being enforced equally with all service providers.
- Customers were regularly going over the heads of some FOMs to solve problems by making direct calls to Steelcase corporate offices. This led to confusion and duplication of effort. It also contributed to degradation of the hard-won relationships between FOMs and their service providers and customers.

The consultant and analysts met several times with FMC leadership to discuss key issues and draft a specific contract to define the performance analysis task and its measurable outcomes. The exceptional clarity of commitment, achieved early on, was due in part to the many "sidebar" conversations the consultant had held with a particularly astute FOM leader/manager. This individual remained a key player throughout the project.

This group (the consultant, analysts, and FMC management) decided to focus initial analysis efforts on the FOM job role itself. The exact responsibilities and measures associated with the FOM position were not clear, even though a corporate job description existed.

To help define the scope of the analysis and guide the project deliverables, the analysts devised a series of focused questions, listed here. (Desired outcomes and measures and steps in the process are in parentheses.)

1 What does the FOM job really look like? (performance model)
2. What things are the FOMs not doing as well as they should to achieve desired results? What things are they already doing well? (gap analysis report)
3. What currently gets in the way of good performance? (gap and causal analysis, including barriers and enhancers to FOM performance)
4. What issues should be dealt with first? (barrier summary report)
5. What is the best—quickest and most cost-effective—mix of solutions to help increase FOM performance? (solution mix recommendations)
6. How well did these solutions work? (evaluation report one year later)

Phase Two: Assessment

The first step in this phase was to agree on desired performance. The consultant and FMC management agreed that developing a performance model would be an appropriate and desired step in providing clarity to the FOM job role.

To accomplish this, the consultant and analysts facilitated several meetings with the vice president, the FOM leader/manager, and other FMC leadership to identify result areas (critical responsibilities and valued accomplishments for the FOM job), competencies (those core competencies critical to the FOM job, such as economic orientation and planning), best practices (what the best performers were doing to consistently achieve results), measures (the clear business and performance measures that were needed), and barriers and enhancers (those factors that were impeding or helping FOM performance). Note: With regard to best practices, the idea here is to clearly document these practices so that others can duplicate them.

FMC leaders identified exemplary FOMs—those individuals who exhibited the best overall performance, both in terms of measures met and in terms of interactions with others, such as teamwork, information sharing, and coaching others. Interestingly, not one FOM was regarded as exemplary in all result areas. For example, an individual might be good at coaching service providers but poor in tracking and reporting key information on a regular basis.

The consultant and analysts interviewed FMC leadership and all FOMs (mostly by phone) paying particular attention to given areas in which each FOM was regarded as exemplary. Each interview took about four hours (two hours to complete and about two to codify the information so that it could be used to articulate behaviors for the FOM performance model). Overall, the interviews took several weeks to complete.

The questions asked during the interviews were specifically designed to uncover information regarding result areas, competencies, best practices, measures, and barriers and enhancers. They are as follows:

1. With regard to best practices related to result areas, the question was, "Can you tell me what you do to accomplish [a given result area]?" In this case, the FOM result areas included a wide range of practices, including select and recommend service providers for inclusion in FMC, assess service provider capabilities, coach and develop service providers, communicate appropriately with co-workers, coach and develop self and others, and "live the Steelcase values."

2. With regard to potential measures of success, the question was, "How do you know that you've accomplished [a particular result area] successfully?"

3. With regard to barriers and enhancers to performance, the question was, "What gets in your way or helps you do your job?"

4. The final question was, "Anything else?" This question often elicited revealing information.

The interviewers then integrated the information during several sorting and collating work sessions that lasted approximately four to five hours each. The result was a working draft of a performance model that specifically defined the result areas, competencies, best practices, measures, and barriers/enhancers to performance for the FOM job (see figure 2). This draft performance model was then validated (with regard to content and measures) and appropriately modified through several meetings with FMC management and the FOMs themselves.

The next step was to identify operational and performance gaps and causes—that is, to compare "what is" with "what should be."

The analysts designed a survey to compare typical behaviors of all FOMs ("what is") against the exemplary or best practices as defined by the performance model ("what should be"). The survey would also be used to clarify the relative importance of specific barriers or enhancers uncovered during the performance modeling process.

Surveys were sent to the FMC management team, for them to rate respective FOMs, and to all FOMs, for them to rate themselves. In all, about 30 surveys were sent out. Respondents were asked to do two things:

1. Rate the frequency and skill with which they felt individual FOMs performed each of the desired behaviors as listed on the model (see figure 3).

2. Prioritize the barriers and enhancers by indicating the extent of agreement or disagreement with work environment statements derived

Figure 2. Performance model.

Result area ...what must be accomplished	Competencies required	Best practices ...how it can be accomplished	Result area measures ...criteria for excellence
Provide initial service provider assessment and selection	• Analysis • Decision making • Information monitoring • Planning and organizing • Relationship building	**Definition:** Select service providers for inclusion into the Furniture Management Coalition using solid, clear criteria. **1. Share in determining the customer's potential service needs and select a service provider network that meets those customer's needs.** • Lead role belongs to AOM and/or AM • FOM role is to clarify the impact of choosing one service provider vs. another who is at or below an acceptable level of competence. **2. Apply key tenets to select appropriate service providers (based on capabilities, pricing, desire, support of FMC, minority business)** • The following criteria is used by the FMC to select is service providers: 1. All dealers are considered. 2. Include dealers currently on the customer product agreement. 3. Identify those that are capable and price competitive. 4. Ascertain who desires to participate. 5. Factor for historical business relationships. 6. Identify geographic alignment and client presence.	✓ **A.** One-page summary of assessment, documented and presented for approval to operations manager and general manager ✓ **B.** Approval is obtained before the customer contract is finalized (any exception to that timing is by prearrangement with management) ✓ **C.** Provide final SP (service provider) assignments ✓ **D.** Execute MSA (master subcontract agreement) ✓ **E.** Execute CSA (customer subcontract agreement) ✓ **F.** Execute certificate of insurance.

directly from interview information based on a scale of 1 to 6, in which 1 = strongly disagree and 6 = strongly agree.

To help ensure consistency of response to these potentially emotionally laden statements, the analysts rewrote all statements as positive statements. For example, the actual barrier of "Needed information usually arrives late" was rewritten as "Needed information usually arrives on time." This allowed respondents to simply indicate their extent of agreement or disagreement with a statement rather than placing them in a position where they had to make a value judgment on the statement itself. This is a subtle but important distinction that resulted in more balanced information because it removed the tendency toward negativity with known issues.

The analysts then collected, analyzed, interpreted, and reported the information in a focused, prioritized format that integrated all information sources (instead of presenting it as a "data dump"). This meant melding a combination of numerical data, written comments, face-to-face discussions, and other information to provide a balanced holistic interpretation. (Note: This kind of interpretation requires a combination of functional maturity in human performance technology, statistical knowledge, systemic thinking, empathy, and a good understanding of the client's world. It is a skill that separates average—or typical—performance analysts from exemplary ones.)

Results of the survey highlighted areas in which the FOMs needed to improve and hinted at key barriers that might be causing the FOMs to underperform with regard to specific goals in associated result areas. The analysis took approximately two weeks to complete.

Next, the consultant and analysts presented key results regarding FOM skills and performance to a selected FMC leadership team.

Overall, while the FMC leadership tended to rate FOMs skill and frequencies slightly lower than the FOMs rated themselves, both groups noted the same general trends. Respondents indicated that the following result areas showed the lowest combined frequency and skill scores:

1. Assess service providers' strengths and provide development. FOMs needed to improve their abilities to lead the development of service provider performance improvement plans to address specific deficiencies, clearly document service provider performance improvement plans, and adequately follow through on such plans.

2. Communicate. FOMs needed to improve their abilities to communicate regularly with FMC leaders, write clear and focused communications, and encourage others to communicate on routine items.

Figure 3. Performance model survey.

1 = Almost Never	4 = Frequently	1 = Little/No Skill 4 = Proficient Skill
2 = Very Infrequent	5 = Very Frequent	2 = Basic Skill 5 = Expert Skill
3 = Infrequent	6 = Almost Always Name _____	3 = Adequate Skill

Frequency of Use	On-the-Job Activities (Best Practices)	Current Skill Level

Select service providers

Definition: Select service providers for inclusion into the coalition using solid, clear criteria.

Frequency of Use	On-the-Job Activities (Best Practices)	Current Skill Level
NA 1 2 3 4 5 6	1. Develop credibility with service providers (to help you give feedback that will be respected).	1 2 3 4 5
NA 1 2 3 4 5 6	2. Assess individual service provider capabilities and capacities by determining if they can provide the required quality and quantity of service.	1 2 3 4 5
NA 1 2 3 4 5 6	3. Clearly document service provider capabilities and deficiencies.	1 2 3 4 5
NA 1 2 3 4 5 6	4. Lead the development of performance improvement plans to address specific service provider deficiencies.	1 2 3 4 5
NA 1 2 3 4 5 6	5. Follow through on service providers' performance improvement plans.	1 2 3 4 5
NA 1 2 3 4 5 6	6. Assess the needs of a given market and compare against collective service provider capabilities and capacities.	1 2 3 4 5
NA 1 2 3 4 5 6	7. Assure that service providers are clear on what's expected of them as written in the *Service Provider Work Instruction Manual*.	1 2 3 4 5

	NA	1	2	3	4	5	6		1	2	3	4	5

8. Clarify and communicate *corporate customer expectations of the FMC* to the service provider.

NA 1 2 3 4 5 6 | 1 2 3 4 5

9. Communicate expectations and results *between FMC and service provider.*

NA 1 2 3 4 5 6 | 1 2 3 4 5

Assess service capabilities; lead performance improvement plans

Definition: Clearly assess service provider performance capabilities, quality, and capacity. Lead development of performance improvement plans to address deficiencies.

1. Develop credibility with service providers (to help you give feedback that will be respected).

NA 1 2 3 4 5 6 | 1 2 3 4 5

2. Assess individual service provider capabilities and capacities by determining if they can provide the required quality and quantity of service.

NA 1 2 3 4 5 6 | 1 2 3 4 5

3. Clearly document service provider capabilities and deficiencies.

NA 1 2 3 4 5 6 | 1 2 3 4 5

4. Lead the development of performance improvement plans to address specific service provider deficiencies.

NA 1 2 3 4 5 6 | 1 2 3 4 5

5. Follow through on service providers' performance improvement plans.

NA 1 2 3 4 5 6 | 1 2 3 4 5

6. Assess the needs of a given market and compare against collective service provider capabilities and capacities.

NA 1 2 3 4 5 6 | 1 2 3 4 5

7. Assure that service providers are clear on what's expected of them as written in the *Service Provider Work Instructions.*

NA 1 2 3 4 5 6 | 1 2 3 4 5

3. Coach and develop. Not enough FOMs had a personal (skill and career) development plan.

In general, respondents rated FOMs highly on their levels of interpersonal skills and their ethical and moral values. They also indicated that FOMs were very adept at "championing the cause" of their respective service providers and at performing tactical, reactive tasks, such as tracking down parts and solving process issues.

However, a combination of factors was found to impede the performance of the FOMs, as follows. (Note: Barriers are organized here according to performance grid categories as shown in figure 1. For example, "grid box 1" refers to the "expectations" box number 1 on the performance grid.)

1. With regard to expectations (grid box 1), expectations and boundaries—latitude of authority, not geographic boundaries—were unclear. In addition, new FOMs were unclear about Steelcase culture.

2. With regard to tools, systems, processes, and resources (grid box 3), the tools to help FOMs select, monitor, and evaluate service providers were inadequate to help maintain profitability. In addition, Steelcase did not have enough dealer business consultants (those who worked in conjunction with FOMs to help dealers' business). Moreover, "customer language" and different ways of doing things made standardization difficult.

3. With regard to incentives and consequences (grid box 4), FOMs were unclear about how to provide negative consequences for low-performing service providers. In addition, few measures and accountability standards existed for sharing information and individual expertise, and measures regarding local customer needs and defined national standards were inconsistent and confusing.

4. With regard to knowledge/skills/attitude, individual capacity, and motives (grid boxes 5, 6, and 7), no real issues surfaced in these categories. The FOMs are all highly skilled and motivated.

Factors that tended to enhance FOM performance centered mostly on the positive aspects of Steelcase culture—such as caring and supporting people (grid box 3)—and on the generally high quality of Steelcase employees (grid boxes 5 and 6). FOMs tended to respect the abilities of their co-workers, and respondents also viewed Steelcase's reputation in the corporate world as a positive.

In addition, some service providers were rated highly for their abilities to provide their own tactical services related to new products, such as installation and warranty repairs.

Phase Three: Implementation and Solutions

Once the strengths and weaknesses of FOM performance were identified, the analysts and consultant led a representative group through a process of matching potential solutions with existing gaps and causes and performing simple cost and scope analysis for each potential solution.

The resulting solution mix was designed to increase the likelihood that FOMs would perform more of the desired key behaviors as indicated on the performance model. Solutions centered on clarifying expectations, documenting processes, and ensuring that appropriate measures and incentives are implemented (see table 1 for the result of this process).

As for carrying out these solutions, the FMC group had primary responsibility for virtually all solution development and follow-up work. The consultant maintained her regular meeting and update schedule with FMC management and followed the general progress of the solutions.

Phase Four: Evaluation

One year later, the consultant and analysts interviewed the vice president, the FOM leader/manager, the newly appointed FOM team leader, and several selected FOMs who were considered exemplars.

These interviews were designed to evaluate the impact of the suggested solutions and were based on a format similar to a portion of table 1 (without the results column filled in). Focused evaluation questions were asked, beginning with the general one of "Compared with last year, how are things this year?" More specific questions related to solutions included the following:
- "Did this solution happen (yes/no)?"
- "What effect did it have (that is, what business or performance metric did it positively affect)?"
- "What behavioral differences or other things have you noticed since the solution was implemented?"
- "What worked? What didn't work?"
- "If a solution was not implemented, is it still worth pursuing?"

The following additional questions focused on the performance model:
- "Did the performance model help create the job clarity originally sought?"
- "Did it help manage performance (performance review process)?"

Table 1. Summary of project issues and solutions.

Desired FOM Result Areas and Job Responsibility Behaviors*	Barriers to Performance†	Solutions	Results and Measurements‡
Select and recommend service providers using a consistent criteria base.	Expectations/incentives (grid box 1): No clearly defined lines of authority to apply true selection criteria.	Define and communicate service provider selection/assessment process.	Process documented. Helped clarify issues with several underperforming service providers.
Assess and follow through on service provider performance improvement plans.	Information (grid box 1): No clear benchmark data to measure past/current performance.	Develop "scorecard" and subteam to establish benchmarks.	Still in process. Held up due to larger corporate integration issues.
	Process (grid box 3): No clear service provider selection/ development process.	Define and communicate service provider selection/assessment process.	Several dealers have documented improvement plans clearly and show specific improvements.
	Process/resources (grid box 3): Dealer alliance group under-resourced to help FOMs regarding development.	VP and manager to meet with dealer alliances group and define roles and responsibilities.	No specific progress made. Issue larger than just FMC (budget and so forth). Alignment gained outside group to continue with this issue.
	Consequences (grid box 4): No real consequences for nondevelopment of service providers.	Specific development measures to be tied to performance review information.	Each FOM has dealer development metrics on individual performance management document.
	Process/linkage (grid box 3): FOMs not formally linked with Steelcase local sales offices.	Implement "sales awareness program" to increase linkages.	Increased linkage. Fewer duplicated efforts. Increased networking.

Act more as a team (communicate; help each other develop).	**Organizational** (grid box 3): No current team leader as catalyst.	Appoint new FOM team leader (player/coach).	Team leader appointed. Increased regular FOM team communication.
Plan, measure, and report more regularly.	**Process** (grid box 3): Service provider selection and assessment process not clarified.	Define and communicate service provider selection/assessment process.	Process documented. FOMs report more regularly on progress made.
Act as the "voice of the customer" in dispute situations.	**Expectations/clarity** (grid box 1): Lack of clarity regarding roles. Customers bypassing FOMs.	Clarify role proactively with customers on a regular basis.	Performance model helped FOMs clarify roles with customers. Customers now tend to contact FOMs first.
Share more key information with one another.	**Tools** (grid box 4): No accountability exists to share information and expertise.	Information-sharing metrics to be placed into each FOM's objectives.	Clearer, more regular sharing of key information.
Spend more time planning, less time fire-fighting.	**Expectations/process/ organization** (grid boxes 1 and 3): FOMs spent 30 percent to 80 percent of their time on activities outside their defined role.	Multiple solutions: FOM performance model and measures; create operations administrator position.	More time devoted to focused work, although still too much fire-fighting is taking place. Operations administrator position still in process.
	Procedures (grid box 3): Procedures to report potential problems are unclear.	Process documentation to outline procedures.	Selection and assessment process defines procedures.
	Resources (grid box 3): Inadequate corporate resources to help dealers; FOMs have to do a lot of "filling in."	Management to address resource issue with dealer alliances group.	Resource issues still exist; discussions are ongoing. This is a larger issue.

* = based on original performance problem statements; † = organized by performance grid categories; ‡ = based on evaluation interviews performed after one year

- "Did it help define individual development plans?"
- "Did it provide any other benefits?"

Results

Results showed that the FMC vice president and the FOM leader/manager were pleased with the intervention and its outcomes, as the following satisfaction statements demonstrate:

- "The return on the individual was sufficiently improved to call it a win."
- "[The process drove us] to really look at what we deliver, realize we are people-dependent, follow processes, and measure results more specifically."
- "The process went well. The pace was good. You delivered what we agreed to in the plan."
- "[This process took] remote individuals [who were] all doing different things and only doing what they knew they did well, and brought clarity to what they should be doing."

Additional positive results included the following:

- The performance model provided increased clarity about the FOM job role. Each FOM now had clear performance metrics, which were adjusted to reflect local market conditions and other specific or unique service provider factors. (The performance model was designed to be an adaptable document.)
- FOMs regularly shared more information with each other.
- Improvements were made to the process of selecting and assessing service providers. A new service provider process document was produced.
- The average amount of time decreased between the recognition of a defect in a service provider and the initiation of development programs to remedy those defects.
- Over 90 percent of the FOMs now had individual improvement plans, as compared with fewer than 20 percent before the intervention.
- Customers (both internal and external) indicated that they knew exactly what they could expect from the FOMs.
- Employee satisfaction among the FOMs increased, as measured by a biannual Steelcase HR survey.

However, several areas didn't see significant improvement. In particular, FOMs were still "putting out fires" more than they would like to, even though this was less of a problem than before. Moreover, some confusion with other FMC job roles and responsibilities still existed.

Conclusion

Three key items contributed to success in this case. First, the consultants met the client's biggest need first in a timeframe that fit their world. Second, the client was committed and continually engaged throughout the process. This included the FOMs themselves as well as "management." Finally, the entire effort was aided by the existence of an inside coach/participant (the FOM leader/manager) who was totally committed to the FMC effort and to the FOMs.

Even so, some things could have been done differently. For instance, the FOM manager felt that the use of the model and measures would have been more effective if similar modeling had been done for the other key jobs within the FMC, such as the account managers and area office managers. Even though focusing specifically on the FOM job did increase performance (and it did so quickly), it lessened the overall impact potential on the larger system by not addressing how the FOM job role fit with other FMC roles and responsibilities and the broader corporate strategies.

In addition, it would have been useful to explain the "performance grid" concept and the systemic view of performance and causal linkages to barriers found earlier in the process.

Finally, it would have been helpful to define and facilitate more regular and specific evaluation efforts, to allow for implementation of any needed midcourse corrections.

Questions for Discussion

1. Why was the internal coach so critical to the success of this effort?
2. What are the strengths of the evaluation strategy used in this case? What are its limitations?
3. Based on what you have read in this case study, what factors need to be in place for successful performance analysis to be completed?
4. What flaws—or potential flaws—do you detect in the data collection and analysis methodology used in this study?
5. What could be justification for having the performance analyst role separate from the performance consultant role?

The Authors

Mike Wykes is the principal performance analyst for Steelcase, Inc. Wykes has been a successful performance analyst, consultant, trainer, instructional designer, and manager for the past 20 years. He holds two master's degrees in educational leadership and HRD. Wykes is a member of ASTD and is president of his local chapter of the International Society for Performance Improvement (ISPI) and has presented and performed workshops both locally and nationally to myriad organizations. His publications include book reviews in *Human Resource Development Quarterly* as well as chapter and case study contributions to books such as ASTD's In Action series. He can be reached at 1969 Jamestown, Kentwood, MI 49508; phone: 616.246.1820; fax: 616.246.1955; email: mwkes@steelcase.com or mwykes@iserv.net.

Jody March/Swets is a performance analyst for Steelcase, Inc. who has worked 20 years within the United States and South America. March/Swets holds undergraduate degrees in Russian language and literature and music performance and education and a M.S. in educational leadership and HRD. During her career, March/Swets has focused on organizational transformation through people and has made key corporate contributions in total quality management/world class performance, business process reengineering, and people development and performance management. She has co-presented nationally at ISPI and locally for ASTD and ISPI.

Lynn Rynbrandt, a performance consultant for Steelcase, Inc., works with members of the executive management team. Rynbrandt helps leaders identify work environment factors that prevent people from realizing business results and helps guide them through the process of implementing viable solutions to removing impediments to performance.

References

Dean, P., and Ripley, D.E., editors. *Performance Improvement Pathfinders.* Washington: ISPI Publications, 1997.

Gilbert, T. *Human Competence: Engineering Worthy Performance* (Tribute Edition). Washington: ISPI Publications, 1996.

Robinson, D.G., and Robinson, J. *Performance Consulting: Moving Beyond Training.* San Francisco: Berrett-Koehler, 1995.

Rummler, G.A., and Brache, A.P. *Improving Performance: How to Manage the White Space on the Organization Chart* (2d edition). San Francisco: Jossey-Bass, 1995.

Stolovich, H.D., and Keeps, E.J. *Handbook of Human Performance Technology.* San Francisco: Jossey-Bass, 1999.

Additional References

Phillips, J.J. *Handbook of Training Evaluation and Measurement Methods* (3d edition). Houston: Gulf Publishing, 1998.

Robinson, D.G., and Robinson, J., editors. *Moving From Training to Performance: A Practical Guidebook.* San Francisco: Berrett-Koehler, 1998.

Rossett, A. *First Things Fast: A Handbook for Performance Analysis.* San Francisco: Jossey-Bass Pfeiffer, 1999.

Rothwell, W., editor. *ASTD Models for Human Performance Improvement.* Alexandria, VA: ASTD, 1996.

Wykes, M. "Performance Analysts at Steelcase" in *Moving From Training to Performance: A Practical Guidebook.* San Francisco: Berrett-Koehler, 1998.

Wykes, M. "Adaptive Performance Analysis at Steelcase." San Francisco: National Conference of the American Society for Training & Development, 1998.

Wykes, M. and March/Swets, J. "Performance Analysis at Steelcase." Long Beach, CA: National Conference of the International Society for Performance Improvement, 1998.

Fish See the Water Last: Organization Effectiveness Assessment

Financial Management

Katherine Donahue

This case study provides an example of a practical approach to identifying opportunities for improvement in operational results, an approach that supports the essential requirement that these actions be successfully implemented. Although the Mercury Group, an outside consulting firm, actively facilitated this organizational effectiveness assessment, the approach differed dramatically from the usual. The entire project—from beginning to measurable, post-project results—took less than 90 days. Employees were actively involved in every step, including project planning; data gathering and analysis; interviews with customers, managers, and employees; brainstorming; and implementation planning and execution.

Background

After more than a year of trying to correct internal problems themselves, senior managers of the application processing (AP) department of a *Fortune* 500 financial management company had come to the conclusion that lack of objectivity from within its ranks was a primary contributor to its inability to resolve declining customer satisfaction ratings from within the department (hence the title of this case study, "Fish See the Water Last").

The AP department eventually realized that to be successful, it needed a knowledgeable facilitator from within the company (but outside the organization itself) to lead the department in an organization effectiveness assessment (OEA). The organization also realized that

This case was prepared to serve as a basis for discussion rather than to illustrate either effective or ineffective administrative and management practices. All names, dates, places, and organizations have been disguised at the request of the author or organization.

an external consultant not only could provide the necessary guidance in its quest to properly identify its problems but also could educate it in the finer points of the factors that drive organization effectiveness and put the department on the path to future success.

This case study demonstrates that the traditional formal study approach of gathering and analyzing copious amounts of data—often at the expense of employee involvement and eventual employee buy-in—is not always the best answer.

The Problems

The AP department was responsible for processing the company's new business applications. For many years, the department had performed the same functions and had done so in the same way. However, in the past several years, volumes had skyrocketed. And despite the fact that additional people were hired to respond to the increase, performance results continued to decline.

The AP department's management summarized its problems as follows:

- Processing time was now four days longer than the industry average.
- The primary customer—the sales organization—reported business lost to competitors due to internal delays.
- Internal customers were frustrated by their inability to learn the current status of an application.
- The employees in this department reported low job satisfaction and high levels of stress.

The AP department's management attempted to resolve these problems by assigning two people to exclusively answer customer calls and by hiring more people. Nonetheless, the department had achieved only minimal improvement. The managers knew the process needed to be changed to accommodate the higher volumes, but they weren't sure how to accomplish it.

Past change initiatives were the result of comprehensive studies that had long periods of disruption and lack of employee involvement—and the resulting outcome of employee distrust. The AP department knew not to repeat that approach. As one manager said, "Somehow, we had to figure out what needed to be done to solve these problems in a short period of time and in a way that would encourage employees to support the change initiatives."

Organization Profile

The organizational unit—targeted during the initiative in this case study, the AP department—reports to a division of a *Fortune* 500 company that sells insurance solutions for its clients' estate planning. The AP department is centrally located to support field sales offices, and its employees are organized in three teams:

1. employees who perform the series of tasks required to process an application
2. underwriters who are involved in some new business applications
3. employees who perform document handling processes.

Key Players

During the OEA, there were three main groups of participants, including a senior organization development professional and the external consultant who became the "project team," and the AP department's employees and managers.

The senior organization development (OD) professional assigned to this project came from the company's HR department and was named as the internal project manager and liaison to the external consultant. With more than 10 years of experience with the company and its OD work and nearly 20 years of experience in the OD field, she was a valuable contributor to the team. Her career emphasis had always been on team building, group interventions, and the design and delivery of training programs to support the operations of the business, but she had no experience in organization effectiveness assessments or in process design. Her excellent reputation facilitated her acceptance as the OEA project manager. She was, in fact, the person most likely to succeed in this position, and the opportunity to gain organization effectiveness expertise was excellent motivation for her to perform the project manager duties to the best of her ability.

An external consulting firm was hired based on its practical approach to assessing organization effectiveness. The consultant's approach happened to be built upon three tenets that fit the department's desired approach and outcome. The three tenets are as follows:

1. Successful implementation of change depends on employees who believe in and are committed to the reasons for the change and to the change itself. Thus, a solution that is 80 percent correct and can be implemented and achieved is better than a solution that is 100 percent correct but is impossible to achieve.
2. Employees know the work, and the job of the intervention team is to help them to articulate their knowledge and experience to form a clear picture of current processes so that a workable solution can be formulated. This tenet also recognizes that employees know that their participation builds the commitment required for successful implementation.

3. It is unnecessary to spend months gathering data and creating voluminous studies and reports that risk the loss of employee acceptance. This tenet is based on the principle that employees distrust studies and results conducted "in secret" over too long a period of time.

All employees and AP department managers participated in the intervention by responding to surveys, personal interviews, and the like.

The Approach

After interviewing the AP department's managers and documenting their perceived opinions as to why their customer service ratings had continued to decline, the project team developed an OEA based on the following events:

- initial communication to all employees in the AP department
- interviews with AP department employees
- meetings with management employees
- interviews with AP department customers
- process mapping
- follow-up interviews with employees
- a systems review
- brainstorming sessions to develop feasible solutions.

Setting the Stage

The initial communication to all employees in the AP department was a memo announcing that an OEA was going to be conducted. The memo described the purpose of the OEA and the general project process. The memo also described the key players who would drive the approach (the project manager, the external consultant, and the AP department employees and managers).

In addition, the memo stated that the OEA would be completed and that any changes would be implemented within 90 days. Most important, the memo stated that employees were free to discuss the project among themselves and that the source of any information shared by individuals during the interview process would remain confidential.

Soliciting Feedback

Interviews with a representative group of AP department employees came next. Representatives were selected from each of the department's three teams, with the goal that each of the three groups of employees would have varied lengths of service and performance levels. (However, no one's on-the-job performance could be less than satisfactory.) Managers who selected the employees were asked specifically not to select those people who were best acquainted with the current process, so that these employees could be selected to do process mapping.

Employees selected to represent the AP department during interviews were encouraged to solicit input, opinions, and feedback from other employees in the department. In the same manner, the other employees were invited to submit email messages to the three selected employees to share ideas about what they believed worked well, what did not, and why.

Interviews began a week after the announcement to give everyone an opportunity to provide input to the employee representatives. The interviews were conducted by the external consultant and attended and observed by the project manager. The external consultant asked the employees the following questions, plus specific questions that were identified during each interview based on previous interviews:

- What does your group do?
- What is working well?
- Why has your department decided to conduct an OEA?
- What is not working well?
- What do you think is the cause of any problems?
- What would you do first to change things if you were in charge?
- What would be the next two items of change?
- Would anyone object to those actions?
- Why?

In summary, the employees said they spent too much time documenting what they did and then reading the documentation every time they picked up an application to complete a step. They were frustrated with what they perceived as constant calls from customers asking for status and not being able to find the appropriate file. They reported that they never felt that a task was completed. They also reported disappointment that when a large case was won, the sales representative was congratulated individually and the AP department was either ignored or congratulated as a group, even though one of them individually may have completed a step in the process that made the difference. They felt it was good that they all had learned every task and could vary their tasks periodically. They also felt that more employees were needed to speed the process. Even so, they did not see any of the processes as changeable.

Identifying Objectives

After the employee interviews, the project team met with the department's management team to identify and prioritize all objectives of the AP group.

For each objective, the managers defined the current performance standard and identified the manager responsible for meeting that objective. They also gathered samples of all reports used to manage the group, including any documentation of the process, and explained the use of each.

The project team then captured the information on a grid, as shown in table 1. The project team reviewed all AP department reports and compared them with the list of objectives and their measurements.

The project team determined that there was no measurement of the overall objective, which was to process applications in a timely manner. For example, not one report measured the progress of an individual application through the process; not even total processing time was tracked. There was no objective for the total time a file was pending, and no report identified applications that had become delayed. There was no objective to monitor time elapsed between each person's handling of the application, and there was no manager accountable for that period of time. Reports measured many results that were not listed as objectives. There was no process documentation other than a procedure manual that was several years old, outdated, and no longer referenced by anyone in the department.

Validating the Objectives

Several AP department customers (field sales representatives) were then interviewed by the project team. Referring to the results on the grid in table 1, the AP department customers were asked to validate each objective, its priority, and its performance standard, and to add to the list as appropriate.

The AP department's customers agreed that the overall objective was to process applications as accurately and as quickly as possible. They added that the AP department should be responsible for identifying any applications that had become stuck along the way so that the sales representative could take appropriate action. The customers were particularly concerned that the people who answered

Table 1. Information grid.

Objective	Standard	Accountable manager	Measurement source	Customer input
				For later use

their calls regarding application status could not immediately access an application's current status.

In fact, the customers were frustrated that nearly every call on a status check meant waiting for a return call, which could take several hours or even a day, and they indicated that they would like to see accountability for regular status reporting.

Mapping the Process

With a list of the AP department's objectives in hand, three employees who were familiar with the process were asked to map the process for the project team's review. These three employees were not the same three who were interviewed initially by the project team. They were asked to get together and map the current work flow, so that the process could be evaluated.

Before they began, the external consultant provided them with two hours of mapping training. They were encouraged to ask the project team for assistance if needed and were free to seek input from co-workers. They were told to not be overly concerned with appearance and to just chart it on paper (rather than learn a software program to chart the flow). They had two days to complete the task.

The employees developing the process maps identified that each application required a variety of additional information to be ordered (such as physicians' reports or lab work to complete the application process) and that this additional information was received as separate pieces of mail during the course of the application process. The current process was an assembly line approach. In essence, the application process was put on hold as employees waited for outstanding information from multiple sources. Between each step, the application was filed as "pending additional information." When information was received, the process then started again and triggered the next action.

Before the rise in volumes, AP department employees could take the time to check the "pending drawer" and proactively pursue missing data while working on another application. But now, too many people were working on applications. It wasn't an easy task to track the status of an application, particularly one that was pending approval and waiting for outstanding information.

Copious documentation was begun to describe every action taken, as it was likely that another employee would complete the next step. Moreover, before an employee could complete the next step, all of the previous documentation had to be read so that the employee could orient him- or herself to the file in question.

Reviewing the Process Flow

Follow-up interviews were conducted with the three original representatives from the AP department, as well as the three who mapped the current process. During the follow-up interviews, the project team reviewed the process flow to ensure complete understanding of each step, why it was performed the way it was, and what the risks would be if it were changed or eliminated. The project team conducted these interviews and, in the process, tested alternative ideas.

Employees laughed when they saw the application process mapped out, especially when they saw the application constantly bouncing from a person to the pending file, back to the person, and back to the pending file. They readily grasped that this was driving the time they had to spend documenting and then reorienting themselves to each file. They clearly understood why, even with two employees assigned to answer status calls from their customers, they could not provide status reports: They had no easy access to the applications.

The employees quickly determined that it would be much better if they could process one file to completion before they began another application. However, they voiced the concern that there was too much work for them to be able to make that switch, based on their mistaken perception that it would take longer than the current application process.

When questioned, they estimated that they spent 10 percent of their time responding to status calls from customers and another 15 percent documenting their actions or reorienting themselves with an application in process.

Reviewing the System

One of the project team's final tasks was to perform a systems review. The team did find that all application actions were logged using a software application that captured data for the reports. However, the system was never accessed to check on an application's status, because no one trusted that data entry was up-to-date. Moreover, a new piece of information might have been received and the application might be in the pending file waiting for someone to work on it. The system was not accessible by the field. And, finally, building a new system was not an option.

Brainstorming

Before the project team could identify potential solutions, team members referred to all of the findings from all of the previous steps and created a list of criteria that any solutions would have to meet.

Based on employee estimates, members of the project team assumed that if they found a solution that eliminated extensive and duplicate documentation, they could free up as much as 15 percent of employee time. If a way could be found to use 5 percent of that saved time to provide proactive application status reports to customers, at least 10 percent more time could be freed up. This would realize an estimated 20 percent improvement in productivity. If the time lost due to filing and refiling the application as it moved through the process could be also be saved, perhaps another 5 percent of employee time could be freed up.

After reviewing and analyzing the information collected and their findings and creating the criteria for solutions, the project team brainstormed potential solutions. The team then facilitated meetings with six of the employees in the original interview cohort who were believed to be the most creative and most able to think both logically and "outside the box."

The project team solicited the employees' ideas and measured each against the established criteria. Once team members defined the ideal solutions, they prepared a presentation to the AP department's managers for approval.

Design Solution

The project team suggested to management that the best solution was to reorganize the AP department into geographically assigned teams. During the information-gathering process, the project team learned that almost all of the employees knew all of the steps and thus knew the entire process. As a result, it would be easy to move to an organization in which employees could "own" an application through completion.

The solution was simple: From the time an application was assigned, the question of who would "own" that application would be clear to both customers and document handlers. This eliminated the need for the application to travel among different people during the process, as each employee would maintain his or her own pending file, and the document handlers could simply route new information to the appropriate person as it came in.

Because it was too expensive to redesign the department's internal systems, the project team proposed that the system capture different information. Fields were redefined (previously, they had been used to capture data regarding unimportant tasks). This allowed an individual application to be viewed and a report to be generated to summarize application status by defined milestones. It also allowed the "case workers" to view the overall status of their applications in process, so that they could determine priorities and keep customers informed.

Members of the field sales offices were told which employees were assigned to their applications and were encouraged to call them directly with questions. The employee team representatives, who also answered their questions, presented the plan to AP department employees.

Obstacles

There were two hurdles to the successful data gathering and implementation of this project plan: initial distrust by employees and management resistance to what would be mostly employee involvement.

Initially, employees were skeptical that the project team would really seek and consider their input. To combat this distrust, the first 20 minutes of every initial interview was spent answering challenging questions posed by the employees. During the first few weeks, the project team was frequently informed of employee rumblings or concerns and of complaints to management. All were met with patient and consistent answers, and distrust died down in less than three weeks.

Managers, too, were skeptical. At first, they were resistant to so much employee involvement, fearing that they were not in control. They had difficulty appearing calm, confident, and positive to employees during the process, which further fueled employee skepticism.

This problem was handled with several group meetings in the first weeks. During the meetings, the managers were reminded that the project team was facilitating the project to ensure that the end result was feasible and not inappropriately masterminded by employees with agendas of their own. The project team also reminded the managers that they would receive frequent feedback on findings and could, like the employees, provide their input.

These frequent meetings allowed the project team to keep its finger on the pulse of management so that probable issues could be predicted and opposition could be met as it arose, instead of during the brainstorming and solutions recommendation process. Of course, the managers were gently reminded that, in the end, they had the power to approve the project team's recommendations.

Implementation

Final buy-in was virtually unanimous. Using reports that showed volumes by geographic locations, management assigned AP department employees to teams. Each team decided how to organize its files and rearrange seating and drafted an announcement to its customers. Members of each team voluntarily came in over two weekends to orient themselves in their new work groups, to distribute applications among themselves, and to load additional data into the system so that they could see application status as of the targeted Monday kickoff.

Results

Fewer than 90 days from the project's start, the department's application processing time not only had been cut in half but also was a full 10 days faster than the industry average. The error rate had dropped to less than 3 percent, and both employees and their field sales representative customers were positive about the results.

Questions for Discussion

1. If individual application processing time wasn't visible, wouldn't it have been valuable to capture this data to know whether only some types of applications were unduly delayed?
2. If the consultant was hired to do the OEA, what was the point of naming the internal project leader and taking her from her regular responsibilities for so long?
3. Didn't all this employee involvement have a major negative impact on the work flow during the eight weeks of the project?
4. Why not select managers as the project team?
5. Wouldn't the decision to select only one employee to map processes for each functional group risk that variations in process would be missed?

The Author

Katherine Donahue, founder and president of the Mercury Group, applies a unique perspective to organizational challenges. Her HR and line management experience, coupled with more than 20 years of effectively troubleshooting organizational development issues, gives her a unique understanding of the interwoven factors that drive operational effectiveness.

Consulting since 1991, Donahue has provided coaching and leadership in organization effectiveness assessments, complex reengineering, process redesign, and change management strategic planning for organizations with 12 to 30,000 employees and for numerous industries.

The Mercury Group has introduced a new tool (called Business Compass) to guide organizations in independently conducting successful organizational effectiveness assessments. Donahue has a Website at www.business-compass.com and can be reached via email at kmercury@mindspring.com.

Managing the Information of an Executive Development Program

Arthur Andersen

Jerry F. Luebke and Susan E. Bumpass

This case study focuses on the development and design of a systemic approach to managing and reporting evaluation data and information for an executive development program. In 1994, Arthur Andersen implemented the Partner Development Program to help partners build and maintain the knowledge, skills, and behaviors they need to be valued business advisors in an ever-changing worldwide market. To provide a framework to facilitate the performance consulting services for the program, a comprehensive program evaluation system needed to be developed. This system not only needed to be directed at the program's impact on the partners' business performance but also had to allow for the systematic gathering, analyzing, and dissemination of critical information for the continuous development and evolution of the program.

Background

Arthur Andersen consists of more than 100 member firms and more than 72,000 people located in 84 countries throughout the world, all united by a single, worldwide operating structure and common corporate culture. Created as a partnership, Arthur Andersen was formed in 1913 and today encompasses more than 4,000 partners. As a global firm, Arthur Andersen is organized into the following four inter-related service categories:

1. *Assurance and business advisory,* which offers business risk consulting and assurance services.
2. *Business consulting,* which offers services related to business planning, change enabling, quality management, and business process improvement.

This case was prepared to serve as a basis for discussion rather than to illustrate either effective or in-effective administrative and management practices.

3. *Global corporate finance,* which offers economic consulting, real estate advisory services, and corporate financial services.
4. *Tax, legal, and business advisory,* which offers international and individual tax services, family wealth consulting, and human capital services.

Change and Challenge

As the world moved from an industrial to a knowledge economy in the 1980s, businesses and corporations found themselves faced with new and more complex challenges in areas such as global competition, communications, and technology. Business executives began responding to these dynamic changes in their markets by looking for new ways to maintain and improve their organizations' competitive advantage and human resource capabilities. Business executives no longer needed simply a technical expert—they also needed someone to help them think through, and ultimately address, the big-picture issues facing their organizations.

Arthur Andersen responded to these shifts in the business environment in two ways. First, the organization began offering a greater variety of business consulting services to its clients. Second, the company began to broaden the way it thought about and delivered regulated accounting and tax services. These changes required Arthur Andersen partners, regardless of their specialty areas, to broaden their skills beyond their defined areas of expertise. Only by understanding the broader context that gave rise to the issues and opportunities their clients faced could they continue to offer technical advice that would be relevant and valuable in the short and long term.

This critical change that Arthur Andersen faced was not only about the acquisition of additional knowledge and skills. This change required extensive redefining of the basic assumptions in delivering professional business services. What was the ultimate purpose of the business services being provided? What were the roles and responsibilities of partners in achieving integrated business solutions for their clients? Who would the partners need to work with, and how would they work with one another and their employees in this new paradigm of professional business services?

In 1992, Arthur Andersen partners participated in a satisfaction survey. Results of this survey, in part, indicated that partners wanted a leadership development program that would:
• focus on working with clients
• help partners meet the changing needs of the marketplace

- address the challenges faced by CEO and CFOs
- provide linkage to the Arthur Andersen strategic business framework and measures.

Based on this feedback, Arthur Andersen leadership identified a task force that subsequently recommended the creation of the Partner Development Program (PDP). An extensive needs assessment study was conducted using both internal and external data sources, and the program opened its doors in 1994 with four courses. The curriculum focused on three competency areas: business insight, relationship management, and leadership.

Program Description and History

The PDP program is positioned within the organization to report directly to Arthur Andersen's CEO. Currently, the program offers 10 courses that employ a variety of learning techniques, such as lecture and small group problem-solving activities, case studies and simulations, and experiential learning. The courses focus on a variety of topics, such as financial management, change management issues, global business strategy, and relationship building at the individual and team levels.

The PDP team is headed by a sponsoring partner who has had significant practice experience and held various Arthur Andersen leadership positions. Additionally, a program director works with the partner in charge and other internal and external resources to develop and coordinate various performance consulting interventions. Three other team members are focused on course logistics and administration of the program. Finally, two program evaluators and three data management specialists work for the program. These individuals are part of an internal assessment and measurement team of about 30 individuals who support various performance consulting projects across Arthur Andersen's training and education groups. These individuals are primarily responsible for working with the program director on the design, development, and implementation of the data collection efforts for the program's performance consulting projects.

In 1996, two years after the program began, it became known that the current CEO would be retiring in a year or two. At that point, a new CEO would be named—a person who had neither ownership nor buy-in to the program. The program's sponsor and director saw the need and value for adopting a more robust evaluation methodology, one that would be able to measure the partners' perceived value of the program as well as the program's impact on key performance measures.

Up to this point, only end-of-course evaluation forms were used to evaluate the overall program. The program leadership was convinced that without more extensive information about the program's performance, there was a possibility that the program could end with the change in CEOs. Initial meetings were set up between the program leadership and internal evaluators to discuss various key features and data sources needed for a new program evaluation system. It also became clear that a much more comprehensive communication plan would be needed to facilitate the use of the information for performance consulting projects within the program and the dissemination of program information to stakeholders and senior leadership.

As a result of these meetings, a formal proposal was developed for the PDP leadership. Three basic objectives were identified to guide evaluation planning and data collection efforts:

1. Determine the program's effects on the attitudes and behaviors of Arthur Andersen partners individually and in teams.
2. Assess the program's impact on organizational concerns.
3. Provide evidence of the program's adoption and determine management issues and problems.

The first two objectives focused on the program's impact, whereas the third objective had more of an internal focus in terms of how effective the program was being managed and how the program design and delivery could be enhanced over time.

One of the first strategies of the new evaluation efforts was to administer a survey to partners who had never attended a PDP course. At this point in time, about 80 percent of all partners had not attended a PDP course. The survey was aimed at determining the reasons why they had not attended a PDP course and what factors would facilitate program attendance. Results from this survey identified critical management, logistical, and communication issues that needed to be addressed as the program moved forward.

Evaluation Framework

The overall evaluation system that was eventually implemented for the program is based on the strategic program evaluation cycle, or SPEC (Luebke, 1997). SPEC provides a framework for tracking and reporting the chain of evidence needed to evaluate an HRD program at three levels or layers of business impact:

- identifying performance enhancement opportunities
- documenting performance enhancement efforts
- monitoring performance enhancement outcomes.

Performance Enhancement Opportunities

The first layer of impact is contingent on the ability to understand and respond to business concerns and individual performance barriers (Brinkerhoff and Gill, 1994). The approach is to start with pertinent organizational outcomes and systematically work down to team and individual performance outcomes.

Two key points of this approach were very attractive to the program sponsor. First, this approach allowed the program to verify the need for training and focus attention on truly important issues within Arthur Andersen. This approach would therefore help control program risks and costs. Second, this process provided an opportunity for the PDP to demonstrate to senior management that it was not only addressing important business issues but was also investigating and discovering insights into business performance issues. This could only be seen as having a meaningful contribution and impact on the overall success of Arthur Andersen.

Performance Enhancement Efforts

The second layer of impact concerned documenting the program's performance of maximizing learning and knowledge transfer of what partners need the most. These efforts focus on tracking the learning performance changes in participants before, during, and after their attendance of a PDP course. Here, effective learning experiences across particular points in time (such as readiness, acquisition/practice, and application) are seen as precursors to successful performance outcomes on the job. In addition, data collection results could be linked to the information collected from the first layer of impact to provide a more insightful analysis into the initial impact of the program on partners.

Performance Enhancement Outcomes

The third layer of business impact, which is related to the success of the first two, concerned actual performance changes in the business environment. These changes are seen as starting with individual partners and eventually accumulating to impact various aspects of Arthur Andersen's organizational performance. The key to this strategy was to examine a number of different business, financial, and HR measures and to build a body of evidence from which plausible conclusions could be drawn regarding the program impact (McLinden, 1995). Furthermore, these outcomes could be linked to the results from the first two layers of impact to provide an overall picture of the program's benefits to the organization.

Data Collection

To evaluate the program at the three layers of impact described above, three corresponding data collection phases were established:

- performance analysis/needs assessment
- training evaluation
- performance evaluation.

Performance Analysis and Needs Assessment

To provide a comprehensive picture of partners' job performance and professional development needs, a number of different data sources and techniques are employed.

At a basic level, informal input from stakeholders continuously is gathered and considered. Even though the overall performance analysis phase can be characterized as "managing by facts," conventional wisdom from senior management, program leadership, faculty members, and other key personnel is viewed as a rich source for developing various hypotheses regarding partners' professional development needs and possible new or revised performance consulting interventions and solutions.

A standard technique for gathering systematic data is to ask partners to complete various assessment instruments. Typically, performance and importance ratings are collected from partners and others regarding partners' competencies and job performance. Gap analyses are then conducted to determine priorities in partners' professional development needs. In addition, interviews with partners and their supervisors have been conducted to supplement the ratings received from partners and others. Another technique used to collect information directly from partners is an ongoing needs assessment at the time of training. Along with the course evaluation feedback that is collected from partners, needs assessment questions are also asked and combined with other available data to determine partners' professional development needs.

A meaningful source of performance data that are examined comes from the various organizational databases that Arthur Andersen has in place. These databases contain detailed information regarding financial performance, client satisfaction ratings, annual job performance summaries, and results from various internal initiatives, such as employee satisfaction surveys and upward feedback ratings. Given that the job performance of the program's target audience has a direct effect on these outcome measures, these databases are closely monitored to understand the current state of the organization.

Another source of data that has been used is feedback collected from a PDP course that provides executive coaching to partners. Briefly, before partners attend this course, they participate in a 450-degree feedback process. They complete a rating instrument that focuses on 50 relationship-building and team leadership practices, as well as 11 client satisfaction outcomes. They also ask peers, ask supervisors, refer to direct reports, and ask clients (the extra 90 degrees in the 360-degree process) to complete this instrument. An outside vendor summarizes the results, and individual reports are distributed and discussed during the course. On an annual basis, the PDP team receives an aggregate data file of the ratings that were collected during the entire year (any personal information that would identify individual partners is removed before the PDP team receives this file). This data then is viewed as a performance assessment, and analyses are conducted to examine how partners' behavior and practices are impacting client and employee satisfaction.

Training Evaluation

Data collection efforts occur before and at the end of each course session. Approximately four weeks prior to attending a PDP course, the partner receives an online survey through the firm's internal email system (Lotus Notes). This survey directs respondents to describe three expectations they have for the course. The respondent also is asked to complete a number of performance and importance ratings concerning course objectives and relevant competencies that are linked to his or her overall job performance measures.

Information gathered from the partners is used in a number of ways. First, a faculty report is generated and given to the faculty a few days before the course begins. This provides a valuable preview for the faculty regarding participants' particular needs and expectations. Second, as mentioned previously, results from the performance and importance ratings of the partners' competencies are viewed as an ongoing assessment of partners' professional development needs. Finally, the performance and importance ratings of the course objectives are used as the "pre" measure in a pre-, during, and postanalysis of partners' rated performance levels (see figure 1).

At the end of every session, partners complete a written end-of-course evaluation survey that contains focused evaluation questions regarding particular aspects of each course. Standard utility questions representing key aspects and outcomes of the training design and delivery also are included for every course. These questions come from

Figure 1. Participants' ratings of course objectives.

Preanalysis		End of Course		Postanalysis*	
Current importance	Current performance	Prior performance	Future performance	Current importance	Current performance

*Data collected two to three months after a session is completed.

an organizational standard evaluation item bank that is used by various training groups within Arthur Andersen. Hence, evaluation results from these items can be compared across various PDP courses and across other Arthur Andersen training programs and courses. These standard utility questions focus on the following areas:

- whether the participants were the right target audience for the training
- effectiveness of the instructional design/learning strategies
- job relevance of course content and activities
- self-perceived learning gains of the participants
- effectiveness of the faculty
- participants' intent to transfer their learning to job responsibilities
- overall training quality.

Finally, partners are asked to rate their prior and anticipated performance of the course objectives. These questions serve as the "during" measure of the analysis of partners' performance ratings. An important aspect of these ratings is that partners' prior ratings of their performance (collected at the end of training) can be compared to their "before" ratings of their performance. This technique gives an insightful perspective of how the training impacted their perceptions of their prior performance.

Performance Evaluation

There are two stages of data collection for performance evaluations. Performance measures are first collected two to three months after partners complete a session. They receive an online survey that directs them to complete rating questions and open-ended questions regarding the following issues:

- their overall satisfaction with the course and the overall program (respondents are also asked their intentions of attending other PDP courses)
- their initial efforts in applying the course content to their job responsibilities (included are open-ended questions directed at de-

scribing individual, team, and organizational performance barriers they may have encountered in the work environment)

- current performance ratings of the course objectives (these ratings serve as the "post" measure in the analysis of partners' reported performance levels).

In addition to the follow-up surveys, telephone interviews with the partners sometimes are completed after a session, depending on particular circumstances. For example, evaluators will call partners within one to two weeks after a session, offering to collect more detailed information regarding their reactions to the course and how they see the course adding value to their professional development.

The second stage of data collection for performance evaluations occurs approximately one year after program attendance. Various organizational databases containing business, financial, or HR data are examined. Data that can be linked to individual partners is extracted and merged together to form special files. Partners' individual evaluation ratings also are merged into these files to allow comparisons between their evaluation ratings and the hard data collected on their performance.

These specially created data files allow the PDP team to compare individual partner results with the overall organizational results collected during the performance analysis phase. The team can also form various research questions and hypotheses regarding program impact that can be tested by conducting various multi- and univariate statistical analyses.

Communication Plan

One of the central issues identified during the initial evaluation planning was how the information would be communicated to key stakeholders. A weakness of the evaluation efforts before 1996 was that the information collected from the program was not systematically getting to the right decision makers and stakeholders who needed to know the progress and impact of the program. As a result, an individual course and annual reporting strategy was designed and implemented.

Standardized course reports are prepared after every course offering. These reports contain the pre-session and end-of-course evaluation results of the individual session and any cumulative results from previous offerings of the course. (Some PDP courses are only offered once or twice a year; others may be held up to seven or eight times a year.) Annual reports for each course are prepared at the end of the year and contain the aggregated pre-session, end-of-course, and follow-up results for all offerings that were held. The main target audiences for these reports are the PDP faculty, sponsor, and team. Moreover, the information contained in these reports is used for the annual planning sessions for the upcoming new course year.

An overall annual evaluation report also is prepared at the end of the year. This report, which is technical in nature, examines the evaluation findings from all PDP courses. Attendance patterns based on participants' regional locations and Arthur Andersen service categories are also examined to determine whether the program is effectively reaching its worldwide target audience. The report also compares the results with the previous year's findings to determine any yearly trends in the data. As part of this reporting process, multiple regression analyses are conducted using the end-of-course standard utility items to determine key drivers of participants' satisfaction with the program. Results from these analyses are also shared with the PDP faculty and course designers to facilitate the process of course revisions and updates. Finally, a summary of the yearly impact analyses is completed, and an internal technical report is written.

Once the annual technical reports are completed, the PDP program director and the internal evaluators meet with a variety of internal specialists in marketing and communications to determine the strategic messages to partners and senior management. The performance analysis and evaluation results are carefully examined to determine the best ways to distinctly and accurately summarize the results in a nontechnical manner for various audiences. For example, evaluation results are included in an annual PDP newsletter sent to all partners. Other communications efforts are created depending on the information needs of particular stakeholders.

Results

Arthur Andersen leadership and various key stakeholders are quite satisfied with the overall performance of the program. Partners consistently indicate that they view the PDP course content as highly relevant to their job responsibilities, and the courses are consistently among the top Arthur Andersen training courses in average training quality ratings. Partners' performance ratings over three measurement periods (that is, before, during, and after) have demonstrated meaningful trends and skill increases.

Furthermore, partners' perceptions of the program's ability to improve their skills in client satisfaction, in retaining and developing others, and in self development are key drivers to their overall satisfaction with the program. Program attendance also has grown steadily every year, with an increasing number of partners attending the program for the first time and others returning to take additional courses.

Results from performance and impact analyses provided insights into the current state of partners' business performance and how the program is impacting aspects of the organization. In fact, recent results from the 450-degree feedback instrument—combined with other organizational client and employee satisfaction data—have provided insights into how partners' behaviors and practices are systematically affecting particular HR and business aspects of the organization's service-profit chain (Heskett et al., 1994). This information has been shared with senior management, and steps currently are under way to communicate this information to a broader audience within the organization.

Finally, one of the most significant accomplishments of the program is that it has the support of Arthur Andersen's new CEO. The senior management leadership team also is supporting proposals and efforts to expand partners' professional development opportunities.

Conclusion

This case study presents the framework used in managing the information of an executive development program. This framework facilitated the performance consulting services surrounding the program and also provided an effective means of managing and reporting the information generated from the program.

Key features of this framework include the following:
- aligning training efforts with organizational performance issues and business measures
- directing evaluation dollars to performance analysis activities that have the highest value of managing program risks
- providing diagnostic measures in tracking individuals' learning-performance changes
- guiding the program information to strategic segments of the organization.

As the program continues, a number of challenges lie ahead. One challenge involves the management and storage of the large amount of data the program is collecting and analyzing over time. With the help of internal specialists in data management and computer systems, current efforts are under way to build a more efficient central database for program data. This new database will allow the PDP team to efficiently track performance data over time and conduct longitudinal analyses of how the program is impacting the organization.

Questions for Discussion

1. This article describes an evaluation system that was used for an executive development program. What other types of HRD programs could benefit from an overall evaluation system?
2. What role (or roles) does a program evaluation play in a program's relationship with its key stakeholders and decision makers? In the design and development of performance enhancement interventions?
3. How have recent advances in technology and data management facilitated performance consulting efforts?
4. A pre-, during, and postanalysis strategy was used to measure self-reported performance changes over time. What are some of the advantages and disadvantages of this measurement strategy?
5. How did the program sponsor and director respond to changes in the organization after the program began? What benefits did they achieve?

The Authors

Jerry F. Luebke is a senior manager with Arthur Andersen's performance and learning group in St. Charles, Illinois. He is responsible for the overall management and technical supervision of various program evaluations and applied research projects. His areas of expertise include program evaluation, employee and client satisfaction assessment, and applied statistical design and analysis. For the past three years, he has directed the application of the program evaluation system for PDP. Recently, the program won a Best Practice Award in Leadership Development from the American Society for Training & Development and the American Productivity and Quality Center (APQC) and was cited for its comprehensive measurement efforts.

Luebke received an Ed.D. in educational psychology from Northern Illinois University. Before joining Arthur Andersen, he taught at the high school and community college levels. He has published articles in a variety of research journals during the past 20 years and has made a number of presentations on training evaluations at national professional conferences. Luebke is a member of the American Evaluation Association and can be reached at 1405 North 5th Avenue,

St. Charles, IL 60174; phone: 630.444.3981; fax: 630.377.3794; email: jerry.f.luebke@us.arthurandersen.com.

Susan E. Bumpass is program director for Arthur Andersen's PDP. During her career at Arthur Andersen, she has managed a group charged with the responsibility of developing products and services to enhance the performance of the Arthur Andersen training function. She has also helped design and develop about 400 hours of technical and nontechnical training across a broad spectrum of competencies in support of the organization's strategies and plans. Bumpass, an ASTD member, represents Arthur Andersen in a forum of companies that are benchmarking and sharing successful internal executive development and training practices. She has made conference presentations at the European Foundation for Quality Management (EFQM), the Association for Educational Communications and Technology (AECT), the International Society for Performance Improvement (ISPI), the International Quality and Productivity Center (IQPC), and corporate university conferences as well as to a wide variety of Arthur Andersen clients. She recently co-authored "Trends in Executive Development," published in *HR Director: The Arthur Andersen Guide to Human Capital.*

References

Brinkerhoff, R.O., and Gill, S.J. *The Learning Alliance: Systems Thinking in Human Resource Development.* San Francisco: Jossey-Bass, 1994.

Heskett, J.L., Jones, T.O., Loveman, G.W., Sasser, W.E., and Schlesinger, L.A. "Putting the Service-profit Chain to Work." *Harvard Business Review,* March-April, 164-174, 1994

Luebke, J.F. "Evaluating the Business Impact of Training." In *HR Director: The Arthur Andersen Guide to Human Capital.* San Francisco: Profile Pursuit, 1997.

McLinden, D.J. "Proof, Evidence, and Complexity: Understanding the Impact of Training and Development in Business." *Performance Improvement Quarterly, 8*(3), 3-18, 1995.

Using AMIGOS to Improve Mentoring Relationships

Sandia National Laboratories

Linda K. Stromei and Patricia E. Boverie

This case study describes the experiences of an external consultant and her client, one of the national laboratories. The case begins with the consultant presenting her proposal to her client and ends midway through the implementation of the pared-down project. Several important lessons and their implications for external consultants are discussed. There are numerous discussion questions and recommendations for future improvement. The story, which is told in narrative fashion with the consultant confiding her frustrations to a colleague, illustrates the importance of professional coaching and feedback. And like all good stories, it has a happy ending.

It is July 1998, and Linda Stromei is about to go to a meeting with her client, Sandia National Laboratories, to discuss her proposal for implementing her mentoring model with their new weapons intern program. She calls her mentor, Patricia Boverie, for some advice.

Boverie asks, "What's your major concern about this meeting?" Stromei replies, "They wanted me to fax my proposal to them so that they could look it over before the meeting. That is fine, but I hope that I get to formally present the model. I really believe that all the components of the model are important."

"Don't you think they will accept the whole model?" asks Boverie. "Actually," Stromei responds, "I am afraid that they will only implement parts of the model, and I worry that when problems arise due to taking shortcuts, well, I might look responsible."

This case was prepared to serve as a basis for discussion rather than to illustrate either effective or ineffective administrative and management practices.

"Go to the meeting with an open mind, present your model, and if they don't use the entire model, you should voice your concerns but still work with them. When organizations start new projects, such as this mentoring program, very often they can't foresee all the complications that might arise. I think you should help them as much as you can and also be ready to guide them through the tough spots," Boverie recommends.

"Thanks, Patricia," says Stromei. "You know, based on my previous association with Sandia, and especially with Andy Rogulich, I know that they are interested in implementing a mentoring program for all of their employees, and the intern program could serve as a pilot program for the rest of the lab."

Background

Stromei is a consultant who worked with Sandia National Laboratories' leadership training program in 1997 and 1998, conducting research and an evaluation of their corporate mentoring program for managers. Based on her research and work with mentoring programs, Stromei developed the award-winning AMIGOS model for formal mentoring programs.

It was during this working relationship at Sandia that Stromei became acquainted with Andrew Rogulich, the program coordinator of the new weapons intern program (IP), who asked her to submit a proposal to implement her AMIGOS model for the interns of this new program. Stromei was asked to put together a proposal and fax it to Rogulich.

Organizational Profile

Sandia National Laboratories (Sandia) is a large research and development national laboratory; its main facilities are located in Albuquerque, New Mexico, and Livermore, California. It is operated by the Sandia Corporation, a Lockheed Martin Co., for the U.S. Department of Energy (DOE). Sandia provides scientific and engineering solutions to meet national needs in nuclear weapons and related defense systems.

Sandia employs about 8,100 employees, 900 of whom are managers, directors, or vice presidents. Approximately 60 percent of Sandia's employees are in technical and scientific positions, and a large percentage of this group holds advanced academic degrees.

A provision of Sandia's most recent contract with DOE mandated the implementation of a mentoring program for managers and senior level technical and scientific staff within two years. Other factors

contributed to the need for a mentoring program. As Sandia was changing its output to meet new challenges in science and technology (even
as it continued traditional efforts in national security), a mentoring
program was sought to "foster agility in the workforce and to provide
a mechanism for developing people to be better able to respond to
changing requirements and complex customer needs" (Stromei,
1998). A large number of Sandia's current employees are eligible for
retirement, and a mentoring program could utilize the expertise of
these employees prior to their retirement.

The Sandia weapons IP is a part of the knowledge management
project at Sandia. It was developed over a two-year period through
research, study, and input from a variety of sources, using a systems
approach. The mission of the IP is to "prepare the future generation
of experts for critical positions in the nuclear weapons stewardship
throughout the nuclear weapons community, in order to perform 'Exceptional Service in the National Interest'" (Stromei, 1998).

The 1997-1998 Sandia evaluation provided quantitative evidence that a mentoring program could accelerate the learning
process and skills transfer (Stromei, 1998). Based on this, a mentoring
component was added to help accomplish the stated objectives of the
intern program, and the four basic areas of emphasis:
1. technical skills
2. general skills
3. history and mission
4. teamwork.

Each intern had a mentor assigned by the home department to
provide the goals and help with the home department business. There
were to be two sets of goals: personal and technical.

Project Design
July 1998

In July 1998, Rogulich called Stromei and asked to set up a meeting to discuss her mentoring proposal. Stromei met with Rogulich
and two other Sandia employees, a corporate training liaison and the
director of the corporate mentoring program. Before Stromei arrived,
these three had met to discuss Stromei's faxed proposal and essentially had already decided what they wanted to do.

When she arrived at the meeting, Stromei explained her proposal
to implement the AMIGOS model, which includes testing, interviewing and matching interns and mentors, training for mentors and in-
terns/protégés, development of goals and objectives and agreements

between mentors and interns, action learning projects with the pairs, and social interactions between the pairs. (See figure 1 for implementation steps in the AMIGOS model.)

Unfortunately, due to time, money and other constraints, Sandia wanted to implement only a small part of Stromei's proposal. Of the overall budget for the IP, less than one-half of 1 percent was allocated to implement the mentoring piece.

Stromei expressed her concerns about not being allowed to implement the full model, and she considered not working with the IP if she were not allowed to implement it fully. However, based on her previous association with Rogulich, she agreed to work with Sandia on a pared-down approach. (See figure 2 for an illustration of which portions of the model Stromei was contracted to implement and which were handled by Sandia employees.)

Budget constraints played a large role in the reduction of initial and ongoing training proposed for the mentors and interns. After the initial meeting, where the structure shown in figure 2 was agreed to, Stromei received an email from the contract writer, advising of additional cuts in the contract. The email stated that yet another piece of the proposal was being deleted, and that the individual coaching meetings were reduced from two hours per mentoring pair to one hour. Again, budget issues were given as the rationale.

Stromei immediately began preparing the training she was to deliver in September, working frantically given the short implementation time between the contract being put into place and the date of the first training. Because the revised contract didn't allow for any advance assessment or needs analysis, Stromei was forced to design her training to accommodate a wide range of personality types and learning styles instead of being able to customize it for the participants.

September 1998

On September 8, 1998, the program orientation for the IP was held. This meeting was attended by the interns, their managers, and their assigned mentors.

This orientation meeting was scheduled for three hours. Most of it was taken up by the program organizers and managers, who provided an overview and introduced this new program. Stromei was given 30 minutes at the end to administer her instruments, the Myers Briggs Type Inventory (MBTI) and the Leader Behavior Analysis II (LBAII). However, many of the interns and managers had left by this point, citing other commitments. Consequently, it was necessary to

Figure 1. AMIGOS model of a formal mentoring program.

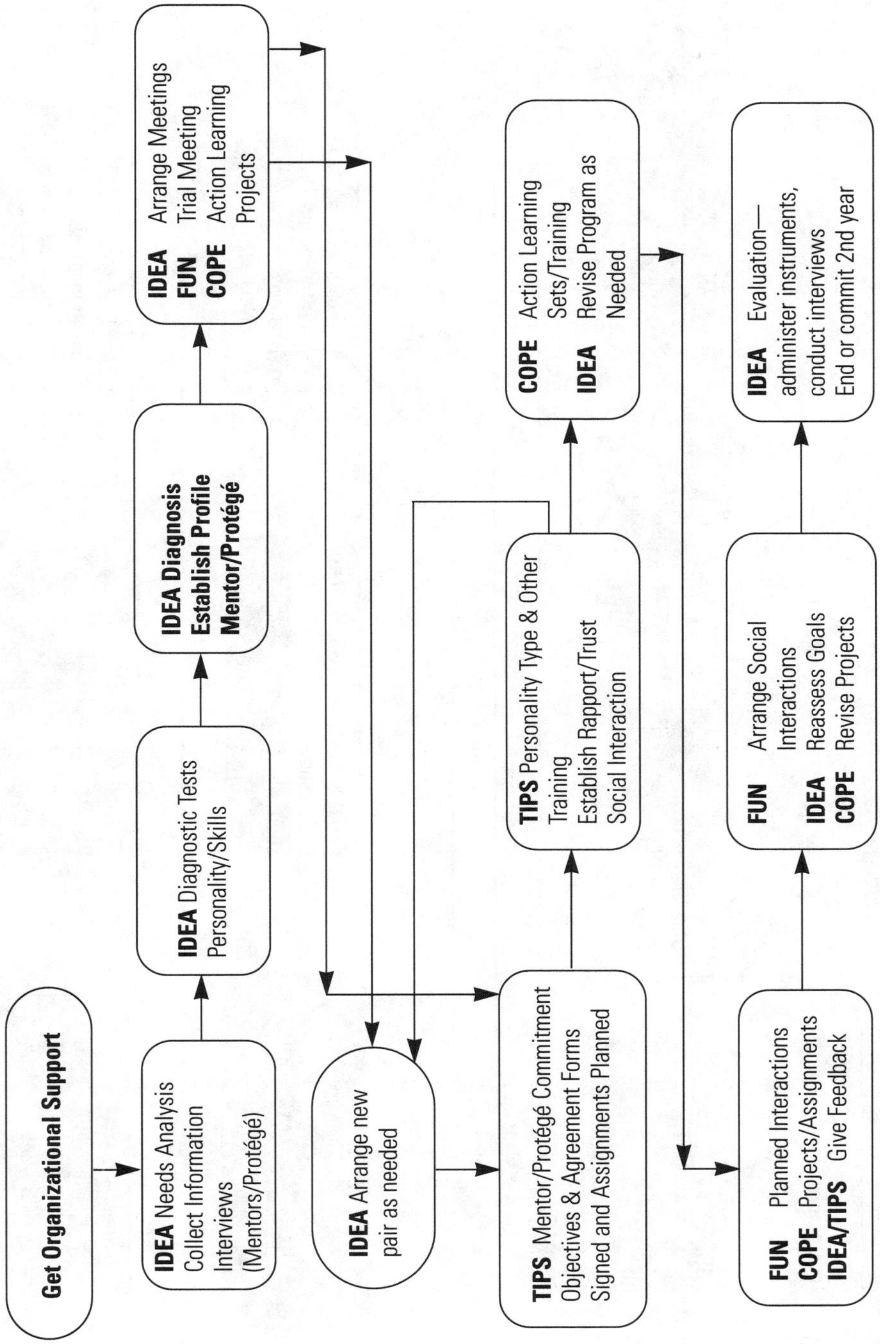

Get Organizational Support

IDEA Needs Analysis
Collect Information
Interviews
(Mentors/Protégé)

IDEA Diagnostic Tests
Personality/Skills

IDEA Diagnosis
Establish Profile
Mentor/Protégé

IDEA Arrange Meetings
FUN Trial Meeting
COPE Action Learning
Projects

IDEA Arrange new
pair as needed

TIPS Mentor/Protégé Commitment
Objectives & Agreement Forms
Signed and Assignments Planned

TIPS Personality Type & Other
Training
Establish Rapport/Trust
Social Interaction

COPE Action Learning
Sets/Training
IDEA Revise Program as
Needed

IDEA Evaluation—
administer instruments,
conduct interviews
End or commit 2nd year

FUN Planned Interactions
COPE Projects/Assignments
IDEA/TIPS Give Feedback

FUN Arrange Social
Interactions
IDEA Reassess Goals
COPE Revise Projects

© 1998 Linda K. Stromei.

Using AMIGOS to Improve Mentoring Relationships   **185**

Figure 2. AMIGOS model of a formal mentoring program.

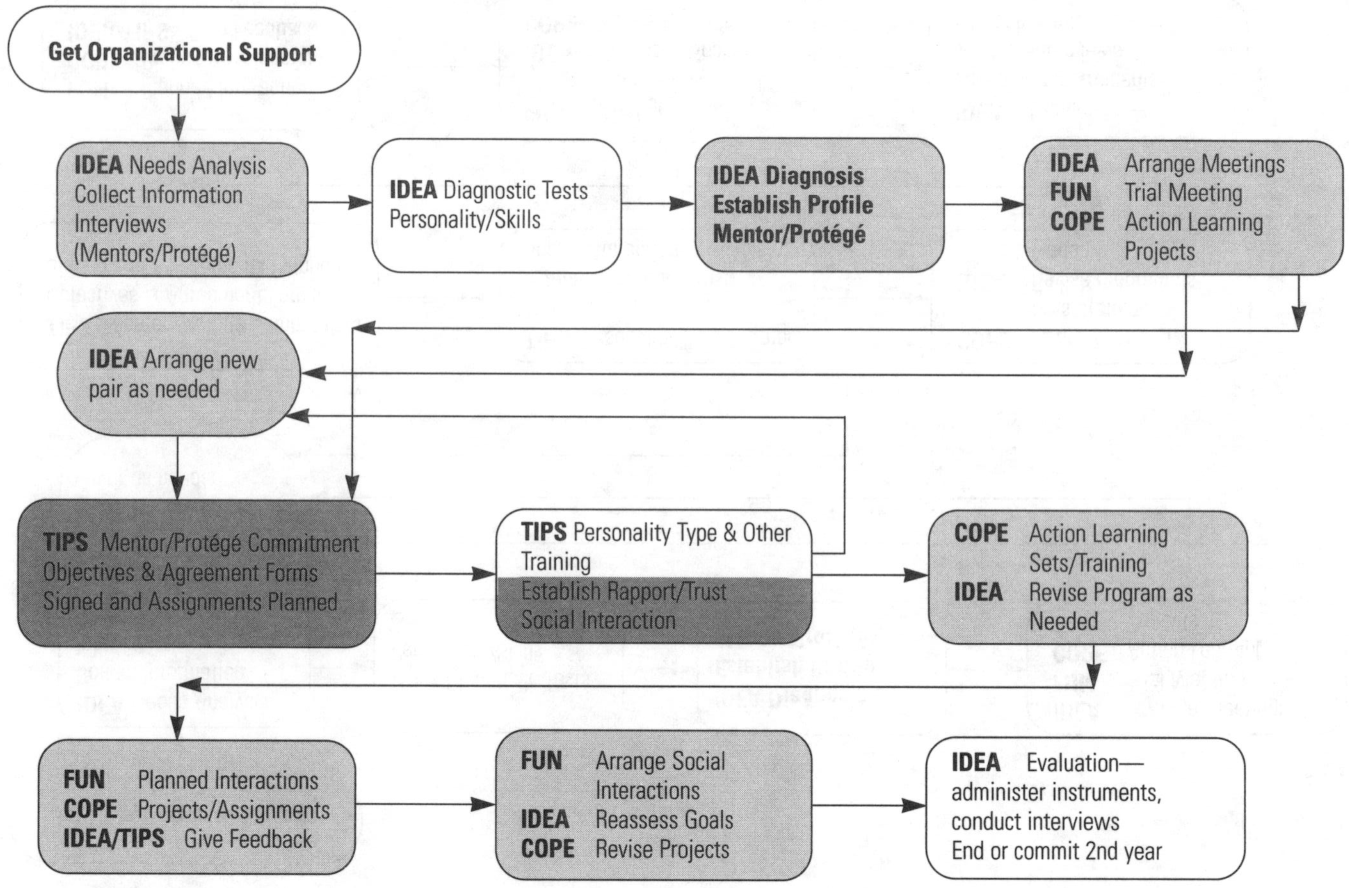

Get Organizational Support

IDEA Needs Analysis
Collect Information
Interviews
(Mentors/Protégé)

IDEA Diagnostic Tests
Personality/Skills

**IDEA Diagnosis
Establish Profile
Mentor/Protégé**

IDEA Arrange Meetings
FUN Trial Meeting
COPE Action Learning
Projects

IDEA Arrange new
pair as needed

TIPS Mentor/Protégé Commitment
Objectives & Agreement Forms
Signed and Assignments Planned

TIPS Personality Type & Other
Training
Establish Rapport/Trust
Social Interaction

COPE Action Learning
Sets/Training
IDEA Revise Program as
Needed

FUN Planned Interactions
COPE Projects/Assignments
IDEA/TIPS Give Feedback

FUN Arrange Social
Interactions
IDEA Reassess Goals
COPE Revise Projects

IDEA Evaluation—
administer instruments,
conduct interviews
End or commit 2nd year

☐ Not implemented; ▨ Implemented by others.

© 1998 Linda K. Stromei.

send the instruments to many of the participants. Many were not completed and returned in a timely fashion; some never were returned.

The first training session for the interns and their mentors was held on September 15, 1998. At this three-hour session, Sandia employees handled training for the objectives and agreement forms. Stromei delivered training on listening skills, learning styles, and mentoring concepts. This session was attended by most, but not all, of the interns and mentors. One mentor and intern participated in this session via an interactive television link from California.

The second and final training session was held on September 29, 1998. This six-hour training session was attended by all but two of the 15 interns and by eight of the mentors, even though Rogulich had stressed that it was essential that mentors and interns attend this session together. This session was to include several exercises that the mentors and interns would work on together to help them get acquainted and begin establishing their working relationship. Thus, the fact that not all of the mentors were there was a source of frustration, especially for those interns who had attended without their mentor.

This session began with a discussion of expectations of the program followed by a mentoring role play. The corporate training liaison went over the technical objective forms, and the corporate mentoring coordinator went over the agreement and objective forms. A box lunch was brought in.

Following lunch, Stromei introduced the results of the MBTI for those who had participated, and she conducted a session on using MBTI in relationships. The group scores on the LBAII were discussed, and each participant who had completed it was given his or her individual scores. This was followed by training on the situational leadership model and how it impacts the mentoring relationship. Particular emphasis was given to the directive and coaching roles of the model, as the ideal mentor needs to be adept at coaching the protégé.

The final activity of the day was a game designed for the mentors to practice coaching their protégés through putting a model together. Unfortunately, some of the mentors had to leave before this final activity, and their interns had no one to work on this project with them.

October 1998

October 1, 1998, was the official start for the technical training portion of the IP. However, according to Stromei's contract, she would have no further contact with the IP, the mentors, or the interns until mid-1999. (At that time, she was scheduled to conduct one-hour coaching sessions with the pairs.) However, she kept in touch via email and phone calls with Rogulich on a regular basis, and she received reports on the program's progression.

November 1998

Stromei spoke with Rogulich about the IP. He mentioned that he had heard varying reports from the interns about how things were going with their mentors; while some mentioned that they were meeting regularly, several said they had not had much contact at all.

Rogulich informed Stromei that he had sent out an informal email survey to all the interns and received replies from ranging from "they meet once a week for lunch" to "they never had seen their mentor in the last three months." Stromei reminded Rogulich that some of the mentors had not attended either of the initial mentoring training sessions and that some didn't complete any of the instruments.

Stromei mentioned to Rogulich that in preparation for her upcoming coaching sessions (scheduled to begin in mid-1999), she would like to give the interns and their mentors some advance notice via email regarding the items to be discussed at these sessions. Stromei thought this would be helpful, especially in light of the fact that the majority of the participants in the mentoring program expressed a preference for introversion (I) on their MBTI—and Is prefer advance notice of topics before meetings.

Rogulich mentioned that the interns were very busy, and that with the holidays approaching, perhaps it would be best to wait until January 1999 to send this out.

Performance Consulting Intervention
December 1998

At Stromei's request, she and Rogulich met to discuss ways to improve the current IP. They decided that they would meet with others to brainstorm ways to rectify the current program's perceived problems and to plan for the next program, which was to begin in October 1999. Due to the end-of-the-year timing, they agreed that the meeting would be held in early January.

Prior to this meeting, Stromei outlined a needs analysis of the situation, using the following performance consulting approach:
1. *Level one.* Before Stromei could plan any intervention, she needed to understand the needs and concerns of the two principal stakeholders (Rogulich and the head of the program, John Hogan) and to work with them to develop a good intervention.

2. *Level two.* What skills were needed? It appeared to Stromei that the engineers and scientists were task oriented; what methods could be used to make them more people oriented?

3. *Level three.* What processes in the program needed to be improved? Stromei decided to set up meetings with the interns and mentors and ask them for their input to this question. (See table 1 for the questions asked in these series of meetings.)

4. *Level four.* On the business level, there were two considerations: What emergency measures could be implemented for this program, and what needed to be improved for the new program that was slated to start later that year?

5. *Level five.* On the payoff level for the organization, the mentoring program was a small piece of a very expensive training program. Initially, less than one-half of 1 percent of the funding was allocated for the mentoring piece of the program. Could Sandia justify allocating more funds for the mentoring piece?

January 1999

Stromei received an email message from Rogulich on January 6, 1999, bringing her up-to-date on what had happened since their meeting in December. He described feedback he had received from the interns about their mentoring relationship. As this was to be a pilot program, it was important to monitor the progress closely, and the program had been under way for three months.

Rogulich reported that the feedback varied widely, from some interns reporting that it wasn't working at all to others reporting that it was working wonderfully. He added that he and Hogan had talked about meeting with Stromei to discuss what modifications could be made to the current group to improve the outcome as well as how to use the lessons learned from this group to improve the new program, which was scheduled to start October 1999. Interestingly, one of Rogulich's findings was that not all of the mentors knew how to mentor, and he felt that was an important piece he would like to see added to the new program. He felt that mentoring training would be something that could be expanded organization-wide throughout Sandia as part of their knowledge management program. Rogulich discussed possible funding sources and indicated that he would like for Stromei to work with someone from Sandia's education and training department to facilitate this added training.

Using the performance based needs assessment as a guide, Stromei met with Rogulich and Hogan on January 13, 1999. At this session, the three discussed issues surrounding the failure of some of the men-

Table 1. Questions for performance consulting intervention.

Questions for Interns	Questions for Mentors
What things are working well for you with your mentor?	What things are working well, or what things did a mentor provide for you that you could provide for your intern/protégé?
How much time are you spending together?	How much time are you spending together?
How regularly do you meet?	How regularly do you meet, or how often do you think a successful pair should meet?
Do you use phone, email, or other creative means of communication?	Do you use phone, email, or other creative means of communication?
Has your mentor gone on any of the planned program field trips with you?	Have you been able to accompany your intern on any of the program field trips, or have you sat in on a class session?
When you meet, do you plan a topic in advance that you want to talk about?	When you meet with your intern, do you think of things to discuss, such as books to recommend, etc.?
Give some specific examples of how you take the initiative in your mentoring relationship.	Give some specific examples of how you take the initiative in your mentoring relationship.
Give some specific examples of how the mentor/intern program has been of benefit to you.	Give some specific examples of how the mentor/intern program has been of benefit to you, or how you think it could benefit you.
What has been your favorite thing about the mentor/intern program so far, and why?	What has been your favorite thing about the mentor/intern program so far, and why?

tors. It was observed that many engineers and scientists were task oriented and that perhaps the current mentoring program did not have enough structure. Stromei reminded them that, as initially proposed, her model indeed had structure, with an up-front agreement, goals, and objectives that she would work with the mentoring pairs to complete. This part of the proposal was not implemented.

The matching of the pairs was also discussed, and it was felt that perhaps this was an area that needed to be changed. The initially proposed model allowed Stromei to be involved in the matching; however, based on the time allotted to put the program together, the intern's department manager had merely been asked to provide a mentor.

The general rule was that the mentors were picked for their technical expertise. However, in some cases, the department managers opted to be the mentors themselves. Stromei advised that this is normally not a good match, given the confidential nature required of a mentoring relationship. Often, it's difficult for a intern/protégé to confide information to his or her manager, as he or she does not wish to be seen as incapable or weak and needing help.

At this brainstorming session, the decision was made to do several things to prepare for the new class of interns (scheduled to start October 1, 1999) and to improve the current class. For the current group and to gain information for planning the new program, Stromei suggested that a series of facilitated lunches be held, two for the interns and two for the mentors. At these lunches Stromei would discuss the following questions, first with the interns and, later, with the mentors:

1. What things are working well for them?
2. How much time are they spending together?
3. Did they plan their topics for the meetings in advance?
4. Who takes the initiative to set up the meetings, the mentor or the intern?
5. Do they use phone or email or another creative means of communication?
6. Did the mentors ever accompany the interns on any of the field trips that are part of the IP?

February 1999

The facilitated lunches were held throughout this month. Two dates were provided for the interns and two for the mentors. Each lunch was well attended by the participants, and all but one of the interns and three of the mentors were able to attend. The participants' answers were recorded on a flipchart. One mentor who could not attend forwarded his comments via email to the project managers.

At the interns' lunches, it became apparent that the success of the mentoring pairs ran the gamut, from meeting regularly every week for lunch to the response of one intern, who jokingly said that he "put his mentor's face on the milk carton and asked, 'Have you seen this mentor?'" (This intern received a new mentor. He reported back that he and the new mentor already had scheduled several sessions, and he seemed to be very enthusiastic.)

After the interns' feedback was gathered, it was decided that a different means of selection for the mentors should be looked at, with the interns having some input into the process. The mentor chosen purely for technical expertise was not the best choice in some instances.

At the mentors' lunches, several of the mentors admitted that they really did not know what they were supposed to do. Most—although not all—of these responses came from mentors who were not at the initial training. One mentor mentioned that he felt the up-front training was a total waste and that the "touchy-feely" stuff, such as the MBTI and the icebreaker, "melted in a puddle." Stromei addressed his concerns and was able to illustrate how it helps to know about the other person's personality preferences and how to deal with them. She further explained that icebreakers are just that—they are meant to help break the ice and to bring a social element to the event.

In addition, Stromei explained that mentoring is a relationship that is not established by merely handing out notebooks with information organized in bullet points. It requires a bonding or trust between the pairs. Icebreakers and other forms of training that allow social interaction are helpful in establishing these relationships.

Table 2 shows the five levels of performance analysis and the needs assessments and outcomes that were derived from the data collection for each level. Although data was not collected from all of the participants, the sample consisted of 94 percent of the interns, and 87 percent of the mentors, which would appear to lend statistical significance to any conclusions based on the data.

Table 2. Five levels of performance analysis after intervention.

Needs Assessment	Outcomes
Level five (organization)	Will develop program for implementing mentoring for entire organization.
Level four (business needs)	Emergency measures instituted for current program; improvements planned for new program.
Level three (program process)	Qualitative data provided basis for current program refinement and development.
Level two (mentors and interns)	More training slated for mentors and interns; handbook/job aid developed for reference; selection process of mentors revised.
Level one (stakeholders' preferences)	Stakeholders have clearer goals for the program and buy-in.

Eventual Outcomes

Based on the performance consulting intervention, Stromei and her client decided that she would put together a handout (job aid) for the mentors. The handout would consist of examples of good mentoring—notably, take the protégés to lunch, introduce them to influential people, suggest books or articles they can read, be available for coaching and feedback, listen to problems, and make suggestions.

Stromei, Rogulich, and Hogan agreed that they would suggest that the mentors become more involved in the classroom sessions and attend the field trips whenever possible.

Stromei then addressed the issue of motivation for the mentors. The suggestion was made to put the mentoring assignment on the performance management report of the mentors so they would get some recognition for it. Other types of rewards were looked at (such as plaques and write-ups in the organization newsletter). Most of the mentors surveyed felt that mentoring was something they could do to give back because someone had done it for them. Other mentors commented that they did not feel that Sandia fully supported the mentoring program because they provided no incentive of any kind for the mentors. Stromei and Rogulich agreed that this area definitely could be changed for the next program.

Other potential changes continue to be discussed. Additional training for both mentors and protégés definitely will be added. In addition, more importance will be placed on the initial agreement forms and the development of goals and objectives, not only for the technical program, but also for the mentoring relationship. Stromei suggested that by conducting initial interviews with the potential participants, possible skills and knowledge areas could be explored. It appears that some mentors do not know how to give good feedback, nor do they have the interpersonal skills needed to teach others. These can be addressed with the planned changes for the new program.

After the facilitated luncheon meetings with the interns and mentors, and after discussing the meeting outcomes, Stromei sent the following email to Rogulich and the corporate training liaison, Michelle Fromm-Lewis:

————-Original Message————-From: Linda K. Stromei
[mailto:lstromei@unm.edu]
Sent: Wednesday, February 24, 1999 9:39 AM
To: Rogulich, Andrew J
Cc: xxxxxx
Subject: AMIGOS model

Michelle and Andy:

Attached you will find my AMIGOS mentoring model, its explanation and the implementation flow chart. These are all copyrighted and are published in my dissertation, which is copyrighted through University Manuscripts International (UMI).

You may or may not remember that I proposed this model for your IP, and due to time, money, and other constraints, we were unable to fully implement it. As we are now seeing, however, through our series of debriefings with both the interns and mentors, validation for full implementation of the model is there; that is, the things we were unable to implement in my model are things that they (mentors and interns) are saying would have helped. I appreciate the support that both of you have expressed to me personally and on my behalf at meetings with others. As Michelle mentioned the last time we met, there is a place for all of us with this project, especially if we all focus on Sandia's overall goal and vision.

I look forward to your feedback. Please keep in mind that the attached flow chart has lengthy explanation for each block, but was purposefully kept brief so it would fit on one sheet of paper.

Linda

Conclusions

Several major lessons were learned in this case. First, proper planning—combined with the organization's vision—is important. Stromei could see that Sandia had broad vision but that it appeared unwilling to allocate sufficient resources to fully accomplish that vision. In cases such as this, either the organization must do what Sandia did, or it will fail to meet its goal. Organizations need to recognize the need to make adjustments to the program in a timely way.

From a consultant's point of view, it is essential to educate clients on the ramifications of the plan under consideration. It is important for the consultant to point out any possible detriments if his or her suggestions cannot be fully implemented.

Stromei felt that by using performance consulting and going in with a planned needs analysis, she was able to see the organization turn the corner toward becoming a visionary learning organization, and she commented on what a delight it was to work with clients who were so willing to change and make adjustments as necessary.

Consultants should be careful not to avoid projects that do not start off with all of their suggestions. Stromei easily could have walked away based on her initial perceptions that she would not be able to fully implement her model, but she realized that by working with the client in a limited capacity, she was able to help them see and facilitate a change in the program. The lesson here is not to let money become the overriding issue in choosing projects.

A lesson for the organization is still evolving. Sandia—as is the case for many government contractors—spends a great deal of money for technical training, which is, of course, important. However, when the relationship of the learners is essential to the skills transfer, as in the mentoring program, allocating funds for these programs also is a sound training decision.

Sandia National Laboratories is to be commended for being a visionary organization. Their overall corporate vision is one that seeks to perform "Exceptional Service in the National Interest." This vision is carried through in the IP, which will benefit not only the participants but our country as well. With this in mind, Stromei was proud that she had the opportunity to work with this program and was pleased to be able to make a difference.

Stromei phoned Boverie to bring her up-to-date on the latest developments. "Well, Linda, it seems like your initial fears about not totally implementing the program were right on target. I think the way you handled the situation was done very well. Now that they are planning on making some changes, and using more of your model, what do you think the next challenge is?"

"I think this may be the challenge—to find a way to convince these scientific and engineering personnel that the social aspect of mentoring will indeed accelerate the learning process. We need to find a way to convince them that learning does not always need to be painful, and it's okay to learn and have fun. By the way, Patricia, thanks for listening; your mentoring of me is what gave me my interest in developing mentors."

"You're welcome, Linda. Thank you for asking me to work with you on writing your case study. It looks like our mentoring relationship has come full circle."

"That's right, Patricia. You know, we should research the stages of a mentoring relationship. That can be our next case study."

Note: As a result of the quality processes used to revise this program, the program was awarded Sandia's Gold President's Quality Award for 1999.

Teaching Note

This case study probably will inspire a lively, instructive discussion. The case is presented straightforwardly and likely will involve little clarification of case content. Depending on the audience, many participants may be able to furnish similar experiences and present their opinions about such situations.

This case should generate a participant-focused discussion—that is, the discussion leader should be prepared to use participants' comments to guide the group into complexities that the case implies rather than states. In order to achieve this, the leader will need the abilities to listen, probe for subtleties, and pinpoint the emerging structure of the discussion with periodic summaries.

This particular case describes a consulting situation in which the consultant is faced with dilemmas as well as issues of personality and organizational culture. After an initial disappointment, the consultant continues to work with the client to a successful conclusion.

This case would be appropriate for training of consultants, organizations that deal with outside consultants, people interested in formal mentoring programs, and curriculum design of training as well as courses in HRD, management, and organizational behavior. It deals with issues of ethics, professionalism, curriculum development, organizational learning, program management, diplomacy, and patience. It could be used in classroom training, as field work, or for a discussion session, and it is especially useful in illustrating the merits of working alongside a client to help the client learn.

Preparing for the Discussion

It's a good practice to ask two participants to open the discussion. This serves several purposes. First, it signals cooperation to the group as a whole. Moreover, having two participants open the discussion provides the leader with not only twice as much material to probe but also a sense of insurance—that is, if the first speaker fails, the second may present more usable material. The discussion leader should stress that the first two speakers are opening the territory for exploration, not providing a complete analysis.

Another factor to consider is the location of the opening speakers. It's best to select participants who are on either side of the room, thus encapsulating the room. It's often a good idea to ask at least one of the opening participants to begin, even before the case is presented. This way participants have fair warning that they should be taking notes.

Guiding the Discussion

The questions listed at the end of this case study are helpful in sparking discussion. Others to consider include the following:

1. What's going on here?
2. What would you advise Stromei to do?
3. Did Stromei do the right thing?
4. How would you describe Sandia's position in this situation?
5. In terms of consulting professionalism, what was Stromei doing well? Did she risk her professionalism at any time?
6. What are some of the problems facing Sandia in regards to this mentoring program?
7. What are some of the problems facing Stromei as she continues to work with Sandia?
8. What underlying issues does this case focus for you?

It is hoped that the group will come up with new and stimulating issues to consider, and it is always good to ask the participants to share similar experiences. The session should be wrapped up with a brief summary of some of the questions the group has posed and finish with a final question to ponder, namely, "What have we learned from Stromei's experiences—and what does it mean for each of us?"

Questions for Discussion
1. Who were the major players in this case?
2. Who are the stakeholders?
3. What was the central issue or problem?
4. What components of a good mentoring program did the program managers understand? What components did they not fully grasp?
5. Describe the relationship between client and consultant. How did it progress and develop? What were some critical issues and situations?
6. What should have Stromei done or said differently at the first meeting?
7. What are a consultant's responsibilities in educating a client ? When should a consultant give up trying to educate?
8. Discuss Stromei's use of performance consulting. What else should she have done?
9. In this case, there was no incentive for the mentors to cooperate. What are some suggestions to remedy this situation?
10. If the organization were to cut resources to the mentoring program again, what should Stromei do?
11. In this case, Stromei found the scientists and technicians skeptical of soft skills training. What is the best way to present this type of training to such an audience and convince them of its value?
12. How can a consultant use performance consulting to bring HRD programs in line with an organization's mission and vision?

The Authors

Linda K. Stromei is president of LINCO, a consulting firm whose clients include organizations in the public and private sectors. Stromei consults in all areas of HRD and instructional design and training and specializes in establishing formal mentoring programs. Stromei is an adjunct professor at the University of New Mexico and Southern Illinois University, where she has taught courses in HR, instructional design and training, adult learning, and learner assessment and evaluation. Stromei, who holds a Ph.D. from the University of New Mexico, currently is the coordinator for the Teaching Assistant Resource Center at the university. Her research interests include skills transfer for formal mentoring programs—in particular, leadership skills transfer and soft skills training for technical employees—as well as the influence of personality types on working relationships. She can be reached at Box 2050, Corrales, NM 87048; phone: 505.890.6095; fax: 505.898.3230; email: lstromei@unm.edu.

Patricia E. Boverie is an associate professor of organizational learning and instructional technologies at the University of New Mexico, where she teaches courses in adult learning and development. Boverie holds a Ph.D. from the University of Texas at Austin, where she studied organizational, social, and educational psychology. Boverie's areas of expertise are in the fields of individual, team, and organizational learning; her current research interests include examining team learning, development of consulting skills, and the social psychology of the distance classroom. Before coming to New Mexico, she co-directed and taught in a graduate program for organization development at Central Washington University. In addition to teaching at the university, Boverie has a private consulting practice.

Reference

Stromei, L.K. *An Evaluation of the Effectiveness of a Formal Mentoring Program for Managers, and the Determinants of Protégé Success.* Unpublished doctoral dissertation. Albuquerque, NM: University of New Mexico, 1998.

Reinventing the HR Function

Redwood Stone Products Company

Jack J. Phillips and Patricia P. Phillips

This case describes a performance consulting project that assessed overall HR practices and recommended performance changes at a medium-size producer of crushed stone products. The areas involved in the assessment included employment and selection, training, job design, compensation, benefits, reward systems, performance standards and appraisal, record-keeping systems, employee relations, communications, safety and health, medical services, environmental, legal responsibilities, and cooperation and teamwork. This case is an example of the findings a thorough, comprehensive performance assessment process can present.

Background

Redwood Stone Products Company (RSPC) is a medium-size producer of crushed stone products, including crushed stone, asphalt, concrete, sand, and gravel. The aggregates industry is very competitive and localized. Efficiency is an important element because the products are extremely price sensitive. Operating in southwestern states, RSPC has been in business for more than 50 years and has a rich history of providing quality products at competitive prices.

In recent years, several change initiatives were implemented at RSPC to improve HR's programs and policies. Most of these initiatives were designed to make RSPC a good place to work, ensuring that RSPC recruited and retained highly motivated, capable employees.

This case was prepared to serve as a basis for discussion rather than to illustrate either effective or ineffective administrative and management practices. All names, dates, places, and organizations have been disguised at the request of the author or organization.

Previous management had focused little on this aspect of the business, and the processes represented a significant departure from the "old" style of management.

The current top management believed that continuous transformation was needed to make RSPC one of the best and most profitable companies in the industry. In addition, management felt that several new HR programs could enhance operating results and the long-term growth of the company. With this in mind, top management commissioned a study to assess overall HR practices and make recommendations for changes.

Objectives

This study had the following objectives:
1. assess the effectiveness of current HR systems, procedures, and practices at RSPC
2. determine the company's level of compliance with state and federal regulations involving employee issues
3. compare HR practices at RSPC with general industry trends and practices
4. recommend changes in the HR function that would improve performance through efficiency, productivity, and effectiveness
5. identify performance improvement projects involving the utilization of HR.

Scope

The variety of functions for this performance improvement project was very broad. Although the traditional view of HR practices has been limited to areas such as employment, training, compensation and benefits, and employee relations, this assessment took a broader view. HR practices are sometimes viewed as involving all of those elements designed to support or protect employees and improve employee effectiveness and efficiency. With this broad scope in mind, this study involved the following functions:

- employment and selection
- employee relations
- career planning and succession
- job design
- performance standards and feedback
- environmental
- compensation
- reward systems

- record-keeping systems
- benefits
- training
- safety and health
- communications
- legal responsibilities
- cooperation and teamwork
- medical services.

In many organizations, the HR function is responsible for improving and coordinating the work of each of these areas.

Methodology

The initial concern was to improve the HR function's effectiveness. With this in mind, it was important to determine the current level of effectiveness and efficiency in terms of actual practice compared with industry standards, as well as to determine the perception of the effectiveness and efficiency by two critical groups—top executives and middle managers.

To conduct a comprehensive assessment, information was gathered using the following four primary methodologies.

1. *Interviews.* The performance consulting team met with all the top managers, a selected group of middle managers, and the HR department staff. During these visits, a variety of issues was explored concerning HR policies, practices, and concerns. In all, 20 interviews were conducted.

The top executives were asked about their perception of the HR function from several perspectives, beginning with their overall opinions of the HR function and its capabilities, results, responsibilities, key issues, concerns, and potential. More specifically, the areas in the bulleted list above were discussed in some detail.

These same issues also were explored with the middle managers. The interviews provided tremendous insight into the senior executives' perception of the function and how it should be operating.

2. *Documentation review.* To help in the assessment of current practices, policies, and procedures, copies of the following documents were secured:

- Documents reflecting the HR mission, vision, and values—employee handbook; safety handbook; benefit plan documents; HR procedures; wage structures; employment processing documents; absence reports; HR systems information; affirmative action audit; and other documents involving employee and HR issues.

- Documents regarding employee work rules—safety records; HR policies, when available; guidelines for salary administration; drug policy; turnover reports; employee files (samples); affirmative action plan, complaints, charges, and litigation; and current HR practices, whether written or unwritten.

3. *External benchmarking*. Several benchmarking projects were explored to compare the performance of RSPC with that of other organizations. The HR effectiveness index from Saratoga Institute in Saratoga, California, as well as an industry-related best practice study conducted by the National Stone Association provided benchmarks for most of the previously listed areas. This allowed comparisons of current performance with that of external practices. The industry-related study was considered most appropriate because of the unique situation and circumstances of the aggregate industry.

4. *Survey*. A final and critical method of data collection was a survey of the management group concerning the perceived strengths and weaknesses of the HR practices and policies at RSPC. Most employees at the supervisor and manager level, including sales representatives, received a copy of the survey (see table 1 for results). The survey explored a variety of issues uncovered in the interviews and in the analysis of the documentation.

The results of the three sources of input were combined, along with the generally accepted practices, to lead to the findings and recommendations.

Survey Results

The questionnaire in table 1 was administered to all supervisors and managers. All told, 77 individuals received the questionnaire, including most of the sales representatives. A few supervisors were excluded when it was determined that their input about the issues would be extremely limited. Questionnaires were mailed directly to respondents with a cover letter explaining the performance consulting project. Respondents were asked to return the completed questionnaire in an enclosed self-addressed envelope directly to the offices of Performance Resources Organization in Birmingham, Alabama.

The response to the survey exceeded expectations, with 63 survey participants responding, for an 82 percent response rate. No attempt was made to code the responses by job grade or location. Therefore, the data represented the opinions of the entire group. The high response rate, coupled with the steps taken to enhance confidentiality, ensured the validity of the process.

Table 1. HR practices survey.

The following survey items address current practices and policies at Redwood Stone Products Company (RSPC). Respondents were asked to be very straightforward with their responses. If a question was unrelated directly to a specific job, the response reflects the perception of the respondent.

For each statement, a check mark was placed under the number that best reflected the level of agreement with the statement, using this format: 1 = Strongly disagree; 2 = Disagree; 3 = Neither agree nor disagree; 4 = Agree; 5 = Strongly agree.

The number next to the heading represents the average for the group. An average rating of 4 to 5 is preferred. Any response approaching a 3 or lower deserves management attention.

Note: The following data reflects the actual results taken from the entire group and is presented to show the specific results. It is important to note that the comments on the questionnaires are not presented. Fortunately, the comments provided a rich source of information both in quality and quantity and provided interesting insights into issues, concerns, and recommendations.

Employment and Selection	3.47
1. When I need a new employee, I am usually able to get a quality candidate to fill the vacancy.	3.39
2. In our local area, we have a variety of sources for new employees (a good pool from which to select).	3.37
3. I am satisfied with the length of time it takes to fill a job vacancy when I have one.	3.12
4. I am usually allowed to make the selection decision for new employees when I have a vacancy.	3.82
5. Supervisors, superintendents, and managers are selected for their jobs based on their demonstrated ability to do the job.	3.65

Training	3.27
6. New employees receive a thorough orientation when they arrive for work.	3.65
7. New employees receive adequate training to perform their jobs in an effective manner.	3.71
8. Training programs are developed for most employee groups.	2.87
9. When training is provided, it is based on the needs of the group.	3.48
10. Supervisors receive ample training to improve skills and job knowledge.	3.02
11. At least some supervisors have individual training plans that outline their development program.	2.90

Job Design	3.57
12. I have a detailed description of my job.	2.78
13. I have a good understanding of my responsibilities at RSPC.	4.16
14. I am encouraged to provide input into major decisions affecting my work area.	3.87
15. I feel that I have complete authority to accomplish my job successfully.	3.49
16. RSPC management values suggestions and input from employees	3.57

continued on page 204

Table 1. HR practices survey (continued).

Career Planning and Succession	**3.12**
17. At RSPC, most employees know what they need to do to move up in the organization.	3.05
18. RSPC does a good job of letting employees know about job vacancies.	3.37
19. Employees usually know about the requirements for other jobs at RSPC.	3.24
20. As a supervisor, I have someone I can talk to about my career development and aspirations.	3.32
21. I am confident that RSPC is interested in helping me manage my career advancement.	3.12
22. I have someone developed to take my job should something happen to me.	3.06
23. For most key jobs at RSPC, potential replacements have been identified and developed.	2.67
Compensation	**2.92**
24. Employees are adequately paid at RSPC.	3.16
25. Pay ranges, grades, and classifications are developed for all jobs.	3.03
26. The job classification system is adequate for managing employee pay at RSPC.	2.86
27. At RSPC, we usually pay for performance.	2.86
28. Employee pay increases provide an adequate opportunity for movement in pay ranges.	2.70
Benefits	**3.62**
29. The RSPC benefits package is adequate.	3.95
30. Employees have a good understanding of their benefits package and what it provides.	3.76
31. When compared with other companies in this areas, our benefits package is competitive.	4.11
32. I have input into which new benefits are provided at RSPC.	2.67
Reward Systems	**2.92**
33. Employees receive recognition for their contributions.	3.23
34. Supervisors and managers receive bonuses based on their performance.	2.85
35. At RSPC, incentive pay plans are utilized to improve productivity and reduce costs.	2.48
36. At RSPC, incentive pay plans are utilized to improve quality and customer service.	2.40
37. Length of service is an important part of employee recognition at RSPC.	3.22
38. At RSPC, a large portion of pay is based on an employee's skills and knowledge.	3.37
Performance Standards and Feedback	**3.04**
39. At RSPC, most employees have measurable goals for their work.	3.19
40. Supervisors and managers have performance measures covering each major area of responsibility.	2.90
41. Performance standards have been developed for most jobs at RSPC.	2.78
42. Employees receive regular feedback on their performance.	3.06

43. The present rating system on the RSPC performance evaluation form is an adequate way to measure employee performance. 2.95
44. The annual performance review is an effective two-way discussion covering major areas of performance. 3.38

Recording-keeping Systems 3.04

45. An employee's personnel file contains very useful and helpful information on an employee's work record and performance. 3.65
46. I can usually locate information about an employee's performance in a timely manner. 3.60
47. I receive routine information regarding the performance of my employees. 3.19
48. Special requests for information about employee performances can be met without much difficulty. 3.33

Employee Relations 3.43

49. The morale of employees is adequate. 3.38
50. The morale and attitude of supervisors at RSPC is adequate. 3.37
51. The turnover at RSPC is at an acceptable level. 3.65
52. Absenteeism is at an acceptable level. 3.68
53. The "employee rep" system is an effective way to resolve employee complaints. 3.14
54. The overall work climate at RSPC is supportive and rewarding for most employees. 3.37
55. RSPC management is genuinely interested in the opinions of employees covering workplace issues. 3.44

Communication 3.42

56. RSPC management has an open-door policy for communicating with employees. 4.05
57. The communication between divisions at RSPC is effective. 2.95
58. The communication between supervisors is effective. 3.55
59. The communication between supervisors and employees is effective. 3.71
60. The communication from top management to employees is effective. 3.32
61. The communication from employees upward to management is effective. 3.17
62. As a supervisor, I am kept informed of major activities and events at RSPC. 3.17

Safety and Health 4.07

63. RSPC is very concerned about the safety and health of its employees. 4.48
64. The safety and health program at RSPC is effective. 4.27
65. The primary responsibility for the safety and health of my employees rests with me. 3.97
66. At RSPC, safety takes precedence over production. 3.87
67. The safety and health department is very effective in communicating and coordinating with me about safety issues and policies. 3.92
68. The safety and health program is flexible to meet the needs of my work unit. 3.94

continued on page 206

Table 1. HR practices survey (continued).

Medical Services	**3.84**
69. The medical services department provides a necessary function at RSPC.	4.05
70. The therapy performed by medical services helps to keep employees on the job.	3.89
71. Utilizing the medical services department is the best way to treat on-the-job injuries at RSPC.	4.02
72. The medical services department is effective at preventing sickness and illness for employees and their families.	3.40
Environmental	**3.89**
73. The management at RSPC is genuinely concerned about protecting the environment.	4.08
74. Most employees are aware of RSPC's commitment to environmental laws and regulations.	3.71
75. The environmental department ensures that RSPC is in compliance with environmental laws and regulations.	4.02
76. The environmental department is very effective at communicating and coordinating with me about environmental issues and policies.	3.76
Legal Responsibilities	**3.04**
77. I am knowledgeable about the employment discrimination laws.	4.10
78. As a supervisor, I receive training on the legal aspects of my job.	3.37
79. At RSPC, we make sure that we are in compliance with all regulations affecting employees.	3.97
80. RSPC has a good track record for hiring and promoting minorities and females.	3.51
81. Employees are treated fairly at RSPC.	3.86
82. At RSPC, favoritism does not enter into HR decisions.	3.22
Cooperation and Teamwork	**3.04**
83. At RSPC, divisions work together as a team.	3.25
84. The HR staff provides me with information and assistance in a helpful manner.	3.52
85. At RSPC, I receive cooperation from all support departments throughout the company.	3.56

Responses indicated that the respondents were frank and candid, although they did tend to be polite with responses. This is not unusual for internal surveys. In addition, because of the positive changes that had been made, many respondents seemed pleased with the results and therefore did not want to give negative input. With these concerns aside, the responses provided some useful information that pinpointed several problem areas. To a great degree, survey responses confirmed most of the issues uncovered in the interviews and in the document review.

Findings and Recommendations

Data was combined from all four collection methodologies to arrive at specific issues and recommendations for each of the functions reviewed. This section only reports those issues that needed attention or discussion. After the identification of the issues, specific recommendations are presented.

Employment and Selection

The employment and selection process appeared to be effective, although a few issues were identified:
- For the skilled jobs, particularly in the maintenance area, the company was experiencing some difficulty obtaining qualified candidates to fill vacancies.
- The time it took to fill a job vacancy was excessive.
- The application form needed improvement.
  The following specific actions were recommended:
- In skilled positions, recruiting sources should be linked more directly with vocational and technical schools. Some of this was already being done, but it needed to be more structured and organized.
- The time to fill a particular vacancy is a measure that should be monitored by HR. The process of monitoring will actually focus more attention on this issue. The average time can be reviewed for potential progress and compared with standards in the industry.
- The application form needs to be redesigned without an address so that it can be used at all locations. Among the needed additions to the application form are company logo, affirmative action statement, employee performance data, and more information about education and training.

Training

Training represented an area where significant improvement needed to be made. Except for safety and regulatory training, there was little effort to build skills and improve the workforce through training and development. This was particularly true for supervisors. The following issues were identified:

- Formal training programs were not developed for most groups of employees.
- Supervisors did not receive training to improve supervisory skills.
- Most of the maintenance and technical employees received on-the-job training, but this was not given in any organized, efficient program.
- The support for external education (tuition refund) had not been consistent.
- There had been no attempts to establish individual development plans for supervisors or high-potential employees.

The following specific actions were recommended:

- Conduct an analysis of supervisor training needs through a questionnaire from supervisors and their managers.
- Organize and conduct a systematic supervisory training program to focus on the most critical needs. Limit supervisory training to small groups to enhance the learning process.
- Initiate individual development plans to develop high-potential employees in the sales and operations areas. This could be expanded to include all supervisors and sales representatives or limited to those who either need additional development or have high potential for advancement. The plan would include significant external programs. For example, supervisors would attend the supervisor training program from the National Stone Association. Sales representatives would attend similar industry programs.
- Consider rotational assignments to give sales representatives an opportunity to understand operations and to give operations supervisors an opportunity to understand the sales function. These could be short assignments of one to two weeks' duration and treated the same as if the supervisor or sales representative was on vacation.
- Connect with vocational schools, equipment dealers, and other sources to develop a more organized approach to mechanical and technical training for the maintenance and shop areas. Because most of the training will occur on the job, present a train-the-trainer program to supervisors and top mechanics to build skills for them to train others on the job.
- Consider a conservative tuition refund program aimed at supporting employees who take courses directly related to RSPC's present and future needs. This could be an inexpensive way to develop employees.
- Develop a formal approach to training assistant supervisors.

- Encourage each major area to develop a training plan for key employees to utilize external programs, on-the-job training, structured rotational assignments, and company programs.

Job Design

There seemed to be no problems with the current job structures for supervisors. They had a clear understanding of job responsibilities and the necessary authority to accomplish their work. They also felt that they were part of a team and were involved in decisions affecting the work unit. Nonetheless, one issue was identified, and that was that supervisors did not have current descriptions of their jobs.

Thus, it was recommended that the company update job descriptions. It helps to have a written copy of what is expected. Also, it can help defend RSPC in the event of legal challenges to the HR system.

Career Planning and Succession

This area needed some attention. Supervisors and other employees did not have a clear understanding of what it took to advance or develop their careers. There were virtually no formal mechanisms in place to enhance career development, and there was uncertainty in terms of top management's attitude toward this process. Specific issues were as follows:

- Employees and supervisors did not know with whom they should talk concerning career development.
- There was no organized way of communicating job vacancies.
- There was no formal succession planning process.
- There had been no formal attempts at early identification of high-potential employees so that their careers could be managed.

The following specific actions were recommended:

- Consider a conservative system for communicating nonmanagement job vacancies. A simple process that lets employees know about vacancies and how they can apply for those vacancies should suffice.
- Address the career development issue in the employee handbook, outlining the procedures to be utilized to discuss career development issues. The employee's direct supervisor is probably the best person for this discussion.
- The HR manager should be tuned in to current and potential vacancies and should serve as a source of career counseling for supervisors and managers for those vacancies (in addition to the individual's manager).

- Implement a simple succession planning process to identify potential replacements for key jobs, particularly top and middle management. This process involves identifying replacements and outlining developmental plans for those employees.
- Implement a process to identify high-potential employees early so that their careers can be developed and managed.

Compensation

Compensation needed significant attention. Although the perception was that employees were adequately paid, the compensation system seemed to have significant problems. The job classification system did not seem adequate. There was a perception of little linkage between pay and performance, and there was some mystery concerning pay increases. Specific issues were as follows:

- For hourly employees, the pay ranges, grades, and classifications were out of date. Ranges were too broad.
- For salaried employees, pay ranges and grades did not exist.
- Although there had been some effort to simplify hourly jobs, there was still room for further simplification.
- The annual merit adjustment was not perceived to be motivational.
- In some cases, there was confusion between the classifications of exempt versus nonexempt jobs.
- Although salary surveys were taken, that information was not communicated to key managers. As a result, there was sometimes a perception of underpayment when it may not have been the case.

The following specific actions were recommended:

- Review hourly pay grades, ranges, and rates. Finalize the changes and publish them.
- Make additional attempts to simplify job titles. There is a definite trend away from specialists to more general job classifications.
- Develop a pay grade and range system for salaried employees.
- Ensure that the merit raises are based primarily on performance. At all times, communicate the philosophy of "pay for performance."
- Ensure that salary survey information is communicated to those who have a need to know. The salary process should be routine (at least annually) and utilized for appropriate adjustments for pay ranges, pay rates, and the amount of increases.
- Jobs that are improperly classified as exempt should be reviewed and changed to the nonexempt classification.
- Consider a pay-for-skills program in the future, in which employees are paid for learning additional skills.

Benefits

Overall, the benefits area received favorable remarks and seemed to be a competitive package. Much improvement had been made in recent years, but a few issues needed to be addressed:

- Short- and long-term disability programs were needed. Although proposals had been reviewed, no plan had been implemented.
- It took too long to process a medical claim. This was probably because the third party payer was based in California.
- Efforts to communicate benefits had not been as effective as they should have been. Employees and supervisors were not fully aware of—and did not fully appreciate—their benefits package.
- Benefit costs were not monitored or reported regularly.

The following specific actions were recommended:

- Review the insurance programs to see if placement with another carrier is appropriate. Some managers questioned the use of the current carrier. Address the issue of process time for medical claims with a definite commitment to reduce the time.
- Move forward with the implementation of short- and long-term disability plans. Most companies have these plans. The short-term plan should be self-funded, and the long-term plan should be underwritten by a carrier. Both are inexpensive but should be favorably received by employees.
- Communicate the benefits package often. It is hard to overcommunicate in this area. Consider a benefits statement that shows the cost of the benefits for each employee. These can be generated inexpensively and sometimes even supplied by the carrier.
- As benefit costs rise, there should be some plans to contain costs. Eventually, employees should share in the cost of their medical coverage.
- As new benefits are explored, supervisors should be involved in terms of determining what is important to the company's employees.

Reward Systems

Along with compensation, reward systems did not seem to be adequate in reflecting what was needed in a progressive company. Generally, employees were not fully recognized for their contributions, and there were few bonuses and incentives tied directly to bottom-line measures. The following issues stood out:

- There was no bonus plan for supervisors or superintendents based on their direct operational performance.
- Incentive plans were not utilized to improve productivity, reduce costs, improve product quality, or increase customer service.

- Length of service was recognized probably more than it should have been.

  The following specific actions were recommended:

- Implement a bonus plan for superintendents and supervisors based on cost control, productivity, appearance, availability, and other operating parameters.
- Try to reduce year-end bonuses unless they are tied specifically to performance measures. The previous bonus scheme was not necessarily tied to performance but was perceived to be based on favoritism and political issues.
- Eliminate seniority bonuses. Reserve bonuses for performance improvement, not for longevity. Recognize seniority through service awards and other public ways to provide recognition.
- Consider a sales incentive plan in which sales representatives are rewarded for volume increases, average sales price improvement, market share gains, and other key variables.
- Consider a gainsharing plan (hourly incentive) in selected areas. The plan should focus on cost reduction.

Performance Standards and Feedback

This area definitely needed improvement. For the most part, performance measures were not clearly defined for supervisors and managers. Also, the quality of discussions to improve performance was not very effective. Specific issues were as follows:

- Supervisors and managers did not have performance measures covering each major area of responsibility.
- Performance measures had not been developed for most jobs at RSPC.
- The present rating system used in the performance appraisal process was perceived to be inadequate.
- The annual performance review process was confusing because of the way it was administered.

  The following specific actions were recommended:

- The entire company needs to focus on additional measurements and reports reflecting performance. HR, finance and accounting, operations, and sales need to improve overall measures and have those measures reflected in performance standards.
- In the operations and sales areas, there is a need for more effective cost statements and statements with operating parameters. Although some progress has been made, additional improvements are needed.
- Each supervisor and manager should have clear-cut measures of accountability for his or her area of responsibility. Included among those would be HR measures.

- Establish a consistent practice for performance reviews in terms of the review dates, the system for review, approvals, and so forth. In addition, the particular form—including the rating system—should be reviewed for potential changes and improvement. After this is established, conduct a brief training session about how an effective performance review should be conducted.

Record-keeping Systems

An important part of the review involved the degree to which records about employees and employee performance were administered and reported to supervisors and managers. Although this function seems adequate, a few issues were identified:

- Very little information was routinely reported to managers concerning employee performance and trends in employee performance. For example, turnover reports had not been developed in two years. Also, absenteeism information, as it was currently collected, was unreliable and was not used as a management tool.
- Employee record keeping had not been automated.
- Employee files needed to be improved. There were too many separate files containing employee information. Consolidation had not been attempted.

The following specific actions were recommended:

- Consider generating a report of HR information to be sent to managers and supervisors. Included in that report would be measures such as absenteeism, turnover, safety records, average wage rate, and average length of service. This information, when combined with operating parameters, would provide each supervisor and manager with a complete statement of operating accountability.
- Consider consolidating employee files into one or two central files, and control the accessibility to the files.
- Move forward with the implementation of the proposed HR software system. It can be useful in reporting a wide range of information (such as job information and evaluation, employee profiles, equal opportunity/affirmative action, employee history, turnover, applicant tracking, wage and salary information, safety and health information, and organizational structure data).

Employee Relations

Employee relations appeared adequate. Morale was good, at least from the point of view of managers and supervisors. It appeared that several improvements had been made in recent years to help the situation. Even so, one issue did surface, and that was that the employee rep system did not seem to be working effectively.

Although it appeared that morale was at an adequate level, additional efforts to improve morale needed to be considered because of its importance, including the following:

- Continue to utilize picnics, barbecues, employee outings, informal recognition, and other special efforts to make employees feel important.
- Because there is an acceptable level of trust with management in terms of employee input, the time is appropriate to implement a suggestion system. This would be a simple suggestion system that allows employees to provide workable, realistic ideas to improve RSPC and be rewarded for their efforts.
- The employee rep system needs changing. Possibly it should be minimized. It was necessary during union organizing attempts but may not be needed today. There is an employee grievance system to help resolve complaints. If the rep system continues, the communication surrounding the process needs to be improved. Department managers need to be informed of issues that are addressed in the meetings.

Communications

Overall, communications appeared adequate. This was an area that had received attention in recent years. Several issues were identified:

- Communications between divisions was not effective. This held true for communications between San Antonio and other locations.
- Upward communications from employees to top management did not seem effective.
- The rumor mill was too strong and active, leaving it as a major source of information at RSPC.

Recommendations included the following:

- Communications between divisions needs to be improved. This issue is addressed under the teamwork section.
- Explore some tools to enhance upward communications. For instance, the suggestion system, as mentioned earlier, can be helpful. Other tools include the following:
  — Consider informal meetings such as "Worker's Voice" to provide employees an opportunity to meet with and talk to upper management. The top division head in each area could conduct these meetings with the lowest level employees in each division, often cutting out

levels in between. Although this makes some managers uncomfortable, it does provide employees an upward channel to the top.

— Consider an anonymous open complaint and comment program, in which employees are asked to submit their ideas, complaints, concerns, and recommendations directly to the CEO. This program is easy to administer and could have a catchy name (such as "Hey Boss" or "Sound Off"). Responses would need to be published within a certain number of days. If they were anonymous, they could be published in the employee newsletter.

— Reestablish the employee newsletter, which was in place at one time. This is a responsibility that could be spread over several different departments but should be coordinated by HR.

— Make attempts to keep supervisors informed about important issues as quickly as possible. Regular meetings with supervisors can help communicate this type of information.

— Make deliberate attempts to undermine and minimize the impact of the grapevine.

Safety and Health

The overall safety and health program seemed to be working quite well. It had good support from the management group, and management got good marks in terms of its commitment to the safety and health of its employees. Only two issues that might need some attention were identified:

• Supervisors may not have been getting rewarded appropriately for safety performance.

• At times, the safety program was not tailored to the needs of specific departments.

The following specific actions were recommended:

• Ensure that safety is a component of a supervisor bonus system, should one be implemented. If not, consider the possibility of increasing the bonus amount for supervisors from the current safety incentive process.

• Consider the possibility of tailoring the programs to each departmental area. Some safety issues are department specific, and the safety program should be flexible enough to adapt to these differences.

Medical Services

The medical services function had a good reputation and received good support for its efforts. It seemed to be fulfilling legitimate and viable needs. Only one issue or concern was identified, and that was that management was questioning medical services' cost-effectiveness and its necessity as an essential function.

The only recommendation is to perform a cost-benefit analysis for the department. This analysis would determine the price for securing services externally and compare them with current medical department fully loaded costs to see whether this is a cost-effective service.

Environmental

The environmental function at RSPC was perceived to be adequately conducted and managed. No specific issues were uncovered.

The only recommendation is that the company continue to communicate with the supervisors about the environmental issues and progress that is made.

Legal Responsibilities

RSPC had a good track record with discrimination charges both in numbers and outcomes. The knowledge of legal responsibilities appeared adequate. Two issues were identified:
- A recent affirmative action audit conducted by the Office of Federal Contract Compliance Programs had revealed significant deficiencies in RSPC's efforts.
- There was some perception of favoritism in personnel decisions that needed to be addressed.
  The following specific actions were recommended:
- The HR department needs to keep up with affirmative action/equal opportunity requirements by maintaining a program, developing support data, and conducting an adverse impact analysis.
- As indicated in the affirmative action audit, there needs to be an additional focus on promoting minorities and attracting females to RSPC.
- Personnel decisions should be based on objective criteria as much as possible, thus potentially minimizing any favoritism in assignments.

Cooperation and Teamwork

Although this seemed to fare quite well, two issues were identified:
- There was a lack of cooperation and teamwork among divisions at RSPC.
- There was a lack of cooperation and teamwork between San Antonio and Houston.

The following specific actions were recommended:

- The lack of cooperation and teamwork must be addressed at the highest level. When top executives work together as a team and respect each other's opinions, the message will be transmitted throughout the organization.
- A team building meeting should be considered to bring top managers together and to utilize a variety of exercises aimed at gaining appreciation for, and respect of, each other's responsibilities, duties, goals, concerns, issues, and so forth.
- The CEO must continue to emphasize and promote teamwork and communication between divisions.

Overall Findings and Recommendations
Role of HR

It is important to review the current and desired role of the HR function in an organization. Historically, the HR function—personnel, as it was called—started as an administrative function where the employee records were kept and payroll was processed. This is the *administrative* role.

The function evolved into a more viable, important part of the organization when a *reactive* role was assumed. Under this role, the HR staff responded to management requests for new programs, policies, and initiatives to improve employee welfare.

Gradually, the function began to take initiatives and develop new programs. In this *proactive* role, the staff developed new programs aimed at improving the efficiency and effectiveness of the organization or at preventing problems. This is perceived to be a preventive posture in the organization.

Finally, a more recent trend is that of a *collaborative* role, in which the function works in collaboration with management to improve the organization, implement new programs, resolve issues, and solve problems. Research has shown that the more an organization moves toward the proactive and collaborative roles with HR, the more effective it will be.

Based on the review of the HR function at RSPC, it appears that the majority of the time of those involved in HR is spent in administrative and reactive roles. The principal focus is on keeping records and responding to specific requests from management. Few efforts are made to initiate new programs or to collaborate with management to improve RSPC. There is a definite need to shift the roles (as depicted in figure 1) from the administrative and reactive to the proactive and collaborative. The function needs to initiate change and to work with management to improve the organization.

Management of the HR Function

How the HR function is managed in an organization makes a significant difference in how well HR policies and practices work. In reality, every manager has HR responsibility, just as he or she has responsibility for cost control, customer service, and quality. The HR staff is charged with the responsibility to coordinate the activities and manage the overall programs.

In some areas, the present management of the HR function has done quite well. The HR staff is knowledgeable about the company and the industry. The relationship with employees, particularly hourly employees, is very good. The administrative skills seem to be effective. However, four areas need additional emphasis to ensure that the function is managed properly:

1. *Focus on results.* There has not been enough of a focus on results from the individual programs and services provided by the HR function. There have been few attempts to relate programs to outputs of sales, cost, quality, production, and customer service. In reality, when any program or service is implemented, there should be some concern for, or connection with, the overall objectives of the company. Even if it is rough, some type of feasibility analysis should be conducted to explore cost versus perceived benefits. A results-based effort needs to be integrated throughout the HR system so that the staff is always trying to link its effort to overall company goals.

2. *Cost control.* Managing the cost of the HR function goes hand in hand with achieving results. This involves tracking and monitoring all costs and comparing them with what has occurred previously and with industry data. For example, one of the most important costs to monitor is the cost of benefits. It is estimated that benefits account

Figure 1. HR role concentration at RSPC.

Role	Current	Desired
Administrative	X	
Reactive	X	
Proactive		X
Collaborative		X

for 25 percent of payroll costs, but there have not been any recent efforts to verify this number or track it on a precise basis. The HR department should be constantly monitoring costs to ensure that the function is managed efficiently.

3. *Relationship with managers.* Although relationships with employees seem adequate, those with managers, particularly senior management, are not as productive. It appears that little mutual respect exists among top managers and the HR manager. In reality, the HR manager should be a partner with top managers in sales and operations. They should work together in a productive work environment to achieve desired goals. This will require HR to consult with line managers and get them involved with issues. At the same time, line managers will need to consult with HR and get the HR staff involved with their issues. This is a first step toward building a partnership relationship and moving closer to the collaborative role, described earlier.

4. *Best practices.* The HR department should constantly observe trends and innovative approaches from other organizations, even in other industries. This is a fast-changing part of business in a complex, constantly changing world. New programs and practices are developed periodically, which can be very effective and productive at RSPC. The HR manager must stay in tune with the latest trends, techniques, and innovative practices and use common judgment to see whether HR can improve RSPC. Part of this process may involve benchmarking certain data with other organizations considered to be the best in the industry.

HR Staffing and Organization

To get the most out of the HR function and meet all of the challenges and issues raised in this study, the function must be adequately staffed. Although no ideal staffing level exists, general guidelines can be utilized. The best rule of thumb is that for every 100 employees, there should be one full-time HR staff member. This figure includes only the traditional HR staff involved in recruiting, compensation and benefits, training and development, employee relations, and so forth. It does not include safety and health, medical services, environmental, or payroll. Using this brief analysis, seven full-time employees would be an adequate staffing level at RSPC. At the present time, five meet these criteria. Ultimately, two employees may be needed as described below.

A recommended approach to an organizational structure is to have a senior level executive responsible just for HR reporting to the

CEO. The current HR manager could report to this executive. This change should focus more senior level attention on this important process. The addition of another employee, focusing primarily on training and development, should ensure that RSPC is adequately staffed and has one of the best HR programs in the industry. Figure 2 depicts this proposed organization.

Questions for Discussion

1. How does the role of external best practices influence each of the areas explored in this case?
2. Which of the four methodologies used is considered the most reliable in providing information?
3. Is the number of recommendations excessive? Explain.
4. How could the recommendations be structured in regard to importance, timing, corporate strategy, operations, and so forth?
5. What other methodologies can be used to assess the current performance of an HR function? What would influence the use of other methodologies?

The Authors

Jack J. Phillips founded Performance Resources Organization, an international consulting firm specializing in HR accountability programs, in 1992. Backed by 30 years of experience in HR and management, Phillips consults with his clients worldwide on issues ranging from measurement and evaluation to productivity and quality enhancement. He has authored numerous books, including *Measuring Return on Investment in HR* (2000), *HRD Trends Worldwide* (1999), and *Return on Investment in Training and Performance Improvement Pro-*

Figure 2. Proposed organizational structure of HR.

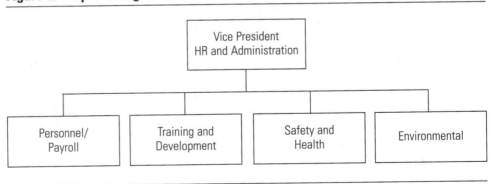

grams (1997). He can be contacted at the Jack Phillips Center for Research and Assessment, Box 380637, Birmingham, AL 35238-0637; phone: 205.678.9700; fax: 205.678.8070; email: roipro@wwisp.com.

Patricia P. Phillips is chairman and CEO of the Chelsea Group, a research and publishing company focused on accountability issues in organizations. She works with organizations to build programs and processes to improve performance and show bottom-line results. Phillips has served as author and co-author for several publications, including *Measuring Return on Investment in HR* (Houston: Gulf Publishing, 2000) and ASTD's Info-line, *ROI on a Shoestring*. She may be contacted at the Chelsea Group, phone: 205.678.9700; email: TheChelsea-Group@aol.com.

About the Series Editor

Jack J. Phillips has more than 30 years of professional experience in HR and management. He has served as training and development manager at two *Fortune* 500 firms, senior HR executive at two firms, president of a regional federal savings bank, and management professor at a major state university. In 1992, Phillips founded Performance Resources Organization, an international consulting firm specializing in HR accountability programs. Phillips consults with his clients in the United States, Canada, England, Italy, Germany, Belgium, South Africa, Mexico, Venezuela, Malaysia, Indonesia, Australia, New Zealand, Hong Kong, and Singapore on issues ranging from measurement and evaluation to productivity and quality enhancement.

A frequent contributor to management literature, Phillips has written more than 100 articles for professional, business, and trade publications. In addition, he has written or edited *The Consultant's Scorecard* (2000), *Measuring Return on Investment in Human Resources* (2000), *HRD Trends Worldwide* (1999), *Return on Investment in Training and Performance Improvement Programs* (1997), *Handbook of Training Evaluation and Measurement Methods* (3d edition, 1997), *Accountability in Human Resource Management* (1996), *Conducting Needs Assessment* (1995), *Measuring Return on Investment* (volume 1, 1994; volume 2, 1997), *The Development of a Human Resource Effectiveness Index* (1988), *Recruiting, Training and Retaining New Employees* (1987), and *Improving Supervisors' Effectiveness* (1985), which won an award from the Society for Human Resource Management.

Phillips holds undergraduate degrees in electrical engineering, physics, and mathematics; a master's degree in decision sciences from Georgia State University; and a doctorate in HR management from the University of Alabama. In 1987, he won the Yoder-Heneman Personnel Creative Application Award from the Society for Human Resource Management. He is an active member of several professional organizations.

Phillips may be reached at the following address: The Jack Phillips Center for Research and Assessment, Box 380637, Birmingham, AL 35238-0637; phone: 205.678.9700; fax: 205.678.8070; email: roipro@wwisp.com.